WRITING
Process, Product, and Power

For Leslie,
A great writing teacher!
Ken Davis

Ken Davis
Kim Brian Lovejoy

Indiana University-Purdue University at Indianapolis

PRENTICE HALL, Englewood Cliffs, New Jersey 07632

Library of Congress Cataloging-in-Publication Data

Davis, Ken,
    Writing : process, product, and power / Ken Davis, Kim Brian Lovejoy.
    p.   ; cm.
    Includes index.
    ISBN 0-13-971011-6
    1. English language—Rhetoric.   I. Lovejoy, Kim Brian.
    II. Title.
PE1408.D243   1993
808′.042—dc20   92-37582
                                                                      CIP

Editorial/production supervision
    and interior design: *Mariann Murphy*
Cover Design: *Bruce Kenselaar*
Prepress buyer: *Herb Klein*
Manufacturing buyer: *Patrice Fraccio/Robert Anderson*
Acquisitions editor: *Phil Miller/Alison Reeves*

 © 1993 by Prentice-Hall, Inc.
A Simon & Schuster Company
Englewood Cliffs, NJ 07632

Printed in the United States of America

10 9 8 7 6 5 4 3 2 1

ISBN 0-13-971011-6

Prentice-Hall International (UK) Limited, *London*
Prentice-Hall of Australia Pty. Limited, *Sydney*
Prentice-Hall Canada Inc., *Toronto*
Prentice-Hall Hispanoamericana, S.A., *Mexico*
Prentice-Hall of India Private Limited, *New Delhi*
Prentice-Hall of Japan, Inc., *Tokyo*
Simon & Schuster Asia Pte. Ltd., *Singapore*
Editora Prentice-Hall do Brasil, Ltda., *Rio de Janeiro*

For Mike Adelstein, Al Crabb, and
Jean Pival

(KD)

For my parents,
Norman and Rita Lovejoy

(KBL)

Contents

CHAPTER SIX

The Process of Writing Words   202

CHAPTER SEVEN

The Process of Handling Mechanics   240

Preface

Writing: Process, Product, and Power is an introductory college writing text that integrates writing as process and as product to empower students as writers.

We have organized the book by seven major features of written products. As we guide students through the writing process, we focus on writing activities and strategies as they relate to each of the major product features. Seven writing assignments, arranged in order of increasing complexity, enable students to develop their writing abilities and to write for real audiences and situations. Each assignment includes three or more samples of student papers for discussion and group work, all written by students of ours, specifically for the assignment. We have found the book especially adaptable to a portfolio approach to teaching writing.

We believe that *Writing: Process, Product, and Power* differs from most writing textbooks in several ways:

- It integrates the process and product of writing by focusing on what writers do as they reflect on the major features of any piece of writing.

- It emphasizes writing as power, enabling students to learn about themselves as writers and thinkers, to engage in problem solving, and to produce effective writing in real situations.

- It defines and illustrates the uses of journal writing throughout the writing process, as a means of reflecting on the student's behavior as a writer, of discovering and shaping ideas for writing, of writing about writing, and of collecting and responding to peer commentary.

- It introduces theoretical concepts in practical ways so that students can easily understand and use them.

- It features a section on writing from research, with a discussion of both print and non-print sources of information.

- It features seven major writing assignments, culminating in a self-reflective essay about the writing course.

- It includes twenty-five student papers for analysis and discussion, reflecting richly rhetorical situations that students can easily grasp. These papers represent a range of abilities, so that students will see papers close to their own level of ability and be able to reason ways to improve them.

In addition to the important people to whom this book is dedicated, we thank our students and colleagues at Indiana University-Purdue University at Indianapolis for their help and encouragement.

Ken also thanks his wife, Bette, and his children, Casey and Evan, for their patience, humor, and love; he also thanks his former students and colleagues at the University of Kentucky, especially Chris Cetrulo. Kim thanks his wife, Mary, and his children Rebecca and Joseph, for giving his life meaning and balance; he also thanks Professor Frank Clary of St. Michael's College, who has long been a source of inspiration.

Finally, thanks go to Phil Miller, Tracey Augustine, and Mariann Murphy at Prentice Hall, and to William Smith of Virginia Commonwealth University, Lucien Agosta of California State University-Sacramento, Molly Wescott of Florence-Darlington Technical College, Patricia Connors of Memphis State University, Ed Davis of Sinclair Community College, Dale C. Brannoa of Oklahoma State University-Okmulgee, and Betty Hart of Fairmount State College for their helpful reviews.

Writing as Process, Product, and Power

A poet visits a writing classroom and invites ten minutes of "freewriting" about an abstract, black-and-white photograph (a conch shell? a sand dune? a nude?); suddenly the room is full of eyes and writing hands, swirling their way down into the curls and turns of the picture. Connie's alert eyes and mind take up the shape, play with it, turn it inside out, then get it down in words on her paper. Cathy looks puzzled, then calm, and sets to work, her Flair pen and her tidy legal pad becoming one—with each other, with the photograph, with the room. David, with relaxed intensity, smiles as he dabs at the page like a painter. (What colors do you paint, David, as you see and resee the picture?)

Susan is cool and professional, her long slim arm holding the page at maximum distance, lest the words get too close. Karen's eyes dance across the turning shapes, dance the shape onto the page, as her dancer's foot shapes tiny circles in the air.

Words come faster now, from poet Liz's scraping of chalk on slate, as her wooden heels walk her *own* words across the floor, across slowly, back quickly, like a typewriter. Barbara, meanwhile, works at the page like a loving artisan, like a farrier shoeing a favorite horse. Hugh's felt-tip pen draws circles and spirals to black out words, replicating the circles and spirals of the photograph. Greg's pencil, yellow and blunt, moves mouselike, gnawing at the words as they come. Bob is writing with his eyes and his bent head, burning the words onto the page like a lens focusing a tiny furnace of sunlight onto a pine board.

Sue leans into her work, letting the words support her through the fulcrum of her plastic pen. Robert, rooted to chair and floor, is a silversmith, shaping his words with pliers and files, crafting glistening wonder from the silver oxide of the photographic paper.

The photograph is multicopied now, transformed into words expressing each writer's unique perspective on the story beneath the photograph. Because each writer is different—in attitudes, beliefs, and assumptions—each views the photograph in slightly different shades of light, illuminating nuances of meaning quite different from others' perceptions. And in the process of communicating their perceptions, they write differently from each other and differently, perhaps, each time they write. So how can we begin to talk about writing—much less learn to write better?

Yet writers *can* learn to write better. And teachers and other writers and even textbooks can help. One way to start that help is by defining *writing*.

In everyday talk the word *writing* is used in at least three different ways. First, it is used as a noun, the name of a *thing*: we can speak of a "piece of writing" as we would speak of a piece of cheese. Second, writing is used as a verb, an activity; we say, "Mike is writing instructions for buying a compact disc player" or "Constance is writing an autobiographical essay." *Writing* thus means both a process and the product that results from it.

A third use of the word *writing*, although perhaps not quite so everyday, is a common one in education, business, and government. In those fields, and others, we talk about writing as a skill, an ability: we talk about the need for improving writing, we offer courses and workshops on writing, and we publish textbooks on writing, like this one. Writing is clearly a *power* that can be learned and strengthened. Moreover, it *gives* power to those who use it well—as students, workers, citizens, and human beings—because it offers a means of expression, a way to use language to achieve our purposes and to communicate our ideas.

This book is about writing in all three senses: as process, as product, and as power. Further, this book has three major goals, each concerned with one of these three ways of talking about writing. This Overview discusses those three goals.

The Writing Process

The first goal of this book is to help you develop your confidence and skill in the writing *process* as a way of communicating—and as a way of learning. So far, you may have thought of writing only as a medium of communication, and certainly that is its major purpose. But writing is also an important tool for learning, and if you are just beginning a college education, that is a useful fact for you to remember. In fact, one of the most valuable activities you can do as a college student—for the sake of both improving your writing and learning your other subjects—is to keep a daily journal of your learning and other experiences.

Using a daily journal to write about your experiences will, for example, reinforce your learning and help you to discover your own questions and points of interests. You've probably been told before that one of the best ways to prepare for an essay examination is to ask yourself possible essay questions and then to practice writing essays in response to them. One of us, in fact, used this strategy when preparing for his Ph.D. written examinations. Though it requires an investment in time, this strategy is particularly effective because it helps you to identify the parts of your subject that you know well and those that you need to review more thoroughly. If you can write about something, you have comprehended it.

Thus, getting into the habit of writing about your learning experiences in the various courses you take in college is one way to become a better learner. You don't *really* know what you know about a subject until you *can* write about it. When you write it down, synthesizing and ordering pieces of information, making connections among disparate ideas, using your eyes, hand, and brain to compose your thoughts in the act of writing, you will have succeeded in learning new information and in discovering new questions to guide your future learning.

Because one of our goals in this book is to help you better understand writing as a process, we are going to suggest that you use a journal to begin thinking and writing about your own behavior as a beginning college writer— that is, to reflect on your own process of writing. Although you have learned most of what you know about written *products* through reading, you cannot learn much about the writing *process* that way. For example, you could read any of the sample papers in this book a thousand times without knowing the number of drafts that the writers produced before writing the final copies that you see in this book.

In fact, one of the main purposes of formal instruction in writing—like this textbook—is to teach you useful things about the writing process that are not apparent from reading the final product.

STAGES OF THE PROCESS

The left-hand column of the chart in Figure 1 is a reminder that writing *is* a process: it is not something that happens all at once. This writing process, as we suggested earlier, is not a rigid, step-by-step activity; it usually involves many twists and turns, much doubling back and leaping forward. Nevertheless, for purposes of learning to write better, it may be useful to think of the writing process as having three stages—stages defined not by what activities are done in them but merely by *when* they occur.

The easiest of the three stages to define is the second stage, which this book calls *drafting*: it consists of everything you do during the time you are actually putting the piece of writing down on paper, or on a computer screen. Drafting is writing the work through once; when it ends, a draft has been completed.

That may sound like the whole writing process, and for some writers, some of the time, it is. When you take a telephone message for a family member or roommate, for example, you very likely just write it down as you

Figure 1 - Writing: Process, Product, and Power

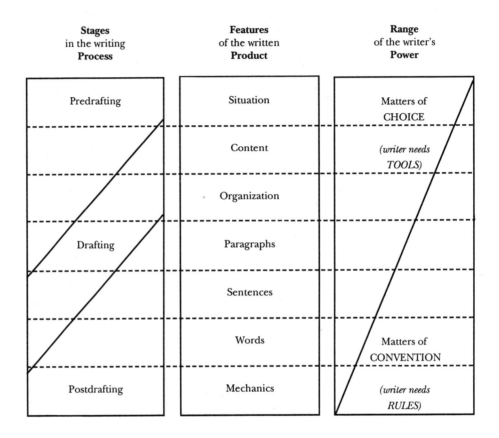

Stages in the writing **Process**	**Features** of the written **Product**	**Range** of the writer's **Power**
Predrafting	Situation	Matters of CHOICE
	Content	*(writer needs TOOLS)*
	Organization	
Drafting	Paragraphs	
	Sentences	
	Words	Matters of CONVENTION
Postdrafting	Mechanics	*(writer needs RULES)*

hear it, and you may not look at it again. Most writing tasks, however, are not that simple and straightforward. In most writing situations, writers do something before they begin that first draft: they think, read, take notes, talk with a friend or colleague, perhaps even outline. For example, one of us likes to list ideas on a page and order them in some way before beginning to write. Some writers talk into a tape recorder and then take notes as they play it back; one of us began his doctoral dissertation that way. Whatever writers do before they draft, that is the first stage of the writing process: we call it *predrafting.* It includes what some textbooks and teachers may call "discovery," "invention," "planning," or "prewriting." *Predrafting* is the preparation for *drafting.*

Similarly, most writers do something after they finish their first draft:

they reread, reconsider, revise. As mentioned earlier, the student-writers who produced the sample papers used in this book reread, reconsidered, and revised several drafts before they reached the final product. That is the third stage of the writing process, the stage we call *postdrafting*. It includes such activities as "rewriting," "revising," and "editing."

Each of this book's seven main chapters is divided into sections on predrafting, drafting, and postdrafting. In this way, the book suggests not just *what* to do to improve the various features of your writing—but also *when* during the process to do it. More will be said about that point shortly.

Of course, it is important to remember that our way of talking about the writing process can only be an approximation of what writers actually do when they write, because all writers compose differently. We have organized the writing process in a way that we think will be helpful to beginning college writers; it should help you to focus attention on particular features of a piece of writing without feeling overwhelmed by all of the variables in a writing situation. As you progress in the course you will, we hope, develop a clearer and more defined sense of your own writing process, first by writing about it in your journal, and second by practicing writing papers for different purposes and in different situations.

YOUR WRITING TIME

Inexperienced writers often begin the writing process by deciding what their first sentence will be, then writing it. At this point, they have completed the predrafting stage and have already begun drafting. They then work their way slowly and laboriously through the draft—planning each sentence, writing it, then reading it back and making revisions or corrections. When they finish the last sentence, they perhaps give the work a quick overall look and then send it on its way. Such writers can be called "one-stage" writers. With little or no time given to predrafting or postdrafting, their writing process consists essentially of a slow, difficult drafting stage.

More experienced writers tend to divide their time more equally among the three stages in the "process" column, perhaps even spending more time at predrafting and postdrafting than at drafting. That is, they tend to do more planning before they actually begin their drafts than inexperienced writers do, and they tend to do more revising and correcting after they finish their drafts. In between, they may do less planning and revising sentence by sentence during the drafting stage: their drafts may be "quick and dirty."

This book will encourage you to divide your writing time that way, and it will provide specific advice on how to do so. By keeping your predrafting, drafting, and postdrafting in proportion, you will have a more efficient writing process and will produce better written products.

One way to understand why this is true is by comparing writing with house building. Imagine a person who decides to build a vacation house on the shore of a lake. On his first visit to the site, he is struck by the view across the water and decides that what he wants most of all in the house is a large picture window. So he drives into town, buys a preframed picture window, and brings it out to the lot. Then realizing that he needs a section of wall to hold the window up, he buys a few boards and a handful of nails, and builds a little wall. But the wall needs a foundation, so he lays a short length of concrete blocks and fastens the wall and window to them. He then paints the wall and window, and hangs curtains. Now he is ready to decide what he wants next in the house—perhaps a bathroom.

No one, of course, builds houses that way: such a process would be an enormous waste of time and money, and it would result in houses that don't hold together very well. But that is precisely the way many inexperienced writers write. Each of their sentences is like the picture window—planned, constructed, and finished before moving on to the next component of the product. The result for the writer, as for the house builder, is an inefficient use of time and an inferior result.

Better house builders, like better writers, divide their time more sensibly. Given a year to build a vacation house, they spend several months before ever putting hammer to nail. They use that time well, defining the needs to be met by the house (How many people must it sleep? Does it need to be heated?), drawing increasingly detailed plans, and buying materials. Then, when actual construction begins, it can go fairly quickly, without frequent stops for further planning, and certainly without interruptions to paint walls or hang curtains. Such finishing activities can come later, in the last several months of the year, as the house is readied for its users.

A second way to understand the need for proportion of the stages in the writing process is to consider the psychology of writing. Within the brain, writing involves two very different activities. One activity is the "mechanical" process of translating ideas into hand motions—the process of thinking, for example, of a small furry animal that purrs, and translating that thought into the hand and finger movements that result in the word *cat* appearing on a piece of paper or a computer screen. That process is an extraordinarily complex one, involving a relatively large section of the brain. We might call that part of the mind the "internal writer."

The other mental activity involved in writing is a more "supervisory" one: looking out at the world and deciding what to say to it, and looking at the emerging piece of writing and deciding how well it fulfills its task. That supervisory function is very much like the role played by newspaper editors: they assign stories, then read and evaluate them. So we might call this part of the writing mind the "internal editor."

Imagine yourself as a newspaper writer, the first day on the job. Your boss assigns you a story, and you sit down at your keyboard. As you hesitatingly type the first words of the piece, you hear a voice behind you:

"What a lousy way to begin a story!" You look up and find that your boss, the editor, is looking over your shoulder, watching you work. You delete the words you just typed and start again. "A little better," the editor says; "let's see where it goes next." You continue, nervously. "What?!" your boss exclaims. "Don't they teach you people to spell anymore?!" And so on. Word by word, page by page, through the story, your editor reads and criticizes as you write.

Few writers could work under those conditions. Yet those are the very conditions that many inexperienced writers impose on themselves. As one-stage writers, they force their internal writer and their internal editor to work simultaneously, with the latter criticizing the former every word of the way. The resulting internal conflict only adds to the difficulty of the writing process and subtracts from the quality of the written product. (Actually, we have internal editors that interfere with all kinds of activities; the poet e. e. cummings was surely speaking of one kind of internal editor when he wrote "since feeling is first / who pays any attention / to the syntax of things / will never wholly kiss you.")

Good newspaper editors, of course, do not read over their reporters' shoulders: they make careful, thorough assignments, then get out of the way. Only after the reporter has produced a draft do they get back on the scene, to make corrections and suggest revisions. Many good writers make their internal editors behave that way too. They learn to make their internal editor do careful, thorough planning in the predrafting stage, then get out of the way during drafting, to let the internal writer do its job without interference. Then at the postdrafting stage, they let their internal editor come back to oversee the revising and correcting.

So to have a more efficient, effective writing process, you do not necessarily need to learn many new techniques. Instead, you may simply need to take much of the planning you are already doing sentence by sentence during the drafting stage and move it into the predrafting stage. Similarly, you may need to take much of the revising and correcting you are already doing sentence by sentence during the drafting stage and move it into the postdrafting stage. As a result of these moves, your written products will almost surely become more successful.

We will suggest several strategies that may be new to you and helpful in the writing process. Use your journal to experiment with these strategies when you begin a writing assignment, and use the strategies that work best for you as a writer. There are many ways to keep in good physical condition, for example, but we do not all practice the same techniques: some of us prefer rigorous walking, others racquetball, others basketball, and so on. The same is true with writing: we do not all use the same strategies when we write. As a beginning college writer, you should experiment with all of the strategies—and more than once—before you make decisions about what works for you and what does not.

Exercises

A. Consider the writing process *you* use. Use the questions below to reflect on your writing behavior. Read each question carefully, and take as many notes as you can. Then, in your journal, write a description of your writing process.

1. How do you prepare for writing a paper? What do you do to get started writing? Do you talk with others about your ideas? Do you read related material? What environment do you write best in? Do you write best at home, at work, in the library? Do you use a certain kind of paper? Write with a certain kind of pen or pencil? Use a word processor?

2. We have described the writing process as consisting of three stages: predrafting, drafting, and postdrafting. Are you usually a one-stage writer, or do you go through various stages? At which stage do you spend most of your time when you work on a writing assignment? Explain.

3. Once you begin writing a paper, how would you describe your composing process? Do you write a paragraph or two, and then rewrite? Do you frequently pause to read what you have written? Do you write a complete first draft and then reread? Do you start with the introduction? In the middle? Do you write for long periods? How often do you take breaks?

4. What do you do when you revise? Do you proofread? Do you change words and correct punctuation? Do you revise often or at different times? Do you make major changes to adjust for focus or audience? Do you have others read and comment on what you have written? Must you see your paper in typed form before you can revise?

5. How does your writing process vary with different writing tasks?

B. The composing process—the act of communicating thoughts and feeling to others—is not unique to writers. Writers, like other "composers," experience the creative process in surprisingly similar ways, whether it be through the medium of words, color, sound, or motion. Visit with someone who is not a writer by trade but who does participate, in some way, in communicating thoughts, ideas, feelings, etc. (e.g., a musician, a dancer, an artist, an actor or actress, a choreographer, etc.). In your journal, describe some of the similarities between your own writing process and the composing process of the person you visited. Focus on the similarities that were perhaps not obvious to you at the beginning.

The Written Product

FEATURES OF WRITING

The second goal of this book is to help you develop your ability to produce successful written *products*, pieces of writing. To be successful as a whole, a piece of writing must succeed in several different ways: it must be well organized, for example, have "good grammar," and be correctly spelled. Most of your past formal instruction in writing has probably focused on these and other features of written products.

However, research about writing suggests that most of what you have learned about written products did not come from formal instruction. Instead, you learned it informally from reading. Every comic book, every newspaper, every novel, every letter you have ever read has contributed to your knowledge of how writing looks, sounds, and "feels." So an important way for you to become a better writer is to keep *reading*.

What formal instruction—like this textbook—can add to your knowledge of written products are new ways of thinking about them. To think of pieces of writing in new ways, you should look separately at the various features every piece of writing has. One way to classify these features is shown in the middle column of the chart in Figure 1. This column lists seven features of any written work, from a one-paragraph memo to a multivolume encyclopedia. These seven features will be the subjects of this book's seven chapters.

The first feature of a piece of writing is its overall sense of the writing *situation*. No written product exists in isolation, created out of nothing. Instead, every piece of writing is written by somebody, for somebody (even if that somebody is the writer), about something, and for some reason. That is, every piece of writing has a writer, a reader, a subject, and a purpose. For example, if you were writing a complaint letter to your apartment landlord about unsafe living conditions in your apartment, you might think of yourself as an "apartment building tenant," your reader as an "apartment building landlord," your subject as "the unsafe living conditions in your apartment," and your purpose as "to convince your landlord that immediate action is needed."

To be successful, a piece of writing must take its writer, reader, subject, and purpose into account; it must meet all the needs of its situation. In your complaint letter, for example, you might succeed in informing your landlord of the unsafe conditions in your apartment, but you may also end up with your name at the *bottom* of a list of tenants whose apartments need repairs. In other words, by not attending to your purpose—one of the components of the writing situation—you might achieve only a portion of what you set out to achieve. Chapter One is designed to help you analyze and clarify the writing situations you encounter as a writer.

The second feature listed in the diagram is *content*: what the piece of writing says. In your letter to your apartment landlord, for example, you would probably describe the location and extent of damage in your apartment, such as the loose ceiling plaster in the master bedroom, the exposed electrical wires under the kitchen sink, or the backed-up sewer line. To be successful, a piece of writing must carry such information, of enough quantity and quality to fulfill its purpose. Chapter Two offers help on collecting information to use as the content of your writing.

The third feature in the middle column of the diagram is *organization*, the order in which the piece of writing is arranged. For example, you may decide that in your complaint letter the best organizational scheme for your descriptive list of repairs is the order of increasing importance. In this way, when your landlord finishes reading your letter, he or she will have in mind the most serious damage and, consequently, will be persuaded to act promptly. The psychological principle operating here is that what comes last in your letter is probably what the reader is going to remember best. Successful writing is arranged in the order that helps it best achieve its purpose, with special care given to what is said in the beginning, middle, and end of the written product. Chapter Three helps you better organize the material you write.

The fourth feature in the diagram is *paragraphs*, the groups of sentences into which most writing is divided. The number of paragraphs in a piece of writing can, of course, vary widely, as you will see when you read some of the sample student papers included in this book. But however many paragraphs you use, a successful written product usually has paragraphs that are organized and cohesive; that is, their sentences are well ordered and "stick together." Chapter Four gives advice on how to achieve these qualities in your paragraphs.

The fifth feature of a written product is the *sentences* themselves. Sentences can vary in length and in style: they can range from short and simple constructions to long and rather complex structures. Successful writing is made up of sentences that are grammatically correct, meaning they are formed according to the rules of standard edited American English. Successful sentences are also purposeful, meaning they are constructed to give emphasis to important ideas and to fit cohesively with the sentences that come before and after them. Chapter Five is designed to help you write grammatical, effective, and coherent sentences.

The sixth feature of any piece of writing is the *words* that compose it. To be successful, each word must have both the right denotation (meaning) and the right connotation (shade of meaning). *Girl* and *woman* both denote someone of the female sex, but they each suggest different meanings. *Girl*, for example, suggests youthfulness and perhaps immaturity, whereas *woman* connotes adulthood and responsibility. It is important, therefore, to be mindful not only of what your words say but also of what your words suggest. Chapter Six provides help with choosing words to use in your writing.

Finally, the seventh feature listed in the diagram is *mechanics*: spelling, punctuation, and other such concerns. It is important that you allow yourself ample time to edit your writing; otherwise, your readers may be distracted by the appearance of your paper and not pay much attention to its content. Revising the mechanics of your paper is one way to make your writing appealing to your readers. Chapter Seven offers help with making your writing mechanically successful.

PRIORITIES IN WRITING

In the middle column of the diagram in Figure 1, the seven features are listed roughly in order of decreasing "size." Although it may not seem to make sense to talk about the "size" of the writing situation, the content, or the organization, these surely are features that involve the whole piece of writing. The other four features do get smaller as we move down the column: paragraphs are parts of whole pieces of writing, sentences are parts of paragraphs, words are parts of sentences, and mechanics are concerned with what happens within and between words. "Size," however, does not equal importance: success in all seven features is necessary for a successful piece of writing, and no single feature is intrinsically more or less important than the others.

Still, the order of the features in the middle column has a significance beyond mere "size." In general, these features are listed in order of priority of *concern*: the order in which, roughly, they must be attended to. Without a sense of the writing situation, for example, it is very difficult to make decisions about content or organization. Without specific sentences and words, it is impossible to determine spelling and punctuation.

PROCESS AND PRODUCT

The relationship between the first two columns of the diagram in Figure 1 is significant. The alignment of these two columns should remind you that certain features of the written product are best attended to at certain stages of the writing process. The overall sense of situation, for example, is probably best considered at the predrafting stage, whereas mechanics should be almost entirely a postdrafting concern. However, as the diagonal lines in the left-hand column suggest, all features may be handled at more than one stage of the process. Writing, after all, is not a rigid, step-by-step activity; as we have seen in the first column of the diagram, it certainly is not. It does make sense, however, to be concerned about some features before others; some writers, for example, are probably held back from writing as well as they can, because they worry about mechanical concerns too early.

You may use these two columns to translate what you know, or are told, about your written *products* into advice for yourself on your writing *process*. Without such translation, you can often go wrong: if, for example, you have problems spelling correctly, you may become so self-conscious while drafting that many other features of your work may suffer too. Instead, you should realize that mechanics is largely a postdrafting matter; you should not worry about spelling while you draft, but learn techniques for proofreading and correcting your spelling at the postdrafting stage. Likewise, if you produce papers that are ineffectively organized, you might consider doing more detailed organizational planning at the predrafting stage of the process.

Exercises

A. In past writing courses you have taken, which features of a piece of writing have been emphasized? Which, if any, have been neglected? Respond to these questions in your journal.

B. The following statements refer to specific features of the piece of writing you just read: the "Written Product" section of this chapter. To which of the seven general features in the middle column of the diagram in Figure 1 does each belong? What are the reasons for your decision?

1. The spelling of the word *successful.*
2. The order of the three main sections: "Features," "Priorities," and "Relationships."
3. The choice of the word *product* instead of the word *artifact.*
4. The structure of the second sentence.
5. The fact that the writing appears in a textbook.
6. The agreement in number between the subject (*order*) and the verb (*has*) in the first sentence of the second paragraph of the "Priorities" section.
7. The way the section begins.
8. The order of sentences in the next-to-last paragraph.
9. The sense (or lack thereof) that the writing was done by two particular authors, with particular personalities.
10. The truth or falsity of the final sentence.

C. At which stage(s) of the writing process—predrafting, drafting, or postdrafting—might each of the following activities be best performed? What are the reasons for your decision?

1. Collecting any information you need for the writing.
2. Getting a beginning sense of your audience.
3. Reviewing a paragraph to see if it has enough transition words.
4. Getting a general idea of how to start and end the piece of writing.
5. Checking for subject-verb agreement.
6. Determining the purpose of your writing.
7. Putting sentences down on paper.
8. Deciding between two words with approximately the same meaning.
9. Deciding the order in which you will present your main points.
10. Making sure a word is spelled correctly.

D. With which features of your written product do you have the most difficulty? For example, do you have problems with content, or organization, or sentences? Write a response in your journal. Afterward, reread the description of your writing process that you wrote in an earlier exercise, and in your journal describe how you could change or develop your writing process to address some of the difficulties that you experience when you write.

The Writer's Power

The third goal of this book is to help you develop your understanding of the writer's *power*. Inexperienced writers may not feel that they have very much power over their writing. Such writers may feel that writing is largely a matter of following rules—*dos* and *don'ts*.

To be sure, there *are* many rules, or conventions, about writing: subjects and verbs must usually agree in number, for example, and most words must be spelled only one way. Not all these conventions make very much sense— no more sense, for example, than the convention that women's coats have the buttons on the left side, whereas men's coats have them on the right side. The conventions of writing, like the conventions of clothing, are simply practices that most people agree to follow.

Writers have the power of choice, however, about many other things. There are no conventions, for example, about precisely how many sentences must go in a paragraph. As the third column of the chart in Figure 1 reminds us, successful writing involves both choices and conventions. Good writers learn which are which.

RULES AND TOOLS

In learning about choices and conventions, writers need both *rules* and *tools*. *Rules* are what we learn to help us follow conventions: "*i* before *e* except after *c*," for example. In the early school years, a considerable number of such rules must be learned—so many that it is no wonder that many students regard writing as *nothing but* following rules.

In later school years, more and more *tools* are introduced: these are pieces of advice that help writers make better choices, not just follow conventions. Tools do not tell writers what they must do every time; instead tools tell writers what they *might* do to make their writing more effective. However, students (and even teachers) sometimes confuse these tools with rules.

For example, many students and some teachers believe that there is a rule against ending sentences with prepositions. To be sure, avoiding final prepositions is good advice, for they often weaken sentences. Yet many good writers ignore this "rule," finding that a preposition is sometimes the most effective way for a sentence to end. So the "rule" is not really a rule at all, but a tool, to be used as needed.

This book will attempt to distinguish tools from rules. Especially in its chapters on sentences, words, and mechanics, it will separate conventions from choices, giving you rules for the former and tools for the latter.

PROCESS, PRODUCT, AND POWER

Just as the alignment of the first two columns of the chart is significant, so is the alignment of the third column with the other two. The diagonal line separating "choices" from "conventions" in that third column reminds us that, in general, choices decrease and conventions increase as we move from earlier to later stages of the writing process and from larger to smaller features of the written product. There are few conventions, for example, about situation and content, but many about words (the dictionary is a whole book of word conventions) and mechanics.

By increasing your knowledge of conventions and choices, or rules and tools in writing, this book will help you develop greater understanding of your power as a writer. And you *do* have power as a writer, in a larger sense as well. Writing gives you the power to move others to action, to express your views in response to an issue, and to accomplish your career goals. Whether you are writing a letter to your landlord, a letter to the editor of a newspaper, or a paper for a history class, writing is power.

THE WRITER'S JOURNAL

One way to develop your power as a writer is to start keeping a writer's journal. In some of the earlier exercises, we suggested topics to get you started writing in your journal and thinking of yourself as a writer. Here we will suggest other ways of using your journal to gain greater control of your writing and a growing sense of your own power to communicate. Of course, you should check with your instructor to see if he or she has specific guidelines—or specific kinds of activities—for your journal writing.

First of all, you might ask: What is a journal? Very simply, it is a spiral notebook, or a binder with looseleaf paper, that the writer identifies as his or her journal. The journal is the writer's work space—where the writer lets ideas flow onto the page in a style and form that meet the writer's needs. Because the content of a journal is intended for the writer and not the reader, it is what you say that really counts, not how you say it.

Occasionally you may be asked to share something you have written in your journal with one of your peers, so at times you may need to write with your peer-readers in mind. Most of the time, however, any writing you do will be for your own purposes as a practicing writer. If what you write is meaningful to you, then it fulfills its purpose. The journal is the home of expressive writing, which is any writing that serves to benefit the writer.

Writing about Ideas. Teachers of writing often require students to write in their journals on a regular basis. You may be encouraged to write about subjects that interest you, about ideas that provoke responses—in short, about anything that you deem important or useful. Getting into the habit of writing in your journal on a regular basis is good for at least three reasons: (1) it gives you continued practice in writing, (2) it enables you to identify some of the topics that interest you and to discover your own thinking on these topics, and (3) it provides a sourcebook of ideas for you to consider when you are searching for a paper topic.

To help students get started writing in their journals, teachers will sometimes provide a list of topics. Then if you are stuck without something to write about, you can review the list and choose a topic that interests you. But finding a topic on your own is not difficult if you have the right mind-set. After all, you are bombarded with information every day, and if you make it a practice to write in your journal routinely, you will train your ear to listen to, and your eye to focus on, potential topics. One day you might summarize a news article you read at the breakfast table or an interview you heard on public radio, another day you might outline some of your ideas for a paper in a history or philosophy class, another day you might react to a stimulating lecture in psychology or respond to a thought-provoking quotation, another day you might write about your experience being confronted by a streetperson asking for change, and the list can go on and on. Writing on a variety of topics in your journal will not only strengthen your skills as a writer but also build your confidence level. You will discover that you do have ideas to share, and as you explore your thinking on a variety of subjects, you will begin to develop a sense of your own power as a writer.

Regardless of what goes into your journal, it should be substantive and lead to greater understanding of the subject—perhaps to some tentative generalization about the topic or about human behavior and events. This is an important point because invariably some students will write about how they spent their Saturday morning, or what they did Friday evening—a kind of itinerary of activities. If you find yourself writing simply an account of your activities—or about anything personal—ask yourself *why*. Why am I recounting what I did on Saturday morning? Why is this important or significant? What is my motivation for writing about this topic? Am I retelling the events of last night to draw some conclusion, to better understand myself or other people, or am I merely filling space on the page? By asking yourself these questions, you will force yourself to bring to the surface the larger meaning that may lie hidden in your subject. In writing about what you did on Saturday morning, you may discover that you are really saying something about your work habits or the activities you value in your leisure time.

A recent student, for example, wrote a detailed description of her bedroom in her journal, and when asked *why*, she said that she really hadn't thought much about why she was describing her bedroom. The topic occurred to her, so she began writing about it. When she began to think about her motivation, she discovered that what she was really saying was that her bedroom reflected parts of her personality. That turned out to be the hidden meaning behind the description of her bedroom.

Writing about Writing. Besides writing about topics of interest, you can also use your journal to reflect on your own process of composing. We have already suggested some exercises to get you started writing about your own behavior as a writer. You should continue to reflect on your composing process as you develop your writing skills.

Your journal is also the place to write about your writing projects. If you have difficulty getting started on a writing assignment, for example, you might use your journal to get your ideas—your thinking—out on paper. Often, it is easier to begin a paper after you have seen some of your ideas on the page. Any predrafting on a writing assignment is appropriate for your journal. Remember that your journal is your own work space.

Your journal is also useful at the drafting and postdrafting stages. For example, if you are in the middle of a piece of writing and you cannot decide what to say next, you can use your journal as a place to clarify your confusion or to solve specific problems. In composition courses, where students spend most of their time writing, the journal can serve as a testing ground for ideas and for problem solving—from lists of information, outlines, charts, and diagrams to longer and more carefully written passages.

Collecting Peer Responses to Your Writing. Finally, many students like to reserve space in their journals for peer responses to their writing. Sometimes your teacher may ask you to write in your journal about a particular topic and be prepared to share it with your peers. And when you begin to exchange drafts of papers, usually not in your journal but on separate sheets of paper, you may still want to use your journal to collect peer responses. By using a part of your journal for your peers' observations and reactions to your writing, you can easily review their comments when you prepare to revise a piece of writing; you can also begin to work out revision strategies in your journal that address some of the concerns your peers raise.

Organizing Your Journal. Because the journal is a place for many different kinds of writing, it is important that you have a system for organizing the content of your journal. Your instructor may have specific guidelines for you to follow. Here are some suggestions you may want to consider:

1. When you write in your journal, consider using only one side of the page; leave the other side blank for your peers and your instructor to record their observations and comments, or for any ideas you decide to add later. An alternative is to write on only the top half of the page, leaving the bottom half blank. Using one of these methods you will have ample space in your journal for peer commentary or for subsequent reflections.

2. Always date each entry in your journal, and give it a topic. If you are writing about an environmental issue, for example, label the entry with a topic—whether it be hazardous waste or chemical spills—and include the date. This method will enable you to find information quickly when you need it.

Also, consider dividing your journal into sections: Writing about Ideas, Writing about Writing, and Peer Responses.

3. When your instructor or one of your peers responds to something you have written in your journal or to one of your drafts, and, conversely, when you do the same for one of your peers, use the same formatting guidelines: date each entry, label it with an appropriate topic (e.g., Response to draft of Essay 1), and sign your name.

4. When you are ready to draft a piece of writing, write it elsewhere than in your journal; save your journal for prewriting, other expressive writing, and peer commentary.

5. Be sure to check with your instructor for other specific requirements relating to your journal.

Exercises

A. Consider the "rules" you have learned about writing. When, and under what circumstances, did you learn them? Have any been contradicted by other teachers or textbooks? Are there any that you have later learned to regard as tools, not rules?

B. In your opinion, is each of the following directives a rule or a tool? What are the reasons for your decision?

1. Spell *receive* with the *e* before the *i*.

2. Have good transitions between sentences.

3. Do not begin a sentence with the word *And* or *But*.

4. Be specific in your descriptions.

5. Have a clear sense of your reader.

6. Put commas and periods inside closing quotation marks.

7. Do not use *principle* to mean "chief," as in "the *principle* idea."

8. Have a clear beginning, middle, and end.

9. Vary the length of your sentences.

10. In general, choose simple words rather than complex ones.

C. To which of the seven features of the written product does each of the rules and tools in Exercise B refer?

D. Describe a writing situation that you have experienced in which you felt or discovered the power of writing.

E. How does a knowledge of your process as a writer help you discover the power of writing?

CHAPTER ONE

The Process of Situating Your Writing

As mentioned in the introduction, no piece of writing exists in a vacuum; all writing occurs within a *situation*. That is, every piece of writing is written by someone; it has a writer. It is written *for* someone, a reader, even if that reader is the writer himself or herself. It is written about something; that is, it has a subject of some kind. And it is written for some reason; it has a purpose. So a writing situation comprises a *writer*, a *reader*, a *subject*, and a *purpose*. In Amy's paper at the end of this chapter, for example, the writer is Amy, a state officer in Future Homemakers of America (FHA); her intended readers are FHA members; her subject is the steps in applying for state offices in the organization; and her purpose is to inform her readers of that process.

Sometimes, less experienced writers forget the importance of the writing situation. They sometimes think of a piece of writing as something that can be good or bad in isolation, without any concern for the world around it. That attitude probably comes from school classrooms, where the writing situation is often a very limited one. In many classroom situations, the only role being played by writers is the role of student, the only reader is the teacher, the only subject is what has been assigned, and the only purpose is to demonstrate knowledge of a subject, in writing that is clear and coherent.

In the world outside the classroom, however, writing situations are far more varied. Writing is done by people in a great many roles: as reporters, salespersons, attorneys, law-enforcement officers, engineers, managers, poets, and thousands of others. Readers vary just as widely, from first-graders struggling through their first textbooks to physicians studying medical journals to keep up with the latest developments in their specialties. The subject matter of non-classroom writing also varies enormously, covering all of human thought and feeling. And purposes for writing vary greatly, as well, from selling detergent to trying to achieve world peace.

The fact that you are now enrolled in a college composition course, and writing papers for an instructor who ultimately must evaluate your written work, may confuse some of you when you begin to think about defining a writing situation. For example, if Amy had not been instructed to imagine a context for her writing, she might have defined her writing situation in the following way:

Writer: Amy, a student in a college composition class.

Reader: My college composition instructor.

Subject: Steps in applying for an FHA state office.

Purpose: To demonstrate my writing ability.

Amy, of course, would have been thinking only of the classroom situation, in which she is writing a paper so that her instructor can evaluate the quality of her written work. And in many college courses that Amy takes, she will be required to write papers solely for the teacher, who is both reader and evaluator. However, teachers of composition and increasing numbers of teachers across the curriculum are beginning to see the limitations of "classroom" writing. They want their students to experience writing in different situations and for different purposes. For example, a history teacher may still require students to write a paper about political reforms in the former Soviet Union, but he or she may go one step further and prescribe a "real life" situation or invite the student to imagine a situation appropriate to the writing assignment. Such an assignment is the following:

You have been selected to join a group of students who will be attending a national conference on the theme of *perestroika*. When you return to campus, you must write a report about recent social reforms in the former Soviet Union; your report will be kept on file in the university library and be required reading for students who enroll in History 290.

It is important to keep the writing situation in mind at all times—even if it is writing a paper principally for the teacher as evaluator. When given a specific writing situation or when asked to define your own, you will need to put the classroom purposes of the assignment in the back of your mind and concentrate on the demands of the specific writing situation. Otherwise, you may produce writing that is not suited to the specific requirements of the assignment—however "good" it might otherwise be.

So only by considering these variables in the writing situation—writer, reader, subject, and purpose—can we even begin to evaluate whether a given piece of writing is successful or not. Amy's piece of writing is successful only to the extent that it helps FHA members apply for state office. Christina's piece of writing—also at the end of this chapter—is successful only to the extent that it informs students about a helpful employment service on the IUPUI campus. A piece of writing that works well for one kind of reader may fail totally with another. Only by considering these variables during the writing process can we produce pieces of writing that do succeed.

Predrafting: Defining the Situation

As the chart in Figure 1 suggests, the writing situation should be almost entirely a predrafting concern. It is possible, of course—and sometimes valuable—just to begin writing without thinking of what role you are playing as a writer, of who your reader will be, or of what your subject and purpose are. But even such exploratory writing has its own implied situation: the writer is writing as a kind of explorer, the reader is the writer himself or herself, the subject is the current content of the writer's mind, and the purpose, perhaps, is to discover possible subjects for other writing tasks. So, even for such seemingly directionless writing, it may be helpful to begin by defining what the situation is. Alternatively, you may already know your subject and have thought about your role as writer and about your reader(s), but you may not have developed a clear sense of your purpose for writing. Any predrafting that you do, then, can be aimed at discovering your purpose. Often, writers need to see their ideas on paper, in tangible form, to develop a complete picture of the writing situation.

For most kinds of writing—letters, articles, reports, for example— defining the situation at the predrafting stage will greatly simplify the writing task. If this activity is postponed until the drafting or postdrafting stage, it will probably mean more revision and hence more time.

If the concept of defining a writing situation is new to you as a beginning college writer, it may be helpful to think for a moment about speech situations instead of writing situations. Every day you participate in different speech situations—talking with your parents, with your children, or with your professors—and each time, perhaps unconsciously, you use language differently. As a native speaker of the English language, you have a wealth of experience using the language in a variety of situations. Much of this knowledge of the language you know intuitively. The way you use language with children, for example, is very different from the way you use language with your roommate or with your teachers. In fact, researchers who have studied the language that adults use with children have termed it "caretaker speech" because of its unique characteristics. With a child, you speak in short, simple sentences with limited vocabulary; with your roommate, you may use idiomatic expressions or slang, and speak in ways unintelligible to children, or for that matter, to most adults not familiar with the current slang expressions. You use language differently—that is, you shift styles—in speech situations because you have developed a sensitivity to the particular speech situation. In a writing situation, you must bring this same sensitivity to bear on the particular writing assignment if you want your writing to be effective.

This process of defining the writing situation can also be subconscious and intuitive; for most experienced writers, this is probably the case. But less experienced writers, and occasionally even very seasoned writers, can profit from consciously and deliberately analyzing the writing situation in which they find themselves. Such analysis need not be particularly time-consuming; for many writing situations, the process of definition may take only two or three minutes: for example, before Christina began writing her paper, she took a minute or two to write down "I will be writing an instructional process about job hunting through the job employment office on campus for current IUPUI students." Those two or three minutes, however, may be the most important minutes in the whole writing process.

That's not to say that the writing process is a linear one. Even after defining the writing situation and writing the first draft, you may need to reconsider the writing situation before proceeding further with your paper. But learning as much as you can about the writing situation before you begin drafting your paper certainly makes the task easier.

THE WRITER: ROLES

The first variable in the writing situation is the writer, so one question to ask when beginning a writing task is, "Who is writing this?" That question may sound absurd: if you are starting a writing task, the writer is *you*. But think about it: all people play many roles in their lives. From moment to moment those roles may change, from student, to friend, to sibling, to employee. Each role brings its own demands: as we have seen, people may even talk differently in one role than in another.

The same is true of writing. As a writer, you will play many different roles. For example, your description of a party in your role as a son or daughter might be very different from your description of the same party in your role as friend, school newspaper reporter, or dormitory counselor. Each role requires that you be conscious of a particular image that you would like your reader to have of you. Let's suppose you are called into the Dean of Students' office for raucous behavior at a dormitory party in your first week of college. The dean informs you that such behavior at campus socials will not be tolerated. She then tells you that she expects a letter from you the next morning describing your behavior at the party and why it is inappropriate. In this letter to the dean, you would probably assume the role of student, one who is mature and responsible, and one who has chosen to go to college for the right reasons. But if you were writing about your experience at the campus social to, say, a friend back home, your role as a writer would not be the same because your purpose and audience have changed.

One structured way to define the role you are playing as the writer of any given piece of writing is to use a model borrowed from the field of systems theory. The model suggests that writers and readers—like all people—are part of various social systems, groups of various kinds and sizes; the model further suggests that there are eight roles a member of such a system can play in communicating information.

To use this model, you first define for yourself the most significant "system" or group that you are identifying with as a writer. This group will often include your readers, but sometimes it will not. Are you writing as a member of a family, a campus organization, a congressional district, or a hobby or interest group? The system can be as small as two people, of course, or as large as a whole society, but by defining the system for yourself, you bring to the writing task an important sense of *community* with your readers, or with others on whose behalf you are writing. After you have identified a social system, then decide which of the following eight roles you, as a writer, are playing within that system. The eight roles are diagramed in Figure 2.

Lookout. The first possible role for a writer is a lookout. Like the lookout in the crow's nest of a sailing ship, a lookout brings information into a social system from outside. The diagram of this role shows an arrow coming into a circle, representing information moving from outside to inside a social system.

In sample 1B, Christina is playing a lookout role as she writes to her fellow students about the procedure for finding a job through the campus employment agency, which she assumes lies outside their immediate shared social system.

Decoder. Sometimes, of course, a lookout can bring information into a group directly. At other times, however, the information must be changed, or "decoded," to make it understandable and usable by members of the group. To maintain the "ship" analogy, the decoding role may be thought of as the role played by the crew member who sees the signal flags of another ship, and translates them into messages for his own captain and fellow crew members. The diagram represents this decoding process with two arrows, one inside the circle and one outside, both arrows connected with a dotted line symbolizing the "decoding" of information.

Although Mike, in sample 1C, is playing a lookout role in writing about the compact-disc player, with which he assumes most readers are only vaguely familiar, it can be argued that he is also playing the role of the decoder. That is, he is sharing his knowledge of compact-disc players so that others less familiar with the new technology can make informed decisions as consumers.

Spokesperson. The first two roles you have seen involve bringing information into a social system from outside; these next two involve the reverse. A

Figure 2 - Writer Roles

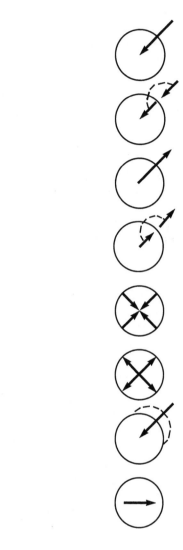

Lookout

Decoder

Spokesperson

Encoder

Pollster

Decider

Memory

Messenger

spokesperson "speaks for" a social system in taking information to the world outside. The captain of the ship, for example, may send an officer ashore at a foreign port to convey greetings and request docking rights. As the diagram shows, this role can be thought of as the opposite of the lookout role.

In the hypothetical example used in the opening chapter, the apartment tenant is being a spokesperson for her family, complaining to the apartment landlord about unsafe conditions in the apartment.

Encoder. This fourth role also involves taking information out of a social system, but this time in a changed, or encoded, form, so that it will be more useful to those outside. On a ship, the crew member sending the flag signals will be putting messages into a "code" for transmission. The diagram shows that this role is, of course, the opposite of the decoder role.

As professional writers and researchers, for example, we are serving in the role of encoders: we are encoding information generated within our social system and are communicating it to you, the beginning college writer, in a way that will be comprehensible and useful.

Pollster. Whereas the first four roles have involved moving information *across* the boundaries of a social system, the remaining four involve moving information *within* those boundaries. One way to move information within a social system is to bring it together to one point. When a writer performs that activity of collecting information, we can call that role a pollster. A ship's captain, collecting advice from the other officers, is playing that pollster role.

If you are working in a collaborative group in your composition class and your instructor asks you to report on your group's discussion, you would be playing a pollster role. You would be listening carefully to the viewpoints expressed in your group and then writing a summary of them for your instructor.

Decider. The reverse of the pollster role is the decider role, sending out information from a point within a social system. A ship's captain, issuing orders to the crew, is playing a decider role.

As a state officer in FHA, Amy is playing a decider role in sample 1A. Although she may not have actually made the decisions about the procedures for applying for state office, as a writer she is communicating those decisions to her fellow members of the social system that is the organization.

Memory. Some writing is done not to communicate information to readers in the present time but to preserve it for future readers; the relative permanence of writing is one of its major advantages over spoken language. A captain writing in a ship's log is clearly playing this role.

Sometimes, writers play a memory role as a follow-up to oral communication. If, for example, Amy had already spoken to members of the FHA organization about procedures for applying for state office, then her paper (sample 1A) simply documents those procedures for future reference. In that case, she can be said to be playing a memory role.

Messenger. Finally, some writing is done just to move information from one point in a social system to another point, as when a crew member is assigned to take a message from one ship's officer to another. Many letter writers are, of course, playing this role.

Suppose you are a student in nursing and are applying for a scholarship offered by your department. In this instance, you would be carrying information about yourself—your qualifications for the scholarship—from one point in that social system (yourself) to another (the scholarship committee).

Naturally, these roles are not clear-cut, and you should feel free to disagree with some of the examples already mentioned. The purpose of this tool, however, is not to establish an objective set of mutually exclusive categories but to help you, as a writer, think in new ways about the many roles you play.

Exercises

A. For each of the roles defined in the preceding list, describe a writing situation in which *you* have played that role. Be prepared to discuss these situations.

B. Using the sample papers at the end of this chapter, list the role(s) the writers may be playing. Be prepared to discuss the reasons for your choices.

C. Tell which role(s) the writer would play in each of the following writing situations:

1. A letter to a friend about your vacation to Aruba.
2. A paper written in your English composition class describing a measuring instrument used in biological experiments.
3. A letter to the editor of a local newspaper responding to an editorial commending the president's education proposals.
4. A note to your teacher outlining the progress made by your collaborative group on a given assignment.
5. A telephone message for a member of your family.
6. A report to your supervisor about a professional meeting you attended.
7. A proposal to the university administrators for longer visiting hours in your student dormitory.

D. As you begin to consider possible subjects for the writing assignment at the end of this chapter, use your journal to write about the possible roles you could play as a writer.

THE READER: KNOWLEDGE, ATTITUDES,
AND EXPECTATIONS

The second variable in the writing situation is the reader, so another question you need to ask yourself when you define your writing situation is "Who is my reader?" Writing, by definition, is done to be read, even if only by the writer himself or herself. Therefore, this question may be the most important question about any piece of writing.

Some writers, however, may not feel comfortable writing for specific readers in the early stages of their writing. Having to write with a view toward the reader may be too restrictive—may, in fact, impede the flow of ideas onto the page. They may prefer to get their ideas down on paper and not have to be concerned with what may or may not be appropriate for the particular reader. For such writers, getting to know the needs of the reader comes later in the writing process.

But a concern for what may or may not be appropriate for your readers cannot be overlooked. At some point, the writer must examine his or her piece of writing in relation to what he or she knows about the readers. Learning as much as you can about your readers will enable you to tailor your writing to suit their particular needs. Suppose you were trying to sell your used car, and you knew that a prospective buyer was interested in a second automobile to commute to and from work in the city. You probably would not call attention to the blasts of sound produced by the oversized stereo speakers mounted behind the rear seat or to the engine modifications designed to increase horsepower. Instead, you would probably point out the quality of the tires, the economical gas consumption, and the overall dependability of the car. That is, you would emphasize those features that you think would most appeal to the prospective buyer.

One of us recently wrote a proposal for a research fellowship offered by an external funding agency. The application stated that the agency was interested in funding theoretical, rather than practical, research. So even though his research study had many interesting practical applications, he wrote the proposal to emphasize ways in which it would contribute to the development of a theory. Knowing what he did about the expressed needs of the organization, he produced what he considered to be a very good proposal.

But writing the proposal was only part of the application procedure. Another part was getting other people in the field to write letters of support, evaluating the research project and its specific contributions. He therefore sent copies of his proposal to various people in the profession who had agreed to write recommendations for him. The application process was now complete. He had done everything according to the guidelines given in the application. He wrote his proposal, selected referees who knew his work well, made certain they each received a copy of the proposal, and mailed the completed application before the deadline. He now had only to wait for the decision.

Weeks later it occurred to him that he had overlooked an important detail: when he mailed his proposal to each of his referees, he forgot to include information about the organization and its particular needs. How will they know what kinds of research proposals the organization is interested in funding? Will their recommendation letters, the supporting information that forms an integral part of the application, reflect the same emphasis on theory that he was careful to express in his proposal? If they do not, then his chances of receiving the fellowship are lessened considerably—all because he omitted information that would have enabled his referees to write with a clearer sense of the readers' needs.

This example demonstrates how important an awareness of the reader is to successful communication. Though the letters of support may strongly recommend the research project, if they do not address the expressed needs of the readers, they will raise questions about the focus of the research project—enough to warrant the project's rejection.

As a writer, then, it is important to consider how well your piece of writing suits your reader(s). Of course, if you have defined your role as a writer, you have already begun to consider who your reader is. But there are still some important questions to ask about your reader(s). Three of the most important questions are "What is my reader's knowledge?" "What are my reader's attitudes?" and "What are my reader's expectations?"

Knowledge. One way to define your readers' knowledge is in terms of their general reading ability. Some readers will simply be able to handle more difficult vocabulary and more complex sentence structures than other readers. Therefore, an article written for the *New York Times* will be very different from an article on the same subject written for the *Weekly Reader*, an elementary school newspaper. In Chapter Six, you will learn a formula for measuring the approximate reading level of your writing.

But an even more important way to define your readers' knowledge is in terms of their understanding of the subject matter of your particular piece of writing. This understanding may not have much to do with your readers' general educational or reading level; you may sometimes be writing to less educated readers about a subject very familiar to them, whereas at other times you may be writing to very educated readers about an unfamiliar subject.

In Mike's introduction to buying a compact-disc player (sample 1C), he assumes that his readers have very little specific knowledge of his subject matter; that, after all, is why they are reading this piece of writing. Conversely, in Amy's paper (sample 1A) about applying for state office in the FHA, she assumes that her readers already have considerable knowledge of the organization; she writes about the process of running for a state office in order to encourage members to accept the challenge.

By considering what your reader already knows about your subject, you can focus more easily on the information you want to add to your reader's understanding of the subject. It may be helpful to think about this distinction in terms of *given* and *new* information. What you can assume your reader already knows is *given*, or *known*, information. The information you introduce to your reader—information you assume is not known by your readers—is *new* information. By keeping *given* and *new* information separate in your own mind when you write, you will have greater control of your focus because you will be writing with a knowledge of what your readers need to know.

Notice in sample 1B how Christina, in her first paragraph and part of her second, begins her paper with information that she assumes is *given*, or *known*, information, and afterward introduces *new* information:

> Mike is a new student at IUPUI. He just registered for classes and is all set to begin in the fall, but he does have one problem: he needs a job.
>
> For Mike, finding a job that will work around his schedule won't be an easy task, but as a student at IUPUI, he has a great resource to help him find a job, and if you are like Mike, it could help you too.
>
> The program is called JOBS, which stands for Job Opportunities for Businesses and Students, and it is located in the Business Building in Room 2010.

Christina uses *given* information as a means of orienting the reader to her subject: the *given* information "sets the scene" for the new information that follows it. In assuming that her readers will easily identify with "Mike," who represents all students faced with the dilemma of having to find a job with work hours that are compatible with a course schedule, Christina succeeds in attracting her readers' attention by using information that is already familiar to them.

Attitudes. Another important question about your readers may concern their attitudes. What will they *feel* about what you are going to say to them? Will they like your message, dislike it, or feel neutral about it? What beliefs, emotions, or prejudices will they carry with them as they begin reading your writing?

In sample 1B, Christina assumes, for the most part, that her readers have a favorable attitude toward her message; otherwise they would not be reading her article. At the same time, she knows that to sustain her readers' interest in what she has to say, she needs to show how the campus employment office can be genuinely helpful. In contrast, someone writing about a controversial issue would assume that some readers would respond unfavorably to the writer's point of view; in an essay proposing mandatory AIDS testing, for example, a writer would need to anticipate opposing arguments in order to write convincingly.

In many cases, of course, writers can assume their readers will be neutral; in sample 1C, for example, Mike can probably assume that his readers will begin with no particular opinion, one way or the other, about his procedure for buying a compact-disc player.

One way to understand the importance of considering the reader's knowledge and attitudes is to consider that any piece of writing must be designed to change the reader's "image" of the world, in small or large ways. The term *image*, first used in this way by the economist and systems theorist Kenneth Boulding, and later adapted by writing specialists Richard Young, Anton Becker, and Kenneth Pike, refers to the "windows" through which all human beings view themselves and their world.

Some of these windows are biological: our sense organs perceive only a very small part of what is going on around us. The philosopher and designer Buckminster Fuller once reminded a lecture audience that information on the current wheat crop in the former Soviet Union was available in that very auditorium, if only there were a way to access it. Satellites were, at that very moment, photographing the crop and transmitting those photographs back to earth. The radio waves carrying those photographs were passing through the lecture hall, and through the bodies of everyone in the hall, but nobody had the right equipment to receive and decode the information. Radio waves lie outside the narrow frequency ranges detectable by human eyes and ears; like much else in our environment, such waves don't make it through our biological windows.

Yet there is much in the world around us that we do take in through our biological windows. What we see in nature, in the classroom, at a rock concert; what we hear and smell our first time camping out in the woods or walking along the beaches of the eastern shore; what we taste when we experience different foods for the first time—all of these combined are a part of who we are as individuals. Our sensory experiences are both similar and different in obvious and sometimes subtle ways.

Other windows are cultural. For example, an Oriental physician looking at a patient literally sees different things than a Western physician; they are simply looking for different things. A Floridian knows only one kind of snow—the wet stuff that falls from the sky and wreaks havoc for travelers—whereas an Eskimo (some would even say a Vermonter) knows many varieties of snow and can even name them. And still other windows are personal: a farmer looking at the clouds in the sky sees them very differently than an artist sees them. So for physiological, cultural, and personal reasons, each person looks at the world through a very narrow window indeed.

Each piece of writing also provides a window on the world; it expresses some of what the writer has seen through his or her window. The reader of that writing thus gets the chance to see the world not only through his or her own window, but also the window of the writer. As a result, the reader's window is shifted or expanded.

When you write to describe or narrate an experience so that your readers can live the experience vicariously and share the emotions associated with it, you are, in a sense, sharing your personal window with your readers. By selecting and ordering details, you are creating a sensory experience for your readers, letting them see and hear and feel what you experienced— whether it's the time you fell through the pond while ice skating, or the excitement you felt when you saw the Rolling Stones in concert.

The fact that you can share your view of the world with other people has two important implications for the writer. First, the knowledge and attitudes expressed in the piece of writing must, to some extent, overlap with the reader's knowledge and attitudes; otherwise the writing will make no sense to the reader and will be rejected. This is an important function of *given* information, as we discussed earlier. But second, the knowledge and attitudes expressed in the writing must, to some extent, go beyond the reader's knowledge or attitudes; otherwise the writing has no purpose. The writing, in other words, must convey *new* information.

So another pair of questions to help you define your writing situation is "What knowledge or attitudes will I share with my reader(s)?" and "What knowledge or attitudes of my reader(s) will I try to change?"

In sample 1C, for example, Mike assumes that he and his readers share a general knowledge of stereo equipment, but that his readers don't share his specific knowledge of compact-disc players. In sample 1B, Christina assumes that she and her readers share a general attitude about the difficulty of finding part-time employment but not necessarily a specific attitude about the advantages of a campus employment service.

Expectations. While the reader's knowledge and attitudes are important considerations in almost any writing situation, the reader's *expectations* are also important. What does the reader expect when reading an editorial or a personal letter or an article in a scholarly journal? Writing with a knowledge of your reader's expectations will usually result in a better product.

We said earlier that one way to become a better writer is to keep reading. The more you read, the more you develop a sense of what good communication is in a variety of writing situations. You may think that when you read you gain knowledge of the subject matter only, but you actually learn a great deal about the kind of written product: you develop expectations as a reader the more you read. For example, even before you begin reading a personal letter, you have certain expectations in mind: you expect it to be written in longhand, to begin with a greeting, to contain news about your friend's activities, to be written in a friendly, informal style, and so on. You would be surprised, in fact, to receive a personal letter that began like this one:

John Williams Smith wishes to extend his greetings to Samantha Johnson, his friend, with whom he has not corresponded in several years.

In fact, knowing what you know about personal letter writing, you would probably infer that your friend is just being funny or that he is on the verge of a setback in his mental stability.

As a reader, you develop expectations for other kinds of writing as well, whether it's a review of a book or movie, an analysis of a poem, a complaint letter, a recommendation, a shopping list, or a research paper. This is all part of the knowledge that you gain by reading.

So another consideration for writers is the expectations of their readers. Two important questions to ask yourself are "What are my reader's expectations?" and "How can I fulfill them?" Although writers usually aim to satisfy the reader's expectations, it is possible, of course, for writers to intentionally exploit certain expectations. But the writer must know what these expectations are and why—for what effect—he or she chooses to exploit them. When readers discover that their expectations are not being met, they can either disregard the material as bad or ineffective writing, or assume that the writer is purposely flouting their expectations—that is, choosing not to fulfill them for some larger communicative purpose. Experienced readers make an effort to understand the motivations behind the choices that writers make.

Let's suppose you're asked to write a review of a movie that you absolutely abhor. Rather than writing about what you disliked about the movie, you might decide on a different approach. You might praise every aspect of the movie using an abundance of superlatives, carefully juxtaposing your evaluative commentary with descriptions that clearly suggest the movie's dullness. Yet you make no explicit mention of the movie's shortcomings. If done successfully, readers of this review would become suspicious of your intent and eventually reason that you are employing irony—that you really mean the reverse of what you say.

Because most writing in college is done to fulfill course assignments, it is important that you read the assignment carefully, noting especially the expectations of your instructor. This is true even if *you* have defined the writing situation, real or imagined. In writing her process description, Christina knew that her instructor expected a clear, well-organized sequence of steps explaining how something is done. She also knew that she would have to write about something that her readers did not already know. These expectations were stated explicitly in the writing assignment.

One final point about your experience as a writer and reader concerns your role as a respondent to your peers' writing. Although you are in college to increase your knowledge in a variety of subject areas, it is also important that you develop further the knowledge and skills that you already possess as a writer and a reader. We have often heard students say that they are not *qualified* to comment on another student's paper. That is the teacher's job, they say, not the student's. What many students may not realize, however, is that the practice of responding to another student's paper is part of the learning process. As writers and readers, you *are* qualified to make observations about writing. Granted, you may feel uncomfortable in this role at first, not because you lack the knowledge, but because you haven't much experience applying what you know to specific pieces of writing.

Responding to another student's paper does not mean you must perform flawlessly; it means that, as a reader, you are offering responses for the writer to consider—some perhaps more helpful than others. But each time you respond to another piece of writing, you will develop your skills as a peer critic, more so than the time before, and your responses will improve in quality. By learning to *apply* your knowledge of written texts, you not only perform a valuable service for your fellow students but also increase your knowledge of written products.

Exercises

A. The letter reproduced below was written by a member of our department. It concerns the Alaskan oil spill and a planned memorial service in Indianapolis. Read it carefully, and then respond to the following questions in your journal.

1. What assumptions does the writer seem to be making about the knowledge and attitudes of her readers? Discuss the reasons for your answers.

2. What is one specific piece of knowledge and one attitude that the writer assumes she shares with her readers? What is one specific piece of knowledge and one attitude that the writer assumes she does *not* share with the readers?

3. What might be the expectations of the intended readers?

Dear Colleague:

I am sure you are by now aware of the recent catastrophe in Prince William Sound, as it is the worst environmental disaster in our country's history. In 1973 I spent a summer on Prince William Sound, working for the Outdoor Leadership School, which ran kayaking courses there in one of the last great wildernesses on this continent. My memories of the months I spent on those waters are still utterly vivid; at the age of nineteen I was fortunate enough to be one of the first non-Eskimos to travel the waters of the Sound in small boats, boats which—by virtue of their very low profile—put us into the most intimate contact imaginable with sea otters, sea lions, seals and whales. These animals were friendly, intelligent, and unafraid. Whales would surface right off the bows of our tiny canvas boats, but never underneath them. Sea otters would paddle by on their backs, pretending to be looking at something on the horizon, but darting intent and curious glances at us as they scooted by just five or ten feet away. The entire environment of the Sound was lush beyond anything that I had experienced before or have experienced since; here was a genuine wilderness, not the small scraps and fragments of so-called wilderness that remain in the lower forty-eight states, but the real thing, teeming with animal and vegetable life, absolutely pristine, utterly non-human.

I have never returned to Prince William Sound, but in the sixteen years that have passed since my summer there it has stayed with me as an important symbol of those places on this earth that the human species has not yet destroyed. So thoroughly impressed was I with the beauty, the wildness, and the lushness of the Sound that I set my second novel, *Bad Guys*, in its waters. I felt that even though most of my readers would never be able to visit Prince William Sound for themselves, that they—and all humans—must be happier for simply knowing it was there.

Now, that happiness had been taken from us. In a recent conversation with the volunteer staff at Prince William Sound emergency hot-line in Anchorage, I was told that recent flights over the Sound had revealed a totally dead landscape. There was no movement in the water. There was no movement in the air. Even the streams which tumble into the waters of the Sound, and which have always attracted bears and deer, even those streams seemed to hold no life. The oil slick itself is now 2,600 miles in diameter, and has moved out of Prince William Sound into the Gulf of Alaska. Most of the animal life has simply disappeared, though dead and dying mammals are to be found on many beaches. The magnitude of this loss is almost incomprehensible.

I am writing now to ask that you bring to the attention of your classes the information on the attached flier. In my conversation with the Anchorage volunteers, I learned that the people of Alaska plan to hold a memorial service for the Sound on Sunday, April 23rd at 2:00. On April 9th they held a vigil, which included the playing of whale songs and of Mozart's *Requiem*; now they have scheduled a memorial. The service in Anchorage will be held on the west end of the city, on the lagoon, and will include five minutes of silence, to listen to the still voices of the Sound. Indianapolis will be holding its own Memorial Service at the same time, in an auditorium at the University of Indianapolis, and I have been asked by Steve Keller, the local organizer, to bring this service to the attention of as many people as possible. Even if you do not normally announce such events to your classes, please make an exception in this case. The time for organization has been short, and the public memory about disaster is often even shorter; the larger the turn-out for the Memorial Service, the greater will be the attention paid to it by the media, and, perhaps more important, the larger will be the individual commitment to do *whatever it takes* to prevent such a catastrophe from ever happening again.

I thank you in advance for your help with this. If you wish to read my letter to your classes, please do so.

Sincerely yours,

Elizabeth Arthur

B. As readers, we develop different expectations for the different kinds of materials we read. What expectations do you have when you read the following:

a movie review
an essay in a popular magazine
a sales letter
a recommendation letter
a grocery shopping list
a news article

C. Choose a subject for the writing assignment at the end of this chapter, and think about what you know, or can assume to know, about your readers. In your journal, write about their knowledge, attitudes, and expectations, and consider how this information will affect what you say in your piece of writing and how you say it.

THE SUBJECT: SELECTION AND SCOPE

A third variable in the writing situation is the subject, what the piece of writing is about. In many composition courses, you may be expected to choose your own subject. Perhaps the best piece of advice about choosing a subject is to write about something you know well—a subject that lies close to your own experiences. Because most, if not all, of the information will come from your own knowledge of the subject, you do not have to be concerned about searching for points to make in your paper; therefore, you can devote your time and energy to other matters.

That does not mean your choice of subject must be limited to what you did during the summer vacation or how you first learned to downhill ski. Although such papers are not uncommon in beginning composition courses, you will be expected to write on other subjects further removed, perhaps, from your own experiences—subjects such as the government censorship of art projects, the issue of gun control, or the controversy over animal research. When Christina began work on the first writing assignment, the process description, she knew that she would have to choose a subject that she knew well but that her readers did not know. These directions were spelled out in the assignment. But her choice of subject was her own. Because she was employed part-time in the campus employment office and was familiar with the operating procedure, she chose to describe the process of how students use the job service to find employment.

Some students may have difficulty coming up with subjects that they know well, and the problem is not that they have lived their adult years in a vacuum. They may simply need a way to get started thinking about what they do know. One of us is reminded of a recent conference he had with his daughter's first-grade teacher. The teacher commented that his daughter had difficulty writing sentences about a picture after the teacher had taken time to talk about it with the class. After working with his daughter at home, he discovered that the problem was not that his daughter lacked something to say; she simply needed a technique to help her isolate pieces of information about the picture from all the information she had stored in memory. Once she learned, for example, how to ask questions about the picture, she had something to say and something to write.

Although this example is far removed from the experience of beginning college writers, it reveals something basic about the learning process: learning, like any other skill, often requires tools or learning aids. Students who have difficulty choosing subjects to write about may need a strategy to help them retrieve information from memory. In Chapter Two, we suggest a strategy to help students inventory the subjects about which they are knowledgeable.

When you choose a subject to write on, always be sure to read the assignment carefully. Some writing assignments, for example, may require you to use outside research in your paper. In such cases, when choosing a subject, you will have to go one step further and check to be sure that your subject has been covered adequately in the research. If it is so recent as not to be treated adequately in books and magazines, you may have to choose another subject or decide whether it is feasible for you to conduct primary research, collecting information by interviewing knowledgeable people on the subject, distributing questionnaires, or using some other survey instrument. Of course, it is always best to get the approval of your teacher before you begin such a project. Chapter Two offers suggestions and guidance for students interested in gathering information from external sources.

In many cases, your subject may already be a "given": the subject matter comes as part of the writing situation. The real question about your subject, then, is not "What is my subject?" but "What is the scope of my subject?" Or to put it another way, "How much of my subject do I need to cover?" These are questions you will have to answer once you have identified your subject, whether it is given as part of the assignment or whether it is your own choice.

No piece of writing can cover any subject entirely: James Joyce, after all, wrote a book of more than six hundred pages, *Ulysses*, describing just one day in the lives of two men and a woman, and still left enough questions unanswered to keep generations of scholars busy. You, like Joyce, have to be selective in what you include.

In Mike's introduction to buying a compact-disc player (sample 1C), he limits a very large subject to several factors that anyone should consider before buying a compact-disc player. Likewise, Amy (sample 1A) could have written on many aspects of FHA, but she chose to restrict the scope of her subject to the steps for applying for a state office in the organization.

We have more to say about restricting your subject in the next chapter.

Exercises

A. Below are the introductory paragraphs of student papers that appear elsewhere in this book. Read each paragraph, and then discuss how you think the writers limited their subjects.

1.   Events in one's life can heavily influence the career goals one may set. Negative situations can either greatly reduce or highly increase one's will to achieve those goals. An unhappy period in my life could have, in fact, kept me from planning for my future. Luckily, however, those events supplied the basis for my decision to become a genetic engineer and they have inspired me to strive towards reaching my goal.

2.   A visitor happening to travel down the winding gravel road that leads to Ceralvo, a tiny community nestled on the banks of the Green River, would find only a few houses and a church that holds services once a year. One might think that Ceralvo has always been a rural residential area; however, the buildings there today are actually the remains of a thriving city of another era.

3.   Man, long considered (at least by man) to be the supreme species on our planet, has had an evolutionary process unprecedented in the animal kingdom. While he has gone from little more than an ape to his present sophisticated form in just a few million years, man's mental evolution has been much more rapid, apparently only over the last few thousand years. But it has only been in the past century that the development has been most rapid. Indeed, many of man's greatest achievements have been only in the past *fifty* years.

B. Using the sample papers at the end of this chapter, choose one of the writers who you think may have limited his or her subject too much, one who you think may have limited his or her subject too little, and one who you think was successful at limiting his or her subject. Be prepared to discuss your reasons for these choices.

C. In your journal, define the boundaries of the subject you have chosen for the writing assignment at the end of this chapter. Explain your reasons for setting these limitations on your subject.

THE PURPOSE: EXPRESSING, CREATING, INFORMING, AND PERSUADING

The fourth variable in any writing situation is the purpose. You will do well to ask yourself before you begin a writing task, "Why am I writing this?" This question, like any "Why?" question, usually has multiple answers; reasons for any action are rarely simple.

In a writing class, one set of answers is imposed by the very fact of the course. In one sense, the purpose for all writing done in writing courses is "to learn to write better," or, perhaps, "to complete the requirement" or "to earn a grade." But more and more teachers and textbooks—including this one—contend that writers can best improve their writing by working within realistic writing situations. You might think of such realistic writing situations as existing at three levels:

1. Writing tasks you would have done anyway, even if you were not taking a writing course. These might include such tasks as writing an autobiographical essay for a scholarship application or a letter to a university requesting information about financial aid.

2. Writing tasks you might not have done otherwise, but which you *can* do for a real, non-writing-class reader and purpose. These might include such tasks as writing your senator about your opinion on upcoming legislation or writing a letter to your local newspaper editor in response to an editorial.

3. Simulated tasks, written *as if* they had non-writing-class purposes and readers. Christina's process description (sample 1B) is in this category, as are all the sample papers in this book not in categories 1 and 2. As we pointed out in Chapter One, many of the writing assignments you will have in college will ask you to imagine a realistic writing situation for your paper.

In general, you will probably learn most from the first kind of writing task. There may not be enough of these at any given time, however, to give you enough writing experience. In this book we suggest writing assignments at all three levels to give you practice in writing and to help you become a better, more confident writer.

When you have chosen, or been given, a writing situation, define your purpose for yourself if it has not already been prescribed in the assignment. One way to do this defining is to consider that writing has four main purposes: to express, to create, to inform, and to persuade.

Writing to Express. Some writing is done just to express the writer's thoughts and feelings, just to get them down on paper. When writers do this kind of writing, they are not concerned about what readers will think; in fact, most expressive writing never gets to readers at all. It exists only in the form of notes, journals, diaries, and the like, intended for reading only by the writer. If it is read by someone other than the writer, a special relationship exists between the writer and the reader so as to make any concern for the way it is written negligible. In many composition courses, for example, students often share expressive writing in their collaborative groups, but usually not until the members of the group have established a relationship of trust with one another.

Because expressive writing is usually not intended for other readers, it cannot really be evaluated or taught; if it allows the writer to express feelings and thoughts, it has done its job. Therefore, this book, like almost all writing textbooks and courses, does not attempt to *teach* expressive writing. However, you *are* encouraged to *do* expressive writing, as part of your total writing process. Especially at the predrafting stage, expressive writing can be an excellent way to define your writing situation, to discover content for your writing, and to explore possible organizations. As you will see in the next chapter, expressive writing can be a learning activity throughout the writing process.

Although most of the sample papers in this book express their writers' opinions or feelings, none has expression as its main purpose, because all are intended for other readers.

Writing to Create. Other writing is done to create works of art. Such "creative" writing is sometimes confused with expressive writing, but their purposes are very different. While creative writing may certainly express the writer's thoughts and feelings, it is—unlike expressive writing—intended for readers. Written products such as poems, song lyrics, short stories, novels, and plays are written for audiences; their purpose is to create works of art that will affect their readers or listeners in some way—by amusing them, or moving them, or just making them take notice. Although such writing can surely be taught and learned, it also lies outside the scope of this book.

Many of the sample papers in this book are, of course, quite creative in their use of language. But none has "writing to create," in this sense, as its main purpose, because none has as its goal the creation of an art work.

Writing to Inform. Although creative writing can inform the reader of the writer's thoughts and feelings, that is not its main purpose. Other writing, however, does have informing as its main purpose. Such writing—constituting, perhaps, most of the writing done in the world—is written to give information to its readers. Informative writing includes shopping lists, interoffice memos, essays, technical articles, textbooks, instruction sheets, and laws.

The sample papers at the end of this chapter, for example, seem to have informing as their main purpose: how to run for a state office in FHA, how to find a job through the campus employment service, and how to buy a compact-disc player. All three papers have as their main purpose to communicate information to their readers.

Writing to Persuade. Only a fine line exists between writing to inform and writing to persuade; for example, Christina's paper on job hunting (sample 1A), although primarily giving information about the process of using the employment service, also seems to have the secondary purpose of persuading the reader to make use of the service. Conversely, persuasion probably cannot be done unless information is communicated. But it is nevertheless useful to consider that writers sometimes have a purpose beyond just the communication of information; they want to change their readers in some way, persuade them to think or feel or do something they have not thought or felt or done before. Advertisements and political speeches have this purpose, of course, but so do many letters and reports and other kinds of writing. An essay to win a scholarship, a letter to get a driveway repaired, one to get a governmental policy changed—all may very well have persuading as their main purpose: persuading their readers to do something.

Exercises

A. Read the following selection from Mortimer J. Adler and Charles Van Doren's *How to Read a Book* (rev. ed. New York: Simon and Schuster, 1972), and decide whether its main purpose is to inform or to persuade. Be prepared to discuss the reasons for your decision.

The Life and Growth of the Mind

Suppose, the test went, that you know in advance that you will be marooned on a desert island for the rest of your life, or at least for a long period. Suppose, too, that you have time to prepare for the experience. There are certain practical and useful articles that you would be sure to take with you. You will also be allowed ten books. Which ones would you select?

Trying to decide on a list is instructive, and not only because it may help you to identify the books that you would most like to read and reread. That, in fact, is probably of minor importance, compared with what you can learn about yourself when you imagine what life would be like if you were cut off from all the sources of amusement, information, and understanding that ordinarily surround you. Remember, there would be no radio or television on the island, and no lending library. There would be just you and ten books.

This imagined situation seems bizarre and unreal when you begin to think about it. But is it actually so unreal? We do not think so. We are all to some extent persons marooned on a desert island. We all face the same challenge that we would face if we really were there—the challenge of finding the resources within ourselves to live a good human life.

There is a strange fact about the human mind, a fact that differentiates the mind sharply from the body. The body is limited in ways that the mind is not. One sign of this is that the body does not continue indefinitely to grow in strength and develop in skill and grace. By the time most people are thirty years old, their bodies are as good as they will ever be; in fact, many persons' bodies have begun to deteriorate by that time. *But there is no limit to the amount of growth and development that the mind can sustain.* The mind does not stop growing at any particular age; only when the brain itself loses its vigor, in senescence, does the mind lose its power to increase in skill and understanding.

This is one of the most remarkable things about human beings, and it may actually be the major difference between *homo sapiens* and the other animals, which do not seem to grow mentally beyond a certain stage in their development. But this great advantage that man possesses carries with it a great peril. *The mind can atrophy,* like the muscles, *if it is not used.* Atrophy of the mental muscles is the penalty that we pay for not taking mental exercise. And this is a terrible penalty, for there is evidence that atrophy of the mind is a mortal disease. There seems to be no other explanation for the fact that so many busy people die so soon after retirement. They were kept alive by the demands of their work upon their minds; they were propped up artificially, as it were, by external forces. But as soon as those demands cease, having no resources within themselves in the way of mental activity, they cease thinking altogether, and expire.

Television, radio, and all the sources of amusement and information that surround us in our daily lives are also artificial props. They can give us the impression that our minds are active, because we are required to react to stimuli from outside. But the power of those external stimuli to keep us going is limited. They are like drugs. We grow used to them, and we continuously need more and more of them. Eventually, they have little or no effect. Then, if we lack resources within ourselves, we cease to grow intellectually, morally, and spiritually. And when we cease to grow, we begin to die.

Reading well, which means reading actively, is thus not only a good in itself, nor is it merely a means to advancement in our work and career. It also serves to keep our minds alive and growing. (pp. 344–46)

B. What would need to be changed in the preceding selection for your answer to be different?

C. In your journal, define the main purpose of the paper you are drafting for the writing assignment at the end of this chapter. How would your paper change if you were writing for a different purpose?

Drafting: Writing for the Situation

If you have defined your writing situation carefully at the predrafting stage, you are well on your way to a successful piece of writing. At the drafting stage, just keep your situation in mind, perhaps by glancing occasionally at notes you made as you defined it. As you put the words of your draft on paper or on a computer screen, keep in mind the role you are playing as a writer; the knowledge, attitudes, and expectations of your reader; the scope of your subject; and the purpose of your writing—to express, create, inform, or persuade.

As you write your draft, you should be cognizant of your own presence in the piece of writing. In some kinds of writing, it may be appropriate for you to use the first-person "I," especially if you want your reader to identify with something you have experienced. When you want to establish a close relationship with your reader, then it is important for you to be visible to your reader and perhaps even to refer to the reader using the familiar "you." In other kinds of writing, however, it may be appropriate for you to use third person and to disguise your presence as the writer; in these situations, the "I" is therefore less prominent and the writer less visible.

That does not mean that you must sacrifice your "voice" when you write, for you do express your own ideas and attitudes regardless of your point of view. If you are writing about protests for democracy in China, for example, you might write a sentence like this one: "The 1989 events in China are a reminder of the benefits of life in a democratic society." This sentence expresses an attitude toward the subject, and it is written in the third person. The emphasis is on the subject rather than the writer. If the writer then decides to relate a personal experience in which his or her freedom was denied or threatened, as an example in support of an idea, it would then be appropriate for the writer to shift to first person, relate that personal experience, and then return to third person to continue the development of the topic or to shift topics.

So it is possible to say what you have to say without always relying on the first person and prefacing all of your statements with "I think" or "I believe" or "I feel." For example, in this book we are writing about the subject of writing, so we often use the third person: we write about defining the writing situation, gathering and discovering content, planning the organization of an essay, and so on. But we are also writing for a particular audience of readers, the beginning college writer, so we frequently use the second person "you" when we are giving advice to you, our readers. And when we want to cite an example from our own experiences, we shift to first person, as we have just done in this paragraph (in this case, the first-person plural "we"). Whatever voice you use, by considering the writing situation as you draft, you will find that the drafting stage will go much easier and result in a better product.

Of course, you will still have many decisions to make in the process of drafting your paper. You may not make all the right decisions, and even if you do, you may not always achieve what you intended in your first draft. Writing *is* a process that requires revision, so you shouldn't expect to get it right the first time. For this reason, it is best to write down your questions and concerns in your journal. For example, if you have tried two or three different ways to begin your paper and none of them seems to fit your particular writing situation, use your journal to record your concerns and to raise questions. In this way, when you share your writing with your peers in the classroom, you will be prepared to direct their attention when they read your paper to specific questions and concerns that you had while writing the draft. You can learn a great deal from other readers when you can help them focus on and respond to particular problems. If you wait until you get to the classroom to formulate your questions, chances are your questions will not be specific enough to evoke meaningful responses.

As you draft, then, always look ahead in the process. Knowing that you will have your draft read by your peers, you can start thinking about how your peer editor can best help you with your writing. In this way, you make efficient use of your time.

Also, if you encounter a problem you cannot solve, take a few minutes to write about it in your journal. Suppose you reach a point in your draft where you don't know what to say next, as often happens—even to experienced writers. Use your journal to work through the problem and to pose possible solutions. You may learn, for example, that you will have to redefine the variables of the writing situation to proceed further with your draft. In other words, you may discover something about the writing situation that you did not know before you started writing your draft. It is not uncommon for writers to go back and reassess the writing situation.

Postdrafting: Checking That the Draft Fits the Situation

When you have finished a draft, and perhaps taken a break before returning to it for postdrafting, you might want to begin the postdrafting by thinking again about the writing situation that you have defined for yourself. If the draft fails to take into account its writer, reader, subject, or purpose, then it may be a waste of time to work on the details of its paragraphs, sentences, words, or mechanics. It may make more sense, in such cases, to redefine the task and begin a new draft. If, conversely, the draft does reflect the writer's role you decided on, if it does seem to take into account the knowledge, attitudes, and expectations of your reader(s), if it does cover the right amount of its subject, and if it does seem to have a good chance of fulfilling its purpose, then you can approach any revising with the confidence that you will have a successful product at the end.

This is also the time to review the observations and reactions of your peer editors. This feedback should be helpful to you in planning your revision strategy. When a peer editor identifies a problem area in your paper, you will have to determine for yourself whether other readers are likely to experience the same difficulty. If they are, you will need to make the necessary revisions to your draft. But remember, especially early in the course, that your peer editors may not always be accurate in their assessments of your draft. Ultimately, you are the one who must decide on what changes need to be made.

As you are preparing to revise your draft, you may find the following questions of some help:

1. What is my role as a writer? What image of myself have I presented to my readers? How have I achieved this in my draft?

2. To whom am I writing? In what ways have I attempted to write

specifically for my readers? What assumptions have I made about my readers' prior knowledge, beliefs, and attitudes about my subject?

3. What exactly am I writing about? How have I defined the scope of my subject?

4. Is my purpose for writing clear? Will my readers understand my purpose as I have expressed it, either explicitly or implicitly, in my paper? How have I attempted to make my purpose clear in my draft?

Assignment 1: Instructions

Assignment: Write instructions for something you know how to do.

In some ways, this is the easiest of the seven assignments: it asks you to write about something specific that you know for readers who do not know it. But this gap in knowledge can make instructions difficult to write: you must always be aware of how much and how little your readers know, and you must be careful neither to confuse your readers by writing over their heads nor to insult your readers by talking down to them.

Sample Papers

(Like all sample papers in this book, these have been written by students in first-year college writing courses and have generally not been further edited for publication.)

Sample 1A (Amy):

Applying for an FHA State Office

Applying for a state office in the Future Homemakers of America is a challenging and rewarding task. It is challenging because you must meet strict requirements and will be up against the toughest competition in the state. It is rewarding because win or lose, you will gain new confidence in yourself as one of FHA's finest members.

The first step is to determine whether you are eligible to become an officer candidate. In order to apply, you must have held an office at the chapter and regional levels of FHA, preferably the same one as the state office you wish to hold. Also, you must have completed your state degree. Other requirements are that you must have a "B" average in school and you must be willing to attend the National FHA meeting the following summer.

After you have established that you are eligible, the second step is to fill out an application. Most of the questions are essay and deal with your experience as an FHA officer and why you feel you are qualified for the position. There may also be questions about new ideas you have for FHA activities. Since the application determines whether you become an officer candidate, you should put much time and effort into your answers.

If you are accepted as an officer candidate, the next step in the process is planning a tentative program for the annual summer leadership camp. This is an important step because it displays your creativity and your organizational skills, both of which are essential in holding a state office. Your program must include a theme for the camp; also, it must include what materials will be covered, who the guest speakers will be, and the type of recreation for each meeting.

Lastly, you must attend the state meeting, which is held one weekend in early spring. During the first meeting open to the entire state association, you will be asked a question and be graded on the content of your answer and how well you present yourself. Next, you must take a written test covering FHA facts. You must also attend several seminars and luncheons with the present state officers. The final criterion is an interview with the candidate committee.

After you have completed the necessary steps in the process of becoming a state officer, the candidate committee makes their evaluations and decides who will compose the next slate of officers. The committee then reports their decisions at the next open meeting. The new state officers must then prepare for an exciting period of maturation and growth. Not everyone gets to be a state officer; however, even if you are not elected, the experience will still be very beneficial to you.

Sample 1B (Christina):

So You Say You Need a Job

Mike is a new student at IUPUI. He just registered for classes and is all set to begin in the fall, but he does have one problem: he needs a job.

For Mike, finding a job that will work around his schedule won't be an easy task, but as a student at IUPUI, he has a great resource to help him find a job, and if you are like Mike, it could help you too.

The program is called JOBS, which stands for Job Opportunities for Businesses and Students, and it is located in the Business Building in Room 2010.

To qualify for the JOBS program, all you need is to be a current IUPUI student, meaning you are currently taking classes, you took classes last semester, or you are registered for classes for the following semester.

When you get to room 2010, which is the Career and Employment Services Office, ask the person at the front desk about the JOBS program, and he or she will tell you who to see. The person who handles the JOBS program is at a desk in the back of the office, and when you go there, the first thing that person will ask you is if you are a current IUPUI student. If you are, he or she will then give you an application to fill out.

The application is pretty straightforward. It asks you your basic name-and-address questions, but the main purpose of the application is to find out what kinds of jobs you are interested in, and what kinds of job experience you have had.

After you finish filling out the application, it goes back to the person at the desk. Now it is time to look for a job.

There is a bulletin board in the hallway outside of the office that lists hundreds of full and part-time positions of every job from general office workers to cashiers. Go out and look on the board for jobs that interest you, but remember, the board only lists the position title and a brief description, so you must copy down the numbers assigned to the jobs you are interested in, and bring them back into the office in order to get a referral slip with more information.

Each student is allowed only five referral slips per day, so make sure that you choose your jobs carefully. Some of the main things you should look at are the rate of pay, the working hours, and the location to make sure it is a job you can get to easily enough.

The JOBS board is updated every day, so if you did find more than five jobs that you are interested in, you might want to come back another day, but always check the board for new jobs added and filled jobs taken off.

When you are finished writing your numbers down, go back into the office and read the numbers off to the person sitting at the desk. He or she will then give you referral slips, which tell you who the employer is, their address, phone number, and how to apply for the job. If, after reading the referral, you are still interested, you may get a copy of the referral to keep. All you have to do is sign the back of the master copy.

With your referral slips in hand, it is now up to you to apply for the jobs yourself. Once you get a job, the office does appreciate it if you would inform them by calling and telling them your name, and which job you got. They need this information so they can take the job off of the board so others don't apply for the same job, only to find that it has already been filled.

As you can see, this program is a very helpful resource for those students at IUPUI who are attending classes and need to find jobs so they can work while attending school, so if you are a student like Mike, and need a job, why don't you go over and check it out?

Sample 1C (Mike):

Buying a CD Player

The newest trend in music listening today is the compact disc player. This is a unit that plays back pre-recorded music by lasers. The reason so many people are becoming interested in CD players is because they give the listener an incredibly true reproduction of the sound. But before you go out and buy one, there are several factors you should be familiar with that will strongly influence your decision of which compact disc player to buy.

The first thing to consider is how much money are you willing to spend. CD players can cost anywhere from $150 to $300, considering the brand name, size, and options desired. These prices are standard; you should be able to find one for less if you wait until a decent sale comes along.

Once you decide the amount of money you are going to spend, you should then look at the different models compact disc players come in. By this I mean that you should decide when you will be listening to your CD player the most, and in turn choose a model that best fits your needs. Say, for example, that you most frequently listen to music while in your car; then you obviously would want one designed to replace your current car stereo. The most popular model, however, is one that hooks up to your home stereo system, assuming your stereo has an auxiliary outlet. There are two reasons this model is the most popular. One is because this model is generally more advanced than the car or portable ones. The other is that the music sounds better being played through powerful speakers rather than headphones or car speakers.

The third model, which may be the most versatile, is similar to the "Walkman" in that you can take it with you wherever you go. The reason this one is the most versatile is because it can also serve as a CD player for both your home and car stereo. You can buy an input wire that connects the portable model to your home stereo for under $10. If your car stereo has a tape player you can also play it through your car stereo. This can be done by purchasing a device that looks like a cassette with a wire coming from one corner. This wire goes into the CD player's headphone jack and the cassette is inserted into the tape deck. The final result of this process is compact disc quality sound from your old car stereo. This adaptor costs approximately $15. You will also need a pair of high quality headphones for the portable model. Otherwise the music would be no different than if you were listening to a cassette. You can get these headphones for about $30. One disadvantage of this model is that it may be broken very easily, because it is portable. Therefore, versatility may not be such a plus.

The next thing you should look at are the options you want your unit to have. The home unit is really the only one that will have a wide selection of options to choose from. The tracking, or searching, option, which allows you to skip from song to song with the push of a button, comes standard on all home units, so you need not worry about it. A wireless remote control is an important option to consider, simply because it is so convenient. If you look hard enough and are willing to pay a little extra you can even get a remote for the car and portable models. "Programmability" is a must for the serious music listener. This function enables you to program the order in which you wish to listen to the tracks on the disc. "Indexing" actually lets you program what part of each song you wish to hear. Many units offer what is usually called the "shuffle" function. What this does is that it randomly picks a song and acts as though it is track one and goes on from there. The "repeat" button is a rather interesting function. It lets you play a song, or a portion of a song, over and over until you press the button again. The portable and car models don't really come with "options," except for the remote. They will come standard with tracking, forward search, and review, just like the bigger home units. Some of these options are quite extravagant, but the others definitely need to be taken into consideration before you actually purchase a compact disc player.

After deciding on the model and options desired, the next decision is what brand to get. The best names to look for are Sony, Toshiba, Akai, Sanyo, Pioneer, JVC, and so on. Sony is probably the best at a reasonable price. There are more expensive brands such as Yamaha that have all the options and will probably last a little longer. In the car and portable models your selection is fairly narrow. The main brands are Sony, Sanyo, and Toshiba, along with some other American names. If you are concerned with "buying American," don't be, because no matter what name it has, it was originally put together in Japan or Korea.

I'm sure you can see how difficult this job can be, with all the different options, models, prices, and brand names to choose from. As long as you follow these instructions, wait for sales, and shop around at several different stores, or possibly consider mail-order, you shouldn't have much trouble finding the perfect CD player to fit your needs.

Discussion Questions

1. Where in these three papers does the writer assume too much knowledge from his or her readers? Where does the writer assume too little? Where does the writer's assumption of reader knowledge seem just right?

2. What organizational patterns have these three writers chosen for their instructions? How effective are these choices?

CHAPTER TWO

The Process of Giving Content to Your Writing

The content of a piece of writing is the information it carries. Whether your purpose is to inform or persuade your readers, you need to *say something*. Content is what your writing *says* about your subject—some aspect of the world around you or within you. If you begin drafting a piece of writing without a clear sense of what you want to say, no amount of time spent on organization, sentence structure, or word choice will make it any clearer—for the writer or the reader. So before you begin thinking about *how* to present the content of a piece of writing, you must first concentrate on *what* you want to say about your subject. This chapter will show you ways of discovering and gathering content for your writing, incorporating it into your draft, and revising it for your readers.

Predrafting: Gathering Content

As far as possible, collect the information you need for your writing at the predrafting stage. While you are still at this stage, you can use the information to make important decisions about the organization of your draft. Moreover, any information you can gather before you draft means that much less interruption at the drafting stage. Once you have something to say, you are well on your way to producing a good first draft, even though in the process of drafting you may discover gaps in your information or the need to shift your perspective.

Before Joe drafted his descriptive essay (sample 2C), he made the following list:

Points

- Special memories (first bicycle, grandma's home)
- the old barn
- exterior appearance (weathered, stained, cracked)
- interior (massive, dark)
- Fun times (sliding on corn, baled hay, a refuge)

Notice that this list shows no concern for features "lower" in the middle column of Figure 1: it isn't organized; it isn't written in sentences; it isn't capitalized uniformly. But it needn't be any of those things: it is written only to help Joe collect the information he needs for his essay, and it serves that purpose well.

Similarly, Christina wrote this list at the predrafting stage of her process paper about how to find a job through the campus employment service (sample 1B):

Fill out application

Look for jobs on bulletin board

Write down numbers

Come in office and get referrals (5 only)

Apply for jobs as employer specifies

Inform school if hired

Because Christina was writing about a process, her list naturally follows a sequential order. She also made each topic parallel in grammatical form (each begins with a verb). But it is still intended for the writer rather than the reader: notice its abbreviated form, with the subjects implied and the definite articles deleted. Christina wrote the list only for herself, to help her begin gathering the content for her writing.

As you begin gathering the content for your piece of writing, you should consider again each of the variables in the writing situation as you have defined them—writer, reader, subject, and purpose. The writing situation, as we said in Chapter One, is your starting point. Having defined your writing situation, you have already begun to think about the scope of your subject—*what* you want to say about your subject. In other words, you have already given a preliminary focus to your investigation. As you gather content for your paper, keep your preliminary focus in mind: in fact, you might even take a few moments to write, in one sentence, what you are interested in saying about your subject. This sentence can serve as your preliminary thesis—a statement of focus that will help you to make important decisions about content, even though your ideas may change as you discover and gather information for your paper. It is only a preliminary—or working— thesis, though, and you should be prepared to refine it as you learn more about your subject and what precisely you want to say about it.

The content for your writing can come from two sources: inside your own mind, in the form of your own knowledge and opinions, and outside "in the world," in the form of information in publications and in the minds of other people. Several tools are available to help you gather both kinds of information.

INTERNAL RESOURCES

All of us know much more than we are aware of at any given moment. Our memories are vast—for all practical purposes, infinitely large—repositories of information and ideas, stored away for years and decades. We retrieve information from that vast storehouse only in small pieces, now and then. For example, you may see someone at a distance who reminds you of a friend you had years before, and suddenly a whole set of memories of that friend— things you had no idea you remembered—come rushing into your awareness.

When you begin a writing task, no matter what its subject, you almost certainly know much more about that subject than you are immediately aware of knowing. What you need to do, then, is find ways to retrieve, from your memory, what you know. In addition, you might need to think about the subject in new ways, so that you can use your past experience with other subjects to help you write about this one.

You are probably familiar with the fact that the cerebrum of the brain is composed of two generally self-contained and self-sufficient hemispheres. It has been long known that if one hemisphere is damaged or even removed, the other soon takes over almost all the functions required for a full human personality. In other words, there is considerable duplication between the two halves of the brain.

But there is also considerable specialization. In most people, for example, the left hemisphere of the brain controls the right side of the body and vice versa. Moreover, and more important for our purposes in this chapter, the left half of the brain generally seems, in most people, to handle linear and analytical tasks, including much of the production of language. The right brain, by contrast, specializes in nonlinear, holistic thinking. This distinction is, admittedly, a rather sloppy one that requires much elaboration and many qualifications before it can be taken literally. But the distinction is helpful in understanding two different ways in which the brain operates. Therefore it is helpful in understanding two sets of tools for gathering information from "internal resources" at the predrafting stage of writing.

"Left-brain" Tools. In very loose terms, the "left brain," as we have said, works analytically and linearly, breaking subjects into parts and dealing with them in a sequence. The brain, when viewed in this way, is like a computer, following a predetermined program, step by step. Several mental tools are available to provide especially useful programs for that "left-brain" computer. These programs, sometimes called "heuristic devices" or just "heuristics," are procedures, or problem-solving strategies, for the "left brain" to follow to realize more fully its analytic potential—to discover more of what it knows. Two especially useful heuristics are the "reporter's checklist" and the "four pairs of questions":

1. *The reporter's checklist* is a tool used by news reporters to make sure they have covered all the important aspects of a news event. If a reporter has the answers to these six questions before leaving the scene, he or she can be pretty sure of not having left out any important information. The six questions are sometimes called "the five *W*'s and an *H*":

WHO?	What person or persons were involved?
WHAT?	What action took place?
WHERE?	In what place(s) did the action occur?
WHEN?	At what time(s) did the action occur?
WHY?	What was the cause or purpose of the action?
HOW?	In what way, or by what means, did the action occur?

You can use this same checklist to become more aware of what you know about the subject of a piece of writing. For any situation involving human activity—and that includes most of what you write—asking and answering these six questions will help you make sure your information is relatively complete before you begin drafting.

Lisa, for example, might have used the reporter's checklist to collect her thoughts before writing her descriptive essay about the Indianapolis Produce Terminal (sample 2B). She could have asked and answered the questions something like this:

WHO?	Me, my dad, the men at the produce terminal.
WHAT?	Trips to the produce terminal, where different produce companies compete in an open market.
WHERE?	At the Indianapolis Produce Terminal, about a one-hour drive from home.
WHEN?	In the early morning before school started.
WHY?	Because Dad needed fresh produce at fair cost to sell to his customers.
HOW?	By arriving there early, knowing how to bargain and for what.

To generate sufficient content for your piece of writing, however, you will need to consider other responses to the six preceding questions. Merely listing a single response to each of the questions will not get you very far. Lisa, for example, would probably devote more attention to the Who? What? and How? questions in her descriptive piece, perhaps even using these questions as starting points for freewriting, a predrafting strategy we discuss in the next section. The value of these six questions is that they help you to focus your thinking on different aspects of your subject to discover what you know about your subject, or some part of your subject.

2. *Four pairs of questions* is a tool for discovering more of what you know about a subject by looking at it in eight new ways—ways you may not think of otherwise. Like the reporter's checklist, this tool is made up of questions, this time arranged in four pairs:

SAME	DIFFERENT
How is this subject like others?	How is this subject different from others?
WHOLE	PARTS
To what larger subjects does this subject belong?	Into what smaller subjects can this subject be divided?
TIME	SPACE
In what time or times does this subject exist?	In what space or spaces does this subject exist?
REASONS	RESULTS
What explains the existence of my subject? What causes it?	What results has it produced? What are its effects?

Mandy, for example, could have gathered material for her description of Rome (sample 2A) by asking these four pairs of questions, as well as further questions they could lead to:

SAME	How is Rome like other cities? How is it like places where my readers live or have visited? What would they find familiar?
DIFFERENT	How is Rome different from other cities? What would my readers find unfamiliar about it?
WHOLE	How is it representative of Europe? Of Italy? Of the Roman Empire? Of the ancient world in general?

PARTS   What are some specific sights in Rome? Some specific
             sections or neighborhoods? What are the streets,
             churches, museums, shops, and restaurants like? What
             are the Romans like?

TIME   What is Rome's history? What survives from earliest
             times? What has stayed the same in Rome? What has
             changed? What is Rome's future?

SPACE   Where is Rome located? What are its surroundings
             like? How is the city laid out?

REASONS   What caused Rome to become a cultural center of the
             world?

RESULTS   What effects has the Vatican had on the cultural iden-
             tity of Rome?

Exercises

A. Choose one of the following sample papers and answer the six questions on the reporter's checklist as the writer of that paper might have
answered them:

1. Joe's description of the old barn (Sample 2D).
2. Christina's process description of the campus employment service
   (Sample 1B).
3. Mike's essay about the compact-disc player (Sample 1C).
4. Michael's description of the Berlin wall (Sample 2E).

B. Choose another of the samples just listed and list questions, based on
the "four pairs," that the writer might have asked before drafting.

C. Choose any subject that interests you—perhaps one you have already
recorded in your journal—and then use the reporter's questions and the
"four pairs" of questions to generate content.

"Right-brain" Tools. Very different from the "left-brain" tools are the techniques of "right-brain" discovery. The right hemisphere, after all, is the victim
of a long-standing cultural bias: we live in a generally analytic, left-brain
culture. So the contribution of right-brain tools is the fuller involvement of
the nonlinear, holistic right hemisphere in the writing act.

As mentioned earlier, language production, including writing, is primarily a left-brain activity. But the left hemisphere works linearly, one step at a
time, along a preset path. The techniques of right-brain discovery are aimed
at freeing the brain from this linear path and letting it think in wholly
different ways. In a sense, they are ways of letting the brain work without
interference by the internal editor described in the Overview to this book.

Three especially useful right-brain tools are brainstorming, freewriting, and treeing:

1. *Brainstorming* is an activity traditionally used by groups to generate creative solutions to problems. Whenever groups work together, members are often reluctant to share creative ideas out of fear of being criticized. To overcome this fear, brainstorming was developed. In a brainstorming session, group members are encouraged to call out ideas as fast as they can but are not allowed to comment on the ideas offered by others. All suggestions are simply recorded on paper or a blackboard; they become, in effect, the property not of individuals but of the group as a whole. Later the group can come back to this shared list and discuss the merits of individual items.

In the writing classroom, brainstorming is sometimes used in group activities, but it is more frequently used by individual students as a method for drawing out ideas stored in memory. Just as other group members can keep potentially good ideas from getting expressed, so too can the internal editor keep potentially good ideas from reaching your awareness. Brainstorming is a means of getting information onto the page, usually in the form of lists. As quickly as ideas occur to the writer, they are written down, with no regard for order, form, or style. There is no attempt on the part of the writer to censor irrelevant ideas or details, for the writer's only concern is to produce information.

If you are preparing to write a description of a place, for example, you might decide to brainstorm for ten minutes, writing down anything you know about the place. It may be particular details that you are reminded of when you think of this place, it may be pieces of conversation you overheard people say when you last visited, or it may be a series of images that you associate, for whatever reason, with this place. You do not try to make sense out of what you have written down until *after* you have completed the brainstorming session.

Then you can review the information and decide if there is a particular mood or dominant impression in the details you have produced. You might discover, for example, that many of the details suggest a mood of darkness and depression. By selecting and ordering details, you can then attempt to create that same impression for your readers.

2. *Freewriting* follows only one rule: write without stopping. To do freewriting, simply write without stopping for a planned period, perhaps ten minutes. If you cannot think of anything to write, write "I can't think of anything to write," until something else comes to mind.

Keep your pen or pencil moving, and write as quickly as you can. Don't stop at any point to think of what to say next; don't stop to read back what you've written; don't stop to correct or change anything. If you are writing on computer, you might even try turning off your monitor or lowering its contrast, so that you don't actually see what you're writing until you've finished freewriting, at which point you can turn the monitor back on.

Your internal editor may resist this freewriting strategy very strongly, but just ignore the internal editor and eventually it will "turn off"; from then on, your writing will seem relatively automatic and effortless.

The result of freewriting will be a page or two of potentially good content for your draft. Now you can go back through that page, cross out what you know you will not need, and underline the particularly interesting

Figure 3 - Tree Diagram

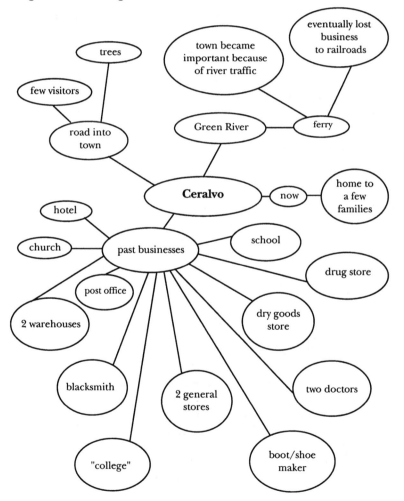

or valuable phrases or sentences. If you think it will be useful, you can even use some of these phrases or sentences as starting points for more focused freewriting.

Joe's first effort at his description of an old barn (sample 2C)—although Joe probably thought of it as a draft—was very close to freewriting: he was concerned simply with getting ideas down on paper, without much concern for their structure or wording. By comparing it with his final copy, you can see how much he improved the essay in later drafts but also how useful this early activity was for him, in getting down on paper ideas and even phrases that he used later:

> A place I know is an old barn on the farmstead where I was born. Many memories of my childhood are formed in or around this old barn. It was a large structure with a large hayloft covering most of the upper portion. A lean to type roof came off of one end and covered a tool shed or storage area and a corn crib. The lower portion was divided into stalls for milking the cows and had many pens where animals could be kept. Many hours were spent in this barn playing, working and just fooling around. In the spring and summer hay would have to be baled and stacked into the loft. A long elevator was used to reach the upper levels as the stacked bales grew higher. This was usually a very hot and sweaty job. When it rained it was fun to spend some of your free time in the tool shed area. Both ends of this area were open so a nice breeze would usually come through it. It was nice to hear the raindrops hitting the roof.

As this example illustrates, freewriting—unlike brainstorming—takes on the appearance of a composition rather than a list of information. Although both activities allow the writer to spill ideas onto the page, they are different in rhythm: brainstorming is jagged and random, whereas freewriting is a free-flowing, continuous expression.

3. *Treeing* is a way to discover what you know about a subject by over-coming your internal editor's normal left-brain insistence on the linear ordering of ideas. Treeing is laying out your ideas on paper in "branches," as you think of them. Begin with the word or phrase that expresses the general subject matter you have defined for yourself; write it in the center of a page. Then draw lines out from it to the words or phrases that it makes you think of. Continue "branching" to new ideas as they occur to you.

Amy, for example, used a form of treeing to gather content for her description of the town of Ceralvo (sample 2D). Figure 3 is based on her rough notes as she thought about what she wanted to include in her writing.

Exercises

A. Choose one of the following subjects and, in your journal, do ten minutes of nonstop freewriting.

1. a process you know how to perform

2. an important experience in your life

3. a place you know

4. a complaint you have

5. a concert or film you have seen

B. Using the same subject, a different one from the list, or one from your journal, draw a "tree" diagram of your ideas on the subject.

C. Choose a subject for the writing assignment at the end of this chapter and do ten minutes of brainstorming in your journal. Write anything that comes to mind about your subject, and work as quickly as you can. When you finish, review the details in your list to discover any patterns or dominant impressions.

EXTERNAL RESOURCES

Collecting materials for writing can take time, especially for the person who is the first to collect material on a given subject. But once information is collected and stored on paper or in people's minds, the task becomes much easier for others. As a writer, you need to learn to collect firsthand information and to access the billions of pieces of information that have been already collected.

In this section, we discuss some of the resources that can provide you with information to add authority and depth to your writing. Some of these resources, such as interviews with experts and informal experimental studies, provide firsthand knowledge; others provide relevant information from printed materials, or publications.

Though you may not be required to write a research paper, one that draws heavily from the available research on a specific topic, you may nevertheless want to incorporate research material into a piece of writing. Most teachers of introductory writing courses would not object to essays that draw on external sources for information, as long as the writer fulfills the writing assignment and makes judicious use of his or her research material. But first and foremost in any piece of writing is the writer's own thinking. That's why it's important for you to examine internal sources to discover what you already know and what you need to know about your subject. Before you attempt to incorporate other "voices" into your writing, you must first listen carefully to your own "voice" so that you can write with confidence and conviction about your subject. As a writer, *you* must be the one in control of your subject, and you must never allow *other* voices in your research to usurp your own voice as a writer.

That is what happens when you string a series of quotations together in your paper without properly introducing them, leaving your reader confused and uncertain about your direction and the way the quotations fit into the argument of your essay. And that is why, for the most part, teachers of introductory composition are wary about students writing from research: teachers want to be certain that you, as a beginning college writer, are confident with your own voice before they introduce the more complex task of weaving research material into a piece of writing.

So when you do use research material in a piece of writing, always have a specific purpose in mind for the research that you present. To do this, you must examine the internal sources of information first so that you have a clear sense of what you know and what you would like to learn about your subject.

In his excellent book *Finding Facts Fast* (2d ed. Berkeley, CA: Ten Speed Press, 1979), Alden Todd suggests three questions to ask yourself as you begin to look for information from external sources:

1. Who would know?

2. Who would care?

3. Who would care enough to put it in print? (p. 10)

Armed with these questions, you can begin your search through two kinds of external information sources: people and publications.

People. Often the best source of information is other people. After all, we learn a great deal from talking to other people. How did you first learn about the most recent innovations in stereo equipment? You probably browsed in stores that sell the product, asked questions of the salesperson, and left with information you did not have when you walked in. Many of your questions about college life, careers, cars, home repairs, courses, teachers, and the like are answered in conversations you have with people. The same is true when you ask questions about topics you write about in college courses or in the work world.

Especially when information is very recent or very specialized, people working in the field will have facts not yet in books or periodicals. Such experts are often happy and flattered to share that information with you. A recent student, for example, who was writing about the controversy surrounding the leg-hold trap, a device used to trap fur-bearing animals, decided to call the author of one of the articles she had read. She had prepared several questions that she hoped he would answer for her. After talking with him on the phone, she ended up with more information than she ever dreamed of getting: he not only responded to her questions but also sent her a three-hundred-page manuscript that he had authored and that was soon to be published. And he was so interested in her project that he took the time to call her a month later to see how she was progressing.

So don't be afraid to approach people, even very busy or well-known people, with requests for information. You can put simple requests in writing, of course. But if time and distance permit, a face-to-face or telephone interview can be useful as well. As the preceding example shows, talking with experts can provide much valuable information. Here are some suggestions for conducting such interviews:

1. *Prepare.* Know enough about your subject to be able to talk about it intelligently. The interviewee will be more likely to offer you assistance if he or she knows that your interest in the subject is more than cursory. Also, read what you can find about the interviewee, as well as articles or books he or she has written. Make a preliminary list of questions.

2. *Break the ice.* Follow your interviewee's lead in exchanging the "small talk" necessary to establish a friendly relationship. But do not draw this process out; with a busy person, be prepared to come right to the point.

3. *Ask who, what, where, when, why, and how questions.* Avoid yes-no and multiple-choice questions; instead ask questions that will draw out additional information. Have a notepad ready to jot down key words and phrases that will help you to reconstruct the interview at a later time.

4. *Listen.* Do not be so concerned about your next question that you fail to hear the answer to your previous one.

5. *Ask follow-up questions.* When points in an answer interest or confuse you, follow up on these points. You can come back to your prepared list of questions later.

6. *Write down what you have learned as soon as possible.* Notes, or even tape recordings, get "cold," difficult to understand, after a time. Translate them into readable form while they are still warm.

Another way to gather information firsthand from other people is to conduct a self-designed study. Much depends, of course, on the time available to you and the nature of your subject. But the study does not have to be complicated, and it can produce very useful information. Suppose you are writing a proposal for more study space in your college dormitory. One way to collect valuable information for your report is to count the number of students using the study room at designated times and the number of students who are turned away for lack of space. It would simply be a matter of tabulating numbers, but the information you collect may be just the concrete data needed to convince administrators that a problem does indeed exist.

Questionnaires and surveys are other ways of collecting information.

They involve more time and energy, however, because you must prepare the material for distribution and then collect it before you can begin to look at the data. Your teacher will be able to direct you to specific sources—experts and publications—for more information about designing these instruments for gathering information.

Publications. Probably more often, however, you will be getting external information for your writing from printed sources, usually books and periodicals stored in libraries. The modern library, whether public or academic, is one of the wonders of our culture, providing information that even the world's richest people could not have obtained a generation or two ago. And this wealth of information is remarkably easy to find and use, even in the largest and most complex of libraries. Here are some beginning suggestions on some of the resources available at a library:

1. *Reference librarians.* The most important resource at most libraries is not a publication but a person: the reference librarian. Although most resources of a library are designed to be accessed directly by users, it would be foolish not to draw on the expertise of this specialist, a person specifically trained in locating information of all kinds and certainly familiar with the resources of his or her particular library. So unless you are quite proficient at using the resources you need, begin your search with the reference librarian. Remember, too, that in some libraries, the reference librarian will be able to answer many questions by telephone.

Some people are shy about asking librarians questions, perhaps out of fear of being thought stupid, but the librarian's job is answering even the simplest of questions. Librarians, in fact, often prepare handout materials specifically for students, such as short guides on how to use specific library resources. When you talk with your reference librarian, ask if such material is available.

2. *Catalog.* The heart of any library is its catalog, the complete directory of the books, periodicals, and other materials that the library owns. (Some libraries may have separate catalogs for its periodicals, with more detailed information about specific volume numbers and issues available). Traditionally, library catalogs have been in the form of cards, usually alphabetized by author, title, and subject. But more and more libraries have converted their catalogs to microfilm or computer memory, making updating more efficient and searches easier and more productive. If your library's catalog is on computer or microfilm, in most cases it will not require special training to access it; you will simply need to become familiar with the help screen on the computer monitor to learn the commands for different searches, or to learn how to operate a microfilm reader.

If your library's catalog is computerized, be sure to ask how much of the card catalog has been entered on computer. A library, for example, may not have completed the transfer of all its holdings to computer memory; it may have everything from 1977 to the present on computer, but everything before 1977 accessible only through the card catalog. If your topic is recent, you will not encounter problems, but if you are writing about some aspect of the 1960s generation, you may have to thumb through the card catalog to locate sources relevant to your topic.

Library catalogs, in whatever form, are absolutely essential for telling you what publications are available and where they can be found. However, catalogs are not always the best place to start when you want to find what materials are available on a particular subject. Subject categories are sometimes too broad for your purpose, and they are sometimes not listed in the same words that occur to *you*. One recent student, for example, was dismayed to find that his university library apparently had no books on "movies"; a reference librarian was able to point out that the catalog listed them all under "motion pictures."

As this example illustrates, the card catalog uses a controlled vocabulary. So when you are not sure of your subject heading, you might want to consult the *Library of Congress Subject Headings*, usually located near the card catalog. This handy reference lists all the headings used in the card catalog. If you are writing a paper about Italian cooking, for example, it will tell you to look instead under "cookery, Italian"; it will also suggest broader, narrower, and related titles as well. So unless you know a particular publication's title or author, you may want to start with a reference book or the reference librarian.

3. *Reference books.* You already are familiar, of course, with several reference books: dictionaries, almanacs, atlases, general encyclopedias, biographical works, perhaps. But most libraries have hundreds or thousands more specialized reference books, and such books are often your very best beginning source of information. Again, the reference librarian will be especially qualified to guide you to the reference books you need. If you are interested in knowing which reference books are commonly used in your particular discipline, you can also check one of the general reference books. These two in particular can be found in most libraries:

Hillard, James. *Where to Find What: A Handbook to Reference Service*. Rev. ed. Metuchen, NJ: Scarecrow, 1984.

Sheehy, Eugene P., ed. *Guide to Reference Books*. 9th ed. Chicago: American Literary Association, 1976.

Because many reference books include bibliographies—or are bibliographies themselves—they can lead you to other books that you can then locate by author or title in the library's catalog.

4. *Circulating books.* Most books at most libraries are not reference books, which must stay in the library; instead, they "circulate," or can be checked

out. Circulating books are usually shelved in areas known as "stacks," which can be either "open"—physically accessible to the public—or "closed"—accessible only to library employees.

If your library has open stacks, you have the advantage of being able to browse through books on related subjects that are shelved together. If your library has closed stacks, you will have to do a more complete search in the catalog, then request the books you want.

5. *Periodical indexes.* The most up-to-date information on many subjects is found not in books but in magazines and journals; you can locate this information with the help of periodical indexes. You probably have already used at least one periodical index, the *Reader's Guide to Periodical Literature*, which indexes articles, by author and subject, in nearly two hundred relatively popular periodicals. But several other specialized indexes exist for more specialized periodicals: the *Social Sciences Index*, for example, covers journals in that field. For help with using a periodical index, thumb through the front matter of the index. Here you will find information about how the reference book is to be used. Otherwise, consult—of course—a reference librarian.

6. *Periodicals.* Periodicals include magazines and journals, issued periodically. The most recent issues in a library will often be "loose," in racks or shelved boxes. Older issues may be collected in bound volumes or microfilmed. In any case, if you know—from a periodical index or other reference book—the title and date of the magazine or journal you want, you should have no trouble finding it, providing the periodical is one that your library subscribes to. Ask your librarian for the location of the serials catalog, a listing of all the periodicals the library receives, and check to see whether the library does have the periodical you need in its holdings. If it does not, the reference librarian may be able to request a photocopy of the material from another library that does have the periodical.

7. *Newspaper indexes.* Articles in several of the world's most important newspapers are indexed in special publications called newspaper indexes. The *New York Times Index*, for example, is issued semimonthly and then compiled into annual bound volumes, with all the articles for a period classified by their subject matter. The *New York Times Index* even includes summaries of major articles, so you can easily read the history of a subject over the course of the year.

A particularly useful index to newspaper articles is *Newsbank*. This index, arranged by subject, lists articles from a variety of newspapers all over the country. Because many of these newspapers do not publish their own indexes, *Newsbank* indexes the best articles and makes them available on microfiche.

8. *Newspapers.* Like periodicals, newspapers can be loose, bound, or microfilmed, although microfilming is the most common way for libraries to store past copies of newspapers. You can access newspaper articles by knowing the name of the paper, its date, and the page number.

9. *Other materials.* Most libraries also contain publications that do not fall into the neat categories of books, periodicals, and newspapers. Many save pamphlets and clippings (often stored in so-called vertical files) on a variety of subjects, and some have special collections of maps, governmental documents, or audio records, tapes, and CDs.

10. *Computer-assisted research.* More and more libraries are now offering automated reference systems that are easy to use and save time. If your library has computerized its card catalog, or a portion of it, it probably subscribes to several computerized retrieval systems for accessing information available in periodicals and other source materials. Each system consists of one or more databases, and their use depends on the particular needs of the researcher. InfoTrac, for example, is one commonly used retrieval system composed of several databases, such as a General Periodicals Index, a Government Publications Index, a National Newspaper Index, and other more specialized databases like LegalTrac and Health Index. Your library may subscribe to one or more of these databases. Ask your reference librarian.

Another computerized retrieval system commonly used is called Silver-Platter. Like InfoTrac, it too consists of a variety of databases covering such general areas as Health Sciences, Health and Safety, Education, Social Sciences, Agriculture, and Business and Technology. One of the databases in Health Sciences, for example, called Sports Discus, is an international sports database covering such areas as exercise physiology, medicine, coaching, counseling, sports medicine, and others. Another widely used database in this system is called ERIC, which indexes the literature of education. Or you may be interested in the database in business called Corporate and Industry Research Report, and the one called PsycLIT, a resource for information in psychology and the behavioral sciences.

Many libraries also have more specialized databases like Abi/Inform, an extensive index of periodical business information about companies and products, business trends, corporate strategies, and management policies and techniques. This more specialized database includes the indexing and abstracting of more than eight hundred business and trade journals.

Many of these databases have certain features in common. All of them include citations to specific articles in periodicals, but many also provide abstracts of articles. This saves you the time of going to the stacks to find out if the article is something you can use.

Of course the advantage of these databases is that they allow you to find information on a subject quickly and easily. Once you locate information that looks interesting to you, you can print what is on the screen and have all the bibliographical information within minutes.

Taking Notes. Whether you are gathering information from people or publications, you will need to record what you find. Many writers find it most convenient to record information on two kinds of cards, called "source" or "bibliography" cards and "note" cards. These cards are just ordinary 3 × 5–

or 4 × 6–inch index cards, though some writers use different sizes or colors to keep their source cards and note cards separate.

Make out a source card for every external source of information you use. Listing information in the form you will be using in your "Works Cited" list or bibliography will make the process much easier. Each discipline has its own particular conventions of documentation, but the bibliographical information is the same. Whenever you write a paper that requires you to use outside material, always ask the instructor which documentation system to use in your paper. The one used here is the Modern Language Association (MLA) style of documentation, used in many of the disciplines in the humanities.

In the case of a personal letter or interview, begin with the name of the person—last name first, a comma, and then first name(s). Identify the nature of the source material (e.g., interview, personal letter), and list the date of the letter or interview. An example follows:

Nichols, Michael R. Interview, January 5, 1991.

In the case of a book, your source card should include the following:

- Author's name (again, last name first; subsequent authors are listed in normal order, e.g., John Smith).

- Book's complete title, either underlined or placed in italics.

- Name of the editor or translator, if any.

- Edition number, if other than the first.

- City of publication (if several are listed, you need record only the first).

- Name of the publishing company.

- Date of publication (usually the latest copyright date).

Here are a few examples of the bibliographical information you would include on a source card for a book:

Peck, M. Scott. *The Different Drum: Community Making and Peace*. New York: Simon and Schuster, 1987.

Bellah, Robert N., Richard Madsen, William N. Sullivan, Ann Swidler, and Steven M. Tipton. *Habits of the Heart: Individualism and Commitment in American Life*. New York: Harper and Row, 1986.

In the case of a periodical article, your source card should include the following:

- Author's name (last name first), if any.

- Article's title, placed in quotation marks.

- Name of the periodical, either underlined or placed in italics.

- Volume number of the periodical, if any.

- Date of the periodical.

- Page numbers of the periodical (list all pages on which the article appears, not just the pages you are taking notes from).

Here is an example of the bibliographical information you would include on a source card for an article appearing in *Time*:

Isaacson, Walter. "O'er the Land of the Free." *Time* 3 July 1989: 14–15.

Record the information you find on separate cards, called "note cards." At the top of each note card, write a word or phrase describing the general subject matter of that card. Then, to key the note card to your source card, write the author's last name; if you have more than one source by the same author, add part of the title as well. When you are ready to take notes on the source material, you will probably use one or a combination of the following types of notes:

Summary. When you summarize a passage, you condense it into a sentence or two, using your own language and sentence structure. Always check to be sure that your summary is an accurate reflection of the original passage but does not use the same words.

Paraphrase. When you paraphrase a passage, you rewrite it in your own words. It is very similar to the summary, except that you restate the passage using about the same number of words as in the original. Both the summary and the paraphrase must always be documented, unless the information is so general as to be considered common knowledge.

Direct Quotation. When you find a passage that is written in a special way, you may decide to copy the passage word for word—quote it directly. To identify directly quoted material, use quotation marks to mark the beginning and the end of a quotation. If you omit words from a sentence when you are quoting it verbatim, use ellipses dots (a series of three periods) to indicate an omission; the sentence parts that remain must fit together grammatically. For example, if you were quoting the preceding sentence, you could substitute "to indicate an omission" with ellipses dots, and the sentence would still be well formed. However, if you used ellipses dots to replace "ellipses dots (a series of three periods) to indicate an omission," the resulting sentence would not be grammatically sound. Also, when you omit parts of a quotation, always check to be sure that you have not changed the meaning intended by the writer you are quoting.

Personal Commentary. Sometimes you may want to make an observation or write a reaction to something you have recorded on your note card. Such commentary is especially helpful when you begin drafting your paper. To distinguish this commentary from other notes on your cards, place this information in brackets so that you know it is not information from the source itself.

Here is a sample note card illustrating directly quoted material from an article appearing in the Indianapolis *Star*:

(Topic:)	Gov't. subsidized art
(Author of article:)	Rooney
(Note:)	"If artists take government money, they have to expect to be subject to the scrutiny and criticism of the Know-Nothings. It's the price they pay for the handout." (p. 14)

Exercises

A. Pair off with someone in the class whom you have not had occasion to meet, and, using the guidelines for preparing for an interview, write a series of questions that you would like to ask this person. Your questions should be designed to elicit information that would be of interest to others in the class. Conduct an interview with the person you have selected, and be prepared to present your findings to the class as a whole.

After the interview, write a bibliography card and a note card, as you would if you were collecting information for a paper.

B. Choose an article, from a popular magazine, that pertains to one of the subjects you have listed in your journal. Write a sample bibliography card and a note card, as you would if you were using information from the article for a paper.

C. Using the same article from a popular magazine, examine the methods used by the writer(s) to introduce information from external sources. Where does the identifying information appear when the writer incorporates material from an external source? Illustrate these methods in your journal.

THE JOURNAL

As you collect information from both internal and external sources, use your journal to create a sourcebook of ideas for writing. One of the best ways to find a subject for a piece of writing is to browse through your journal. Of course, the value of this particular strategy depends on the quality and quantity of your journal entries. If you recall, your journal is the place for you to "think on paper"—to record the ideas that interest you, the topics that intrigue you, and the hobbies and activities that occupy your leisure time. It is also the place for you to ask questions, to explore, and to experiment with ideas.

Think of your journal as a storehouse of ideas, much like a stock room in a department store, where all the merchandise is stored temporarily until it can be moved out onto the shelves for buyers to purchase. Like a stock room—closed to the public—your journal is your own reserve space to do with as you please. It serves the purpose of the writer, not the reader. But like most stock rooms, if it is to serve its purpose, it must be monitored closely, updated regularly, and organized efficiently. Your journal will be a useful sourcebook for you as a beginning college writer if you can find information in it quickly when you need it.

To start thinking about the subjects that interest you, try formulating a question that focuses your thinking on some small part of reality, and then respond to the question in your journal. Some examples of questions follow that tend to call forth lists of items rather than paragraph-length responses. Remember that the purpose of such questions is to help you to list familiar subjects. If a particular subject from your list catches your attention and seems appropriate for a particular assignment, you can develop it further, using the strategies we discussed earlier in this section.

What issues do I feel strongly about?

What courses do I like/dislike the most?

What do/don't I enjoy doing in my free time?

What was most/least rewarding about high school?

What social events do I like or dislike?

What are the worst/best part-time jobs?

What social issues am I most/least likely to follow in the news?

What kinds of movies, books, videos, and so on do/don't I enjoy?

What are the places that I have visited that have been most/least enjoyable?

These are just a few questions that could generate lists of potential subjects. You will no doubt have other questions of your own to ask as well.

Another way to generate subjects for pieces of writing is to be more attentive to your own everyday experiences. When you read something interesting in a newspaper or popular magazine, write about it in your journal. If you don't have time to write at length, then at least jot down the idea so you can add to it later; you may have an opportunity to investigate the topic and learn more about it in a future assignment. Think also of the variety of topics that you hear discussed on television news programs, or the discussions you have with your peers about teachers and courses, registration procedures and academic fees, the cost of textbooks, dormitory visitation hours, the state lottery, athletics, or the like. These are all potential subjects for future papers. If you develop the habit of writing in your journal regularly, you will have an ample supply of subjects to choose from.

That doesn't mean that your journal will write your paper for you. It will very likely produce a subject and perhaps even a focus, but you will still need to learn the process of generating information. So when you browse through your journal looking for subjects to write about, don't be too quick to dismiss a subject from consideration just because you cannot immediately think of what to say about it. You may have lots of information stored in memory, but it just may not be accessible to you at the moment. Gathering content for a piece of writing does not happen instantaneously; it requires thought, planning, and a good deal of writing, all of which often lead to important discoveries about your subject.

Some of the strategies we discuss in this chapter may be more helpful for you than others, but you will not know that until you experiment with them in your own writing.

THE PRELIMINARY THESIS

A preliminary thesis is a sentence that states the writer's main idea in his or her piece of writing; it serves as a guide for the writer, not the reader. Once you have gathered content for your piece of writing, either from internal or external sources, or from both, you should now be able to see your thesis in a new light: Does it say what you want it to say? Will it serve as a guide to your reader, letting the reader know where you are heading in your piece of writing? In some situations, depending on the nature of the writing, you may not have to alter your preliminary thesis, but in most cases, you will need to revise it to reflect what you have learned in the process of gathering content for your piece of writing. Gathering content is part of the process of writing, and most writers must stop periodically to reflect on the process they are engaged in and how each step in the process affects what they are trying to say.

Your thesis should introduce the reader to your topic and should say something about the topic. Suppose you are writing a letter to the youth director of a summer camp to apply for a position as a counselor. Your preliminary thesis may look something like this:

> I want to focus my letter on specific courses that I have taken in school as well as on my work experience, because both these areas relate directly to the job I am applying for.

You can see how this sentence would be very helpful to the writer. But in the process of discovering content, the writer may learn that it was the course work in art and psychology that is most applicable to the position of counselor, and that it was the part-time job working with underpriveleged children that most qualifies him or her for the position. When this writer is ready to draft a letter, he or she may then formulate a thesis that looks something like this:

> My coursework in art and psychology and my work experience with underpriveleged children make me an excellent candidate for the position of youth counselor in your summer program.

Now the writer has produced something that the reader will find helpful. The thesis sentence lets the reader know what the letter is about; it previews the content of the letter for the reader.

Mandy's descriptive essay (sample 2A) written for a tourist magazine provides another good example. This is the opening paragraph of her essay:

> Looking out an open window of an ancient building, one sees the crooked street pathways of a very unique city. These streets are crowded with historical sites bringing to life beauty, culture, and a past age. You probably have heard that Rome contains beautiful history, but until you experience it for yourself, you will not realize the truth of this statement.

Without even looking at the rest of her paper, you know that it will focus on the rich history to be found in certain places in Rome. Mandy, however, wanted to define her focus even more, as evidenced by the first sentence in the paragraph immediately following the introduction:

> Rome contains art galleries, ancient ruins, and many other tourist sites, but one particular site which impresses tourists is St. Peter's Cathedral.

But not all essays have thesis sentences like Mandy's that you can point to in the essay. A thesis sentence may be implicit rather than explicit. When you are writing a description of a place, for example, you select details to create a particular impression of the place for your readers, but you may not state—or tell—your readers, necessarily, what that impression is. Instead, you might want your readers to infer your meaning from the choice of details you have presented. Mandy *tells* us that we will be impressed by St. Peter's Cathedral; there is no doubt about the impression that she wants to leave with her readers. Conversely, Lisa's description of the Indianapolis Produce Terminal (sample 2B) is much less explicit. She embeds her descriptive details in a narrative—a story—whose action centers on the Produce Terminal. But she does not tell us what her impressions are; she uses her details to convey her impressions.

So, in some cases, it may be appropriate to express your thesis implicitly rather than explicitly.

Exercises

A. Choose any two of the essays at the end of this chapter, and determine whether the thesis in each essay is explicit or implicit. Does the thesis accurately reflect the content in each essay? If not, write a thesis sentence that more effectively states what the writer is attempting to say. If the thesis is implied, then identify any inconsistencies in the writer's focus that make it difficult for you to infer the writer's thesis.

B. In predrafting your description of a place, the writing assignment at the end of this chapter, you probably have already begun to use some of the strategies we have discussed for generating content. Review the content you have collected for your description of a place, and then, in your journal, formulate a preliminary thesis to guide you in drafting your piece of writing. What central impression or mood do you want to create for readers of your piece of writing?

Drafting: Expressing Content

After you have gathered content for your paper, you are ready to begin drafting. Having examined your preliminary thesis, you can begin writing the content of your paper, knowing that as you write you have a focusing thought—a central idea. If you find yourself veering off your subject as you write, you will need to get back on course; however, if what you are writing seems interesting and relevant, albeit unexpected, then keep writing. Get the information down on paper, and later you can review it and decide whether it will be useful to you. As much as possible, try to maintain the focus you expressed in your preliminary thesis.

Keep your journal close by in case you want to jot down questions or concerns that occur to you in the drafting process. But do not interrupt the drafting process and lose your train of thought; instead, wait for a convenient juncture and then take some time to reflect. After you have completed the draft and given it a rest, you can refer to the questions in your journal to plan your revising strategy as well as to invite reactions from your peer respondents.

As you draft your piece of writing, you may be using information you have gathered from external sources. Sometimes you will be putting this information in your own words ("summarizing" and "paraphrasing" it); other times you will be quoting it directly from your source. If you have to interrupt your draft to find more information, rather than stopping and losing momentum, make a brief note about the information you want to insert so that you can do so later, and then continue drafting. You will probably make more progress in your writing if you can complete a first draft. You can always add more information later in the postdrafting stage.

Whenever you use the exact words of your source, whether that source is a person or a publication, be sure to identify those words as a direct quotation. As a rule of thumb, indicate a direct quotation whenever you directly quote three or more consecutive words from your source, but even one or two words, if they are used in a particularly original way, should be indicated as a direct quotation.

Normally, indicate a direct quotation by using quotation marks. However, if the quotation is more than eight to ten typed or written lines long, don't use quotation marks. Instead, indent the entire quotation from the left margin; if you are typing, the indentation should be ten spaces, and the quotation should be double spaced, just like the rest of the piece of writing. By double indenting the direct quotation, you create a separate block of text. This formatting technique, used in place of the quotation marks, lets the reader know that you are quoting directly from a source.

Whether you are quoting a source directly or not, you must indicate, for your readers, who or what that source is. In most writing, this "citation" or "documentation" process can be done informally, simply by naming the source in the writing itself. Your readers will thus be assured of the source of your material, even if you have not given them enough information to check it easily on their own. Examples of informal documentation can be found in almost any popular magazine, like this example excerpted from an article titled "Reflections After the Cold War" by Richard J. Barnet (*New Yorker*, January 1, 1990, pp. 65–76):

> In the United States, verbal attacks on Japan make good politics. In Japan, America-bashing is at least as popular, especially after clips of United States congressmen taking sledgehammers to a Toshiba cassette player were relentlessly rerun on Japanese television. "While one can always find an American voice of reason to counter every act of Japan-bashing in Washington," the Washington correspondent for the Japan *Times* Ayako Doi writes, "it is hard to find a Japanese who would publicly counter America-bashing in Japan." The new focus on the United States-Japanese relationship is feeding hostility in both countries, because the problems underlying the relationship are not being adequately addressed. . . . Some public-opinion polls already show that popular sentiment in the United States is more concerned with the popular threat posed by Japan than with the military threat posed by the Soviet Union. (73–74)

Notice that the writer of this passage cites the author (Ayako Doi) and the source (*Times*) of the direct quotation but not the title of the article, the date of its publication, or the pagination. Moreover, in the last sentence, he draws on data from public-opinion polls, but he does not identify which ones or where they can be found. This informal method of documentation is appropriate for readers of the *New Yorker*, who are primarily interested in reading for information and entertainment. If the article were written for an academic journal, however, readers would expect full documentation.

Therefore, in academic writing, you must document your sources more formally, so that your readers can easily check your citations, if they should desire to do so. Traditionally, this documentation was done in footnotes or endnotes, but now most scholars and teachers use "parenthetical" documentation, like that recommended by the MLA. In MLA style, you simply put the author's name and the page number in parentheses at the end of the quoted or paraphrased material; your reader can get more complete information from your "Works Cited" list at the end of your piece of writing. (We explain the procedure for setting up a "Works Cited" list in the postdrafting section of this chapter.)

If we were using information from the excerpt quoted above in an academic paper, we might document it in this way:

> Richard J. Barnet, in a recent article appearing in the *New Yorker*, asserts that political tensions are mounting between the United States and Japan, "especially after clips of United States congressmen taking sledgehammers to a Toshiba cassette player were relentlessly rerun on Japanese television" (73).

Because we already mentioned the author's name in introducing the quotation, we did not need to repeat it in the parenthetical citation. We included only the page number on which the quotation appears in the article. If readers need the complete documentation, they then refer to the "Works Cited" list for the article by Barnet.

We also could have introduced the quotation without mentioning the author's name, as in the following:

> A recent article appearing in the *New Yorker* asserts that political tensions are mounting between the United States and Japan, "especially after clips of United States congressmen taking sledgehammers to a Toshiba cassette player were relentlessly rerun on Japanese television" (Barnet 73).

Because we have not mentioned the author's name in our introduction to the quotation, we have included it in the parenthetical citation at the end of the quotation. However, if the author's last name is not enough to identify the particular source in the "Works Cited" list, we would have to include the first name, and perhaps a title or partial title as well.

When you finish drafting, remember to write questions in your journal for your peer critic. If you wait, you are likely to forget the questions that will be most helpful to you in revising your draft. Write questions that will produce substantive responses. If you write, "Does the quotation I use in the first body paragraph illustrate the point I am arguing in this paragraph?" you are asking a "yes-no" question, which may not be very helpful. But if you write, "How does the quotation function in the first body paragraph?" you are asking for information and not simply a "yes" or a "no."

Postdrafting: Revising Content

The postdrafting stage is the time for you to look critically at what you have produced in your draft. If possible, allow yourself enough time, when you work on a paper, to set your draft aside for a day. By doing this, you can evaluate your draft more objectively, as though you were reading it for the first time.

Having produced a draft of your piece of writing, you should have a clearer conception of what you want to say. Start, then, by reexamining your thesis. If it is stated explicitly in your paper, does it state the focus of your piece of writing in clear, precise terms? Do the key words reflect the emphases in your piece of writing? If your thesis is implicit, does the content of your piece of writing lead the reader to infer it? If you're not sure, ask your peer editor to read your paper and to write what thesis he or she thinks you're implying. In this way, you'll know whether you have maintained a consistent focus.

Also, review the questions and comments you made in your journal while drafting your piece of writing, as well as the reactions and observations you received from your peer editors. This information should help you plan a revising strategy that will lead ultimately to a more effective product.

At the postdrafting stage, when you revise for content, you ask yourself if the content is accurate, if it is complete enough to accomplish your purpose, and if it is relevant to your focus. Surprisingly, though, revising the content of a draft is what many beginning college writers spend the least amount of time doing. *Revising* to them simply means correcting a misspelled word, choosing a better word, or adding a mark of punctuation. Although all of these revisions to a draft are important and necessary to effective communication, they should not—and often cannot—be done effectively until the writer has first asked himself or herself important questions about content. As we said in Chapter One, readers have expectations when they read a piece of writing, including expectations about content, and it is the writer's responsibility to fulfill these expectations.

H. P. Grice, a language philosopher, has developed a theory of conversation that has implications for writers. Knowing how Grice's theory works may help you better understand what your readers' expectations are and how you can revise the content of your writing to meet these expectations.

Grice theorized that when two people engage in a conversation, they agree to cooperate—to talk with each other—by having a purpose for talking. They do not necessarily announce what that purpose is because it is often tacitly understood. Once the purpose is clear, according to Grice, speakers must observe four rules of conversation. One rule, for example, is relevance: what is said must be *relevant*. Think, for instance, of the last time a friend shared something important with you, and you responded with a comment about Monday night's football game or something else completely unrelated. What happens in this situation when your response is not *relevant* to the purpose or direction of the conversation? Well, your friend either becomes angry and stops communicating with you, or looks at you with an expression of disbelief and says, "What did you just say? Are you listening to what I am saying to you?" Fortunately, one of the advantages of a speaking situation, unlike a writing situation, is that you do often get an opportunity to recover when you violate a rule. Oftentimes, a simple apology ("I'm sorry; I wasn't paying attention") will bring the conversation back on course and allow the speakers to continue cooperating. In a writing situation, however, the writer has no opportunity to make amends for lapses in communication.

The three other rules of conversation that Grice describes are quality, quantity, and manner. Quality refers to the truth and accuracy of what you say, quantity refers to the amount of information you give relative to the purpose, and manner refers to the way you present your information, such as its organization or its clarity of expression. As with the rule of relation, when speakers unknowingly break these rules, they risk a breakdown in communication.

You can see how closely this parallels writing and the relationship between writers and readers. Writing, like speaking, is a cooperative effort: writers cooperate with readers by attempting as best they can to fulfill their readers' expectations, and readers cooperate with writers by reading to understand or discover the meaning the writer is communicating. But unlike speakers, writers must attend to the rules and avoid unintentional violations because the reader is not present to ask clarifying questions. If the writer fails to define a key term (a violation of the rule of quantity—not giving information that is needed), for example, the reader is not present to ask, "What do you mean?" or "How are you defining that word?" The result of repeated rule breaking on the part of the writer is poor writing—a failure to communicate meaning.

In this context, Grice's four rules can be helpful to the writer in the postdrafting stage. They can serve as a revising checklist, in fact, enabling the writer to organize important questions for revision and to anticipate the expectations of his or her readers. In what follows, we demonstrate how three of Grice's rules—quality, quantity, and relevance—can help the writer revise the content of a draft—what the writer *says* to his or her readers. Although these three rules are by no means mutually exclusive, they can help the writer focus on different aspects of content in the postdrafting stage. The fourth rule—manner—will be discussed in a later chapter.

RELEVANCE AND QUANTITY: REVISING BY ADDING AND DELETING

As rules for revision, relevance and quantity complement each other. Relevance directs your attention to the relevance of ideas, examples, and details to your purpose and your readers. When you use examples to support an idea, you check to be sure that they are well suited to your readers. You ask yourself, "Is there another example that would be more relevant and better suited to my readers?" "Or are there details that would be more relevant to my purpose?" Quantity, in a sense, solves the problems that relation uncovers. It refers to the amount of information necessary to accomplish your purpose. It invites questions like, "How much information will my readers need?" "Am I giving enough examples to convince my readers that what I say is indeed true?" "Am I giving too much information?" In answering such questions, you either develop your ideas more fully, adding new details, or you eliminate extraneous detail, information deemed unimportant.

For example, the content of a piece of writing must be detailed enough to provide new information to its reader. Consider this paragraph from a draft of Mandy's description of the city of Rome:

> Any tourist entering Rome for the first time will experience the sense of its deep history. This sense of deep history can be experienced in several places. A place exists for any interest one might have. One I personally enjoyed is St. Peter's Cathedral, where the Pope has services. This cathedral, with its beautiful stained glass, large sculptures, and immense altars, gave me the sense of history. I felt as if it were another age and I was the out of place object. If one doesn't enjoy this site then Rome has art galleries, fountains, and ancient ruins to offer. There are thousands of historical spots in Rome and each brings to life a different part of history that one can enjoy.

Mandy was moved by what she experienced in Rome and wanted to share her feelings with her readers, but she did not provide enough new, specific content to make that sharing happen. The paragraph provides very little real information; in fact, it could probably have been written by someone who had not been to Rome at all and who knew only a bare minimum about the city. At the postdrafting stage, Mandy added considerably more information (quantity) about St. Peter's Cathedral; this new, detailed information—especially when accompanied by a change in point of view from "I" to "you"—helps the reader see and feel what the writer saw and felt. Read her final copy (sample 2A) to see the difference.

At times you (like Mandy) may discover the need for this greater detail only after you have written a draft. When you produce a draft, you translate ideas into words on a page so that you have something concrete and tangible in front of you. Then you can invite your internal editor to peer over your shoulder at what you have produced—to examine your content for relevance and quantity.

In Lisa's draft of her essay about the Indianapolis Produce Terminal, she experimented with her concluding paragraph because her ending seemed too obvious and not really relevant to what she was attempting to accomplish.

Her internal editor was at work. Here is the draft of her concluding paragraph:

> Just then I spotted my dad leaning against a skid of boxes, speaking with a salesman. They stood very close and almost seemed to whisper, a ritual I didn't understand. Dad grimaced and pulled a box from the middle of the stack. I watched closely as he opened the lid and stuck his face down on the grapefruit and sniffed. He smiled then and nodding his head he pulled a wad of bills from his pocket. I turned and headed back to our truck to watch our orders being loaded and wait. I knew he would meet me there soon and we would head back west, dropping me off at home so that I could get ready for school and learn reading, writing, and arithmetic. I felt very safe that day riding on that old truck seat beside my dad, and very much a part of his life.

Lisa wondered whether the last sentence was even needed; she thought her readers could perhaps infer that idea from the details provided in her description. And in the sentence with the words "reading, writing, and arithmetic," again she questioned whether she was being too obvious in relating the significance of this experience in her life. In both cases, as you will see by comparing her draft with her final version, she deleted this information (i.e., reduced quantity) because she felt it was more information than was needed.

QUALITY: REVISING FOR ACCURACY

Quality focuses your attention on the accuracy and truth of the information you provide your readers. It leads you to examine your evidence and the way in which you have interpreted it. Quality is especially important when you are using external sources because it requires that you evaluate your sources of opinions, your "experts," for credibility and bias. As a writer, it is your responsibility to make fair and judicious use of source material.

In academic writing, for example, your readers will pay attention to the publication dates of printed material that you borrow from in your piece of writing. They will check to see if your research material is up to date, especially when your subject gets lots of attention in the research. If you are writing about abortion and you incorporate information from sources no more recent than the late 1970s, your reader will naturally question whether you are writing with a knowledge of the more recent Supreme Court amendments to the *Roe v. Wade* ruling.

Likewise, if you have conducted an experiment as a means of gathering information for a piece of writing, your readers will expect you to provide information about your methods. This information, in academic writing, enables the reader to evaluate the evidence you have gathered.

Relevance, quantity, and quality are key words that can easily be committed to memory to guide you in the postdrafting stage of your writing. If you think of your writing as a transaction between you and your readers, and you plan your revisions in anticipation of your readers' needs and expectations, you are more likely to produce successful writing—writing that is clear, complete, and effective.

PREPARING A "WORKS CITED" LIST

If your writing was done for an academic situation and if you have cited external sources, you will need to provide the complete information your readers need to locate those sources. In MLA style, this is done in a "Works Cited" list, an alphabetical list, by author, of the citations in your piece of writing. This list of sources follows the text of your paper. It includes only those works cited in your paper. In general, each source in the list includes the same information listed earlier for "source cards," arranged in alphabetical order by authors' last names. The first line of each source in your list begins at the left margin, and all subsequent lines for each source are indented five spaces.

Because you will be writing papers in other courses, remember that documentation procedures vary from discipline to discipline, so it is always best to ask which method is used in the discipline in which you are writing. Although the bibliographical information is basically the same regardless of the discipline, the way this information is presented does vary across disciplines. Many excellent research manuals are available in your library, and your reference librarian can direct you to them.

Exercise

In your journal, list three questions to help your peer reader evaluate the content in your piece of writing. Begin your questions with information words like *what, where, when,* and *how* so as to avoid yes-no questions.

Assignment 2: Description of a Place

Assignment: Describe a place you know.

Describe a familiar place that you know so that your readers can share the feelings you have when you go to this place. Gather as much content as you can, and then select the details that will help your readers to experience the place as you do. What impression of this place do you want your readers to have after reading your paper? Consider especially what words you can use to convey best your specific sensory perceptions of the place you are describing. How can you make your reader see, hear, or smell what you saw, heard, or smelled in this place?

Sample Papers

Sample 2A (Mandy)

[An article for a tourist magazine]

Looking out an open window of an ancient building, one sees the crooked street pathways of a very unique city. These streets are crowded with historical sites bringing to life beauty, culture, and a past age. You probably have heard that Rome contains beautiful history, but until you experience it for yourself, you will not realize the truth of this statement.

Rome contains art galleries, ancient ruins, and many other tourist sites, but one particular site which impresses tourists is St. Peter's Cathedral. As you walk through the archway into the entrance hall of this incredible structure, you immediately feel as if you have entered another age. It looks quite different from anything found in America. The huge spacious rooms and high ceilings seem to engulf you. You walk on marble floors worn by thousands of feet. These floors still give vivid impressions of swirling creamy designs combining ivory white with strings of sparkling gold. While you walk, your eyes are finding bold sculptures and immense altars symbolizing sacrifices and images you can not begin to understand.

Traveling on through the cathedral, you enter halls lined with large stained glass pieces. One can only stand in awe of these pieces with their glittering pictures, shimmering from the streams of cascading sunlight. The glass looks like rainbows thrown together as images or colors splashed in an array of pictures. This stained glass would definitely be in an art museum if it weren't part of the cathedral.

During a visit to St. Peter's, your experiences lead you to imagine a service there. One can just see the Pope standing before the congregation in his elaborate robe, hands folded, reciting a prayer in Italian. His voice echoes off the walls in the large room like God speaking to his people. It all just jumps to life inside St. Peter's.

As before, Rome has much more to offer you than just St.

Peter's. The art museums, ancient ruins, and fountains are just as much fun to explore. St. Peter's is just an example of how impressive an aspect of Rome can be. Rome is an exceptional city, and you will enjoy the beautiful history it provides to a tourist!

Sample 2B (Lisa)

[A piece for a rural magazine]

The relentless ringing in my ears wrestled me from sleep. Still lying in bed groping in the darkness for the source of this irritation, I relaxed when the ringing ceased—but not for long. "Hustle up," my dad whispered as he poked his head through my bedroom door. "The early bird gets the ripe tomatoes, you know." Still in the dark, I grabbed for the sweat-shirt and jeans I knew were folded neatly on the foot of my bed. Hearing the engine of the old Ford one ton explode into action, I scrambled into my clothes and tore out of the house, half running, half stumbling, just a little afraid of being left behind.

The sky we were driving toward lightened, but since we were making good time, the sun never appeared on that one-hour drive to the Indianapolis Produce Terminal. In the cab I used a flashlight to count and straighten stacks of bills. I felt very adult-like as I placed rubber bands around each stack of $100, and listened intently as my father explained the details of that day's marketing.

Our bodies rocked from side to side on the squeaky truck seat, as we bounced and bumped along the rough stone driveway leading to the Terminal gate. Disregarding a red flasher sign that read "ALL DRIVERS MUST STOP AT GATE," we rumbled along between the two open-faced truck docks. They must have been two city blocks long and they faced one another with high fences at each end, enclosing all the trucks and trailers in between like the walls of a fort. Their long open fronts were punctuated by coal stoves and flues, rising from floor to ceiling like black columns. Signs on the roof above each section proclaimed the company name of the occupants below. Caito and Mascari, Bova Fruit Co., Mery Guliano, Independent Potato Co., The Banana Kings—I read each name under my breath as we passed by, as if memorizing them all.

My dad spied an opening and backed up carefully, squeezing our Ford between two trailers, until we bumped gently against the rubber stoppers on the dock. I hopped out of the truck landing on some already mashed tomatoes sending red gooey pulp and juice squirting up my pant legs. Not at all disturbed by this, I chose a path back to the dock, taking great delight in carefully stepping on every green bean, lettuce leaf and other pieces of garbage strewn about the gutter. Smashing my way back to the dock I waited anxiously for my father, who had taken the stairs, to come around and pull me up on the dock with him. I felt very small and insignificant standing between those trailers, drowning in the hum of their refrigerator units.

At nearly 6:00 A.M., the marketplace was a flurry of activity. Hustling and bustling down the aisles were produce buyers of various descriptions, vying for the attention of dark complected salesmen wearing fedoras and smoking cigars. Old men in tattered clothes pulled skids stacked high with boxes and crates through the crowd, shouting warnings as they went. "Comin' through now! Little bit a room please. Comin' through!"

Feeling the chill of an October morning, I stopped at the coal stove, where a few old white-headed men gathered daily, observing their sons and grandsons handling the business which they had thrived on for years. Sitting in their armchairs, they reminded me of kings on thrones, ruling their kingdoms. I stood silently, remembering conversations that I had overheard between my father and grandfather which gave clear testimony of their great respect for these patriarchs of produce. Warming my backside, I shut my eyes and breathing deeply tried to distinguish all the heavy aromas which pervaded the area. Strongest were the scents of pungent citrus and spicy apples. Also I noticed the unmistakable musk of onion and an occasional waft of rotten potatoes.

Warmed up a bit, I took a walk along the main aisle, dodging busy adults who took no notice of me. I loved to look at each company's display. Always showing their biggest and best produce, they offered my eyes a kaleidoscope of color and a beautiful array of shapes and sizes. Boxes were lined up neatly on a slant, containing bright yellow and orange citrus alternating between various shades of red and green apples. A row of lettuce and other salad vegetables along the top included every tint of green imaginable. Intermittent cases of smaller fruit—deep purple grapes, grass green avocados, hairy little kiwis—made the large fruit look even larger. The display was seasonally framed by bunches of Indiana corn hanging all around and bordered at the bottom by earthen colored squash bulging out the tops of bushel baskets. Indeed the marketplace was a scene to awaken the senses.

Just then I spotted my dad leaning against a skid of boxes, speaking with a salesman. As always they stood very close and almost seemed to whisper—a ritual I didn't quite understand. Dad grimaced and pulled a box from the middle of the stack. I watched knowingly as he opened the lid, stuck his face down on the grapefruit and sniffed. His nose could easily detect moldy fruit in the bottom of a box. He smiled then and nodding his head pulled a wad of bills from his pocket. I turned and headed back to the truck to watch our orders being loaded and to wait. I knew that he would meet me there soon and we would head back west, dropping me off at home so that I could get ready to go to school.

Sample 2C (Amy)

[An article for a county historical society newsletter]

A visitor happening to travel down the winding gravel road that leads to Ceralvo, a tiny community nestled on the banks of the Green River, would find only a few houses and a church that holds services once a year. One might think that Ceralvo has always been simply a rural residential area; however, the buildings there today are actually the remains of a thriving city of another era.

During the mid-1800's, water travel was the most popular form of transportation; consequently, many cities sprang up along rivers where they would have easy access to water routes. Ceralvo was one of those cities. Ceralvo grew very quickly because the ferry boats that docked there brought new people to the area. The ferry was also responsible for bringing supplies which were stored in several warehouses built along the river.

The city had nearly all of the institutions one would expect to find—a post office, two general stores, a dry goods store, a church, and a school. Ceralvo also had a hotel, a drug store, and three tobacco factories where tobacco was stored and traded. The city was home to such professionals as a blacksmith, a cobbler, and two doctors. Ceralvo even had a college, although it consisted of only a handful of students taught by a professor.

During the early part of this century, river travel declined due to the increased popularity of railroads. Because river travel was the life blood of Ceralvo, the city met with hard times. It was at this time that several businesses, such as the dry goods store, moved to the growing city of Owensboro. Families and professional people also moved to more prosperous cities around the state. The final, crippling blow to the city was the flood of 1937, which wiped out most of what remained in Ceralvo.

Sample 2D (Joe)

[A reflective piece for an agricultural magazine]

Childhood memories usually occupy a very special place in your mind. Some of them may be warm images of special times as you were growing up. Possibly your first bicycle or maybe a special toy or doll you had a certain closeness to. Many memories can be of places, like those of your grandparents' home, their antique furniture with doilies seeming to cover every table, or of their old pot-bellied stove, radiating heat from its reddened sides.

A place which returns many memories to my mind is an old barn that stood on the farm where I was born. It was a very large structure with siding that had been weathered and cracked by the many years of harsh summer sunshine, and the bitter cold of winters. Years of rain had rusted many of the nails, leaving dark brown stains, streaked into the grayness of the siding. Some of it had fallen to the ground. Off of one end of the barn, a gently sloped roof extended over an open area. A long corn crib ran parallel to the barn and supported the outer end of this roof. Each wooden shingle of this roof seemed to be trimmed with a soft, green moss.

A grassy mound of soil rose to the second story of this barn. By walking up this hillside, you could reach the upper section of the barn. Opening two large doors reveals to you a large open area. A few tiny holes in the roof let the sunlight pierce the darkness of this hayloft. Allow a few minutes for your eyes to adjust to this darkness and you can see that a massive skeleton of large wooden beams surrounds you. Each beam still carries the axe marks where someone had shaped them by hand. Wooden pegs hold them solidly together. By autumn, bales of hay would occupy much of this space.

Descending the ladder leads to the lower portion of the barn. It is divided into many stalls. Planks of wood, some of them two feet wide, were used to make the walls of these pens. This lower section of the barn is where the cows were milked, and where other animals could be kept separate.

Many hours were spent in and around this barn, working and playing. In the spring and summer bales of hay would have to be stacked into the loft. This was usually a very hot and sweaty chore. Fall was the time to harvest the corn. It would fill the crib (a long rectangular area) from its floor to the roof. Feeding and tending to the animals was a daily task.

Playing on a mountain of baled hay, or sliding down a golden pile of corn would be something any farmboy would recall. The barren ground beneath the basketball goal tells of the endless hours spent playing ball here.

This barn could also be a refuge when you needed time to relax. You could spend a still moment watching purple barn swallows, their tails forking out to a V-shape, as they would dart through an open door or window, to a nest among the beams in the ceiling. Or you may sit in the comfort of the loft, with the fresh smell of new mown hay, and watch for the old barn owl to return to its nest that you have discovered. Many times it was nice to stretch out on a soft bale of hay and listen as the raindrops played their music on the roof.

Sample 2E (Michael)

[A description for a textbook]

At the end of Seventeenth of June Street, Strasse des 19 zu Juni, lies a fourteen foot wall, the Berlin Wall. This is the most famous part of the Wall that was built by Russia and East Germany to "keep out Western influence." The Berlin Wall was built about three decades ago, separating East and West Berlin. Since then it has become synonymous as the landmark that divides Western and Soviet Bloc countries.

There it stands, a concrete slab that horrified and shocked the world. The physical aspect of the wall is frightening. The part seen by most tourists is a tall, cold, gray wall with an ominous guard tower standing behind it. Through the darkly tinted windows of the tower a high powered machine gun is unmistakably seen in a small porthole. The Wall itself looks as if it has a million stories of struggle to tell; its pock marked, graffiti ridden surface is accented by large red signs telling people to keep behind the metal railing.

Climb up the small platform overlooking the Wall. What is there to see? An obstacle course of death: barbed wire, deep sand, trenches, land mines, and dog tracks where the Germans run fierce German Shepherds trained to kill. The atmosphere is a mockery of freedom.

Look past the Wall and barbed wire. Look toward the blurred bleakness of the East. Old cars and new military vehicles loaded with soldiers carrying AK47s zip through the crowded streets. People walk along briskly, dressed in dark colors and old clothing. Minding their own business they hurry through the crumbling buildings as soldiers suspiciously glance about. Their world is one of busy and wary watchfulness.

On the Western side there is an ominous reverence for the Wall. Visitors and tourists speak in hushed voices and toss nervous glances toward the guard tower. Watch the faces of the people looking toward the East. What do you see, sadness?

A man begins waving and shouting in German, "Hallo, Hallo!" On the Eastern side an old man waves back. The old man shouts out something but the other does not hear. A tear runs down the man's cheek as he turns sadly away. Look back over to the East. Soldiers are already forcing the old man to leave.

This is the Berlin Wall. These are the emotions of the Berlin Wall. What will its future be? Will it remain or be destroyed? Only our future generations have the power to make that decision.

Discussion Questions

1. Which of the five places described seems most real to you? Which seems least real? What word choices contribute to these effects?

2. What differences in sentence structure do you see among these five writers? What effect do these differences have on your response to the descriptions?

3. As you probably noticed, these sample papers are untitled. The writers chose to write their papers for small magazines or newsletters, and often in such situations, the copy editor of the magazine or newsletter decides on an appropriate title for the piece. The copy editor often counts character spaces before deciding on an appropriate title. What titles do you think would be appropriate for these pieces of writing?

CHAPTER THREE

The Process of Organizing Your Writing

One of the most difficult things about writing is that it is linear. That is, it consists of one word, phrase, or sentence after another; it is typically read in a "straight line," starting at the beginning and proceeding to the end. Thought, on the other hand, is often not linear. What we know about a subject, we know "all at once," as a complex of simultaneous, interconnected ideas. Converting nonlinear thought to linear writing is one of the most difficult and important activities in the writing process.

In an early episode of the "M*A*S*H" television series, an unexploded bomb lands in the compound, and Hawkeye and Trapper are assigned to defuse it. A bomb-defusing manual—a piece of writing—is located, and Colonel Blake, safely behind a sandbag bunker, reads it aloud through a bullhorn.

"First you need a wrench," he reads. Hawkeye and Trapper find one. "All right, now, place it gently on the nut just above the locking ring and loosen." They do. "Now, rotate the locking ring counterclockwise." They figure out which way is counterclockwise and rotate it. "Now, remove the tail assembly." They do. "And carefully cut the wires leading to the clockwork fuse at the head." Snip. Snip. "But first, remove the fuse. . . ."

The resulting explosion dramatizes the problem of linearity in writing. The writer of the manual knew the subject but failed to consider the order in which readers would be reading it. The result was a less than effective piece of writing. An effective piece of writing is organized: it has its information in the order that best serves the reader's needs and the writer's purpose.

If you doubt your ability to achieve effective and purposeful organization in your writing, you may find it helpful to think of some of the ways you employ organizational skills every day in a variety of situations. Consider, for example, what you do when you first get the day's mail. Do you randomly open the pieces of mail, or do you select certain pieces to open first? You probably organize the pieces of mail without even thinking about it, opening the personal letters first, then perhaps the bills, and finally—if at all—the junk mail.

You employ these same organizing skills when you plan your day's errands, read a newspaper, or write a shopping list. When you look at the morning or evening newspaper, for example, you probably read certain sections first, depending on your purpose or interests. Or when you write a shopping list, don't you tend to group items—dairy products, meats, canned goods? You can easily imagine the confusion you would experience in today's more expansive grocery stores if you did not organize your shopping list—or at least know the way grocery products in the store are organized. You would spend literally hours walking from one end of the store to the other, and back again, looking for each grocery item on your list. Though your method of organizing will vary with different purposes, the strategy itself is always the same: you organize to accomplish your needs and satisfy your purposes.

As you can see, you use your organizational skills each day to function in the world. Your organizing skills, in a sense, are your survival skills. Every day you manage the events and details of your life to accomplish your needs, and in a writing situation, you manage your ideas—your written work—to communicate effectively with your readers.

So, to learn how to organize your writing effectively and purposefully, you can start by applying the organizational skills that you use every day. As you read this chapter, think of the organizational strategies we illustrate and discuss, not as new material, but as an extension of the knowledge you already possess.

Because much of this knowledge is intuitive, you might try consciously relating these strategies to common situations in your own experience. When you read about time order, for example, think of various processes you engage in routinely—like getting dressed in the morning, planning the evening meal, mixing the baby's formula, and changing the oil in your car. Likewise, when you read about classification as an organizing tool, think of your record collection and the way you may have organized your records into groups; or when you read about analysis, another organizing tool, think of your car or compact-disc player and the particular features that influenced your decision to buy it. By relating these various organizational strategies to your own experiences, you will play an active part in your learning and have an easier time applying this knowledge to the management of information in your writing.

Predrafting: Planning the Organization

As the diagram in Figure 1 suggests, the best time to consider the organization of a piece of writing is at the predrafting stage. As you define the situation for your writing and gather information for its content, you will no doubt begin to form ideas of how that information should be organized: how it can be presented most effectively for your readers' understanding.

Planning the organization will be easier for some kinds of writing and more difficult for others. For example, in describing a process, once you have identified the steps or stages, you may not have to think much about the organization; the order in which you listed the steps or stages of the process at the predrafting stage may in fact be the order you follow when you draft your piece of writing. In other kinds of writing, however, you will need to devote more time and thought to organization. In writing an autobiographical piece, for example, about the events in your life that contributed most to your career interest, you may at first decide to follow a chronological order, as you would in describing a process. You may discover, however, that a chronological ordering of events may not be the best organizational plan to achieve your particular purpose. In this situation, then, you would organize the content of your piece of writing differently. You might decide to begin with the least important events and progress to the most important ones, or you might choose to relate specific events to others in your life, regardless of the time sequence. Each piece of writing will be different because the variables in the writing situation *will vary*—sometimes only in subtle ways, other times in more obvious ways.

Before you begin drafting, you may find it helpful to sketch the organization of your ideas on a separate sheet of paper that you can refer to as you draft your piece of writing. A formal outline—with Roman numerals, capital letters, and so on—is not necessary, unless it helps you better conceive the organization of your writing. But an informal outline, perhaps just in the form of a numbered list, can be very helpful for many writers, in giving them a sense, before they begin drafting, of the order in which they will present their information to their readers.

At the predrafting stage of writing her instructions for applying for state FHA office (sample 1A), Amy wrote the following informal outline:

Application
    qualifications
    requirements

Tentative program
    topics to be covered
    guest speakers
    theme
    recreation

State meeting

Stage performance

Test

Interview

As you can see, Amy was able to produce a tentative outline of the topics and subtopics that she wanted to address in her piece of writing.

Developing an informal outline at the predrafting stage is often an effective way to prepare for drafting a piece of writing. But it also requires a good deal of planning. As a beginning college writer, you might find it difficult at first to plan the organization of your piece of writing before you actually begin drafting; your attention to the variables in the writing situation as well as to the content of your piece of writing may in itself be overwhelming. If this is the case, then simply start drafting; your ideas will take shape as you draft, though perhaps not in a way that will completely satisfy you or your readers. But once you have produced a draft, you can then go back and look more critically at the organization of your writing. So organization may not be a conscious step for you in the predrafting stage. But at some point, if your writing is to be effective, attention to organization must become a deliberate step in the process of communicating your ideas to your readers.

Whether you make an informal outline for your writing, or allow your ideas to take shape as you draft, you need to consider the three parts of any piece of writing: the beginning, the middle, and the end.

BEGINNINGS: MEETING THE READER

It is not entirely accurate to say that the "beginning" is a "part" of every piece of writing. Certainly not all pieces of writing have a clearly identifiable section we can label with the noun "beginning." But all pieces of writing "begin" somewhere, and that verb reminds us that "beginning" is an activity involving the piece of writing and its reader.

The beginning is where the reader starts, and so it has a very important role in the piece of writing. If you remember, from Chapter Two, the list that Joe made before he began drafting his descriptive piece about the old barn (sample 2C), you may recall that in that preliminary list, he already recognized the importance of a beginning for his writing. An idea occurred to him, and he wrote it down.

• Special memories (first bicycle, grandma's home).

Joe knew that he wanted to describe an old barn that was a center of activity for him as a child, and by generalizing from that experience in his life, he was able to place his subject into a larger class—special memories. Moreover, he had even begun to think of particular examples of special memories that he could use in his beginning.

The beginning of a piece of writing is the starting point for the reader: it is the space in which the writer prepares his or her readers for the subject and focus of the piece of writing. It is like the lobby of a hotel that you enter for the first time. Everything about the lobby—its appearance, its style, its size—is often indicative of the type of accommodations and quality of service you can expect when you register as a guest. You form your first impressions on entering the lobby, just as you form your first impressions on reading the beginning of a piece of writing. The beginning is where the reader first meets the writing, discovers what it is about, forms a first impression of it, and decides whether to read on. So the beginning must

1. Define all or part of the writing situation for the reader.

2. State or imply a clear thesis, or focus—what the writer wants to accomplish.

3. Give a favorable first impression, making the reader want to keep reading.

One very important thing to remember about the beginning of a piece of writing is that it doesn't have to be the first thing the writer writes. That is a great advantage of writing over speaking: the order of composing doesn't have to be the same as the order of receiving. In speaking, you cannot take back your words once you utter them, but in writing, you can compose your thoughts in any order because you have the privilege of revising and editing to your satisfaction. Sometimes you may even find it easier to skip the beginning at the drafting stage and come back to it after you have drafted the middle of the piece of writing. Many writers do this because they often discover ideas for beginnings in the process of drafting their piece of writing.

Even though Joe had a general idea of how to begin his piece of writing about the old barn, for example, he actually composed the beginning only after he had written several complete drafts of the rest of his essay. Only at that point did he know the specific details that he wanted to include in his beginning paragraph.

> Childhood memories usually occupy a special place in your mind. Some of them may be warm images of special times as you were growing, possibly your first bicycle or maybe a special toy or doll you had a certain closeness to. Many memories can be of places, like those of your grandparents' home, their antique furniture with doilies seeming to cover every table, or their old pot-bellied stove, radiating heat from its reddened sides.

To orient his readers to the subject of his paper, Joe begins by writing about childhood memories in general, first about memories of "special times" and then about memories of "places." In doing so, he invites his readers to reflect on their own special childhood memories and thereby establishes a common ground with his readers. Using a few selected examples and images, he achieves his purpose by creating a mood appropriate for his reflective essay.

Once he has engaged his readers, he then introduces, in the next paragraph, his specific focus:

> A place which returns many memories to my mind is an old barn that stood on the farm where I was born.

The opening paragraph, then, functions to set the proper mood and to involve readers in a nostalgic look at childhood memories. The thesis, or focusing sentence, tells readers what the piece of writing will be about, the key words being "the old barn" and "returns many memories."

Christina (sample 1B), if you recall, used a similar strategy in her essay about the campus employment service. To introduce her subject, she describes a new student on campus, named Mike, who is faced with particular circumstances—a full schedule of classes and a desperate need for part-time employment. Most students can easily relate to these circumstances.

> Mike is a new student at IUPUI. He just registered for classes and is all set to begin in the fall, but he does have one problem: he needs a job.

Christina knew that if her readers—college students—could see a part of themselves in Mike, they would be more inclined to continue reading her piece of writing. In an earlier draft, however, her beginning was not nearly as compelling.

> Finding a job can sometimes be a long and disappointing task. You can search for months and months and keep coming up with dead ends.

At the postdrafting stage, Christina revised this lackluster beginning and effected a more personal and direct appeal to the readers' needs. Like Joe, she creates a situation that she knows her readers will more easily identify with, and only then does she introduce her focus.

> For Mike, finding a job that will work around his schedule won't be an easy task, but as a student at IUPUI, he has a great resource to help him find a job, and if you are like Mike, it could help you too.
>
> The program is called JOBS, which stands for Job Opportunities

for Businesses and Students, and it is located in the Business Building
in Room 2010.

In his essay about buying a compact-disc player (sample 1C), Mike takes
a more pragmatic approach in his beginning. Because he assumes that most
of his readers may not have heard of the compact-disc player, he is careful to
take the time to orient his readers to his subject. After first introducing the
subject of his piece of writing, the compact-disc player, he briefly defines
what it is and tells why it is "the newest trend in music listening today,"
ending the paragraph with a sentence expressing his focus and his purpose.

> The newest trend in music listening today is the compact-disc
> player. This is a unit that plays back prerecorded music by lasers.
> The reason so many people are becoming interested in CD players is
> because they give the listener an incredibly true reproduction of the
> sound. But before you go out and buy one, there are several factors
> you should be familiar with that will strongly influence your decision
> of which compact-disc player to buy.

Michael does not see the need to "sell" his subject, as Christina does, and so
his beginning is matter-of-fact. He is not promoting the sale of CD players, as
Christina is promoting the benefits of the campus employment service. He is
merely sharing information with his readers so that they can make an informed decision if they should decide to purchase a CD player. But like
Christina and Joe, Mike ends with a focusing sentence that prepares readers
for what will come in the middle of his piece of writing: "several factors" that
will "strongly influence" one's selection of a CD player.

One pitfall to avoid when planning the beginning of a piece of writing
is "overintroducing." Constance began the first draft of her autobiographical
essay (sample 2C) like this:

> It was a terrifying experience, blindfolded, tied up, and placed
> in a bathtub. I hear the door lock and feel the darkness. At the age
> of five, I am alone and frightened. The cruel captors are outside the
> door laughing and whispering. I suppose they are making plans,
> more plans for punishment. The door unlocks; I am lifted from the
> tub; a feeling of dread washes over me. What now? Once again my
> three brothers have taken advantage of being left to babysit me, their
> "baby sister."
> I have pondered about my various intellectual and cultural
> experiences. I have wondered what in my life has had such an
> awesome impact upon me? What has exposed me to various facets of
> life? One simple reply—brothers.
> I suppose that in a "normal" family (whatever that may mean),

one does not always get the opportunity to see the world in different colors.

Perhaps I should make an introduction? Before my illustrious entrance into this world my parents had three boys: Don, Jeff, and Chris. Each in his own way seems to typify a very separate culture.

One problem with this beginning was its length. Because it constituted almost a fourth of the entire draft, it seemed out of proportion, forcing the reader to go a fairly long way to get to the essence of the essay. But a more serious problem was the lack of unity in this beginning. It seemed, in fact, almost like four different beginnings, with four different tones, each in its own paragraph: a suspenseful anecdote, a philosophical meditation, a sociological reflection, and a dramatic fanfare. Constance was "overintroducing" her writing.

At the postdrafting stage of her process, Constance revised her beginning to look like this:

It was a terrifying experience, blindfolded, tied up, and placed in a bathtub. I hear the door lock and feel the darkness. At the age of five, I am alone and frightened. The cruel captors are outside the door laughing and whispering. I suppose they are making plans, more plans for punishment. The door unlocks; I am lifted from the tub; a feeling of dread washes over me. What now? Once again my three brothers have taken advantage of being left to babysit me, their "baby sister."

Perhaps I should make an introduction? Before my illustrious entrance into this world my parents had three boys: Don, Jeff, and Chris. Each in his own way has had an awesome impact upon me. Each has exposed me to various facets of life, facets that I, alone, would never have realized existed.

This beginning does a much more effective job of introducing her essay: the first paragraph creates interest and encourages the reader to read on, whereas the second paragraph clearly introduces the purpose and focus of the essay. Although Constance was able to make this revision at the postdrafting stage, she could probably have saved some time by planning more carefully while predrafting. As a developing writer, however, she needed to see her beginning on the page before she could find a way to make it better.

Exercises

A. Choose three of the following sample papers and evaluate how well their beginnings perform each of the three functions listed earlier:

1. Amy's instructions for applying for FHA office (sample 1A).

2. Mandy's description of Rome (sample 2A).

3. Lisa's descriptive essay about the Indianapolis Produce Terminal (sample 2B).

4. Kathy's autobiographical essay for admission to nursing school (sample 3A).

5. Amy's autobiographical essay (sample 3B).

6. John's autobiographical essay (sample 3D).

B. Write new beginnings for three of the sample papers just listed. Be prepared to discuss any improvements you have made.

C. Choose one of the essays you have written in the course, and apply what you learned in this section about beginnings to your own essay. In your journal, experiment with two or three different ways to begin your essay, and then test each version on your peer readers to see which one is best suited to your writing situation.

MIDDLES: GUIDING THE READER

The middle of the piece of writing is its reason for being: it guides the reader through the subject matter to fulfill the writer's purpose. It is the space in which the writer develops and amplifies the central idea, or focus, introduced in the beginning. If, from the reader's perspective, the beginning of a piece of writing is, as we said, like entering the lobby of a hotel, then the middle of a piece of writing is like checking into the hotel, dining in its restaurants and cafes, enjoying its recreational facilities—in short, experiencing firsthand the quality of its accommodations and service. This combined experience would either prove or disprove your initial impressions of the hotel. Similarly, readers consider the middle of a piece of writing as the writer's attempt to affirm, through an orderly presentation of supporting material, the central idea established in the beginning. Whereas a hotel guest might ask, "Is this hotel what I thought it would be?" a reader of a piece of writing is likely to ask, even if only subconsciously, "Does this middle section maintain and support the focus that the writer introduced in the beginning?"

Middles can be organized in a variety of ways, but these organizational plans are essentially of three kinds: those that "imitate" the subject itself, those that "conceptualize" about the subject, and those that persuade. As you study these various ways of ordering the content of a piece of writing, remember that these orders do not occur in isolation. They are almost always used in combinations with other ordering strategies. Together they operate at different levels within a piece of writing. One ordering strategy, for example, may function to frame the whole piece of writing, while other orders may serve to organize the content in a sequence of paragraphs, in a single paragraph, or in a few contiguous sentences.

By learning to identify these ordering strategies and their function in a hierarchical system of orders, you will eventually write and read with greater awareness of the role organization plays in communicating meaning to readers.

Imitative Organization. Some subjects are already organized linearly, so when this natural, linear organization seems best for the reader and purpose, the writer need only imitate it in the piece of writing. The "M*A*S*H" technical manual is a good example. There was already an order of steps for defusing the bomb; all the writer had to do was write down the steps in that order. This does not mean, however, that the writer has a simple, essentially passive role to play in this process. As the "M*A*S*H" episode illustrates, the writer must still be very careful to get the order right.

The two most common imitative organizations are time order and space order.

1. *Time order*, often called chronological order, is the order of events in time, usually from earliest to latest. Time order is particularly appropriate when recounting something that happened in the past or when giving directions for a process.

Amy's instructions for applying for FHA state office (sample 1A) are organized in time order, step by step through the process. So is John's autobiography (sample 2D), although the other autobiographical essays (2A, 2B, and 2C) are not necessarily organized this way.

When you choose time order, make sure that it is the most helpful organizational pattern for the reader. Some inexperienced writers overuse this pattern, describing almost every subject in the order they learned about it. Although time order may be helpful as you are getting your ideas onto paper, serving a preliminary purpose for you as writer, remember that it may not be the ideal mode of organization for your readers. Most readers will not be interested in knowing the order in which you learned about a subject.

2. *Space order* is the order of objects, or parts of objects, in space, perhaps from left to right, or from top to bottom, or from outside to inside, or the reverse of any of those orders. Space order is particularly appropriate in writing physical descriptions, as in descriptions of a place.

Michael's description of the Berlin Wall (sample 3B) is principally organized by space order; he first shows us the wall as we would see it as we approach, then takes us onto the wall and gives us the view from its top, first east, then west. But notice that Amy's description of the town of Ceralvo is organized not in space order but in time order; her overall approach is not so much geographical as historical.

Especially important in spatial order is the writer's control of point of view. For example, if you are describing a place like a historic building, you may locate yourself outside the building and describe its exterior, but you would not describe its interior unless some part of it could be seen from your vantage point. If you wanted the reader to see the interior of the building, you would have to shift your point of view—your vantage point. Otherwise, your description would be confusing to your reader. The reader needs to know when your point of view changes. Notice how Michael prepares his readers for a change in vantage point in this paragraph from the middle of his piece of writing about the Berlin Wall.

> Climb up the small platform overlooking the Wall. What is there to see? An obstacle course of death: barbed wire, deep sand, trenches, land mines, and dog tracks where the Germans run fierce German Shepherds trained to kill. The atmosphere is a mockery of freedom.

Likewise, in his description of the old barn, Joe begins by describing the outside of the barn and then takes the reader with him as he moves to the side of the barn, up a grassy hillside to the second-story level, and through two large doors leading to the inside, detailing his perceptions as he moves. When he enters the two large doors of the barn, only then does he describe how "a few tiny holes in the roof let the sunlight pierce the darkness of this hayloft."

Of course, space and time order may also be combined. If you are narrating a story, you are not only relating events in time but also perhaps describing people and places, using sensory details and images to make the scene come alive for the reader.

Because Lisa's description of the Indianapolis Produce Terminal is set in a narrative context, she uses time order to organize the narrative—her trip to the Indianapolis Produce Terminal—and space order to describe the people and the place once she arrives there. Here is one paragraph that exemplifies how she combines time and space order.

> At nearly 6:00 A.M., the marketplace was a flurry of activity. Hustling and bustling down the aisles were produce buyers of various descriptions, vying for the attention of dark complected salesmen wearing fedoras and smoking cigars. Old men in tattered clothes pulled skids stacked high with boxes and crates through the crowd, shouting warnings as they went. "Comin' through now! Little bit a room please. Comin' through!"

Conceptual Organization. Many subjects, of course, are not organized linearly. Even for some that are, a linear, imitative organizational plan may not serve the reader's needs or the writer's purpose. For these remaining subjects, a "conceptual" plan is necessary. That is, the writer must impose a new order on the subject, an order that the writer conceives as best meeting the needs of the writing situation. Four of the most common conceptual plans are cause-and-effect, classification-and-analysis, comparison-and-contrast, and definition.

1. *Cause-and-effect* organization is just what it says, an account of the cause(s) for something or an account of the effect(s) of something. When examining causes, you look back in time and ask, "What caused X to occur?" When examining effects, you look ahead in time, relative to the event, and ask, "What has happened as a result of X, or what would happen if X occurred?"

If you got into your car one morning and discovered that it would not start, you would probably consider the possible *causes* before calling a mechanic for assistance—an empty gas tank, water in the distributor, loose or corroded battery cables. Conversely, if you had your car at the service garage for an engine tune-up and had just picked it up, you would probably listen carefully for any unusual sounds coming from the engine—for any *effects* that might indicate poor engine performance.

Either cause or effect can be presented first in a piece of writing, depending on the writer's purpose. The middle section of Amy's autobiographical essay (sample 2B) has a cause-and-effect organization: she describes her father's illness, then describes the effect it had on her professional goals.

When organizing your material in cause-and-effect order, be sure to avoid the logical fallacy called *post hoc, ergo propter hoc* (after this, therefore, because of this)—the assertion that just because Event B came after Event A, it was the effect, or result, of Event A. Another common problem associated with cause-and-effect is oversimplification, or attributing a single cause to an effect when there may in fact be multiple causes.

2. *Classification and analysis* are ways of organizing information by dividing it into categories or parts; technically, classification consists of dividing a group of things into categories, whereas analysis consists of dividing one thing into parts, but the principle is the same for both. In both cases, you are helping the reader understand the whole by understanding the parts or categories that make it up.

Constance's autobiographical essay (sample 2C) is organized in this way, dealing with the influence of each of her three brothers, in order. In writing about her past experiences, she uses her three brothers as "categories" to frame her experiences, enabling the reader to follow her discussion. Similarly, if you were writing a review of a movie or concert, you would analyze your subject by first dividing it into parts and discussing these parts, which together would make up your evaluation of the movie or concert.

Suppose you are writing a paper about the sport of skating. As part of your discussion you decide to write about the different kinds of skates, so you classify your subject—skates—into three categories: hockey, figure, and speed skates. In describing how these skates are different from each other, you might then divide the subject into its parts, such as the shape of the boot, the length and design of the blade, and particular construction features.

By organizing your information in this way, you are making the writing task easier for yourself and also assisting your readers' comprehension.

When classifying a subject, be sure that your categories are governed by the same principle of classification. We can classify students as freshmen, sophomores, juniors, and seniors—each category being an academic level or rank based on total number of credit hours; however, if we add part-time students to these four categories, then the principle of classification shifts from academic level (determined by total number of credit hours) to academic status (determined by number of credit hours within a semester). If distinguishing between full-time and part-time students is important to the writer's purpose, then the writer must keep these two levels of classification separate. The following sample outlines show both classification schemes combined but ordered to reflect different emphases:

Sample Outline 1

FIRST-LEVEL
CLASSIFICATION: FULL-TIME STUDENTS

    Second-level
    classification: Freshmen

                         Sophomores

                         Juniors

                         Seniors

FIRST-LEVEL
CLASSIFICATION: PART-TIME STUDENTS

    Second-level
    classification: Freshmen

                         Sophomores

                         Juniors

                         Seniors

Sample Outline 2

FIRST-LEVEL
CLASSIFICATION: FRESHMEN

    Second-level
    classification: Full-time students

                         Part-time students

FIRST-LEVEL
CLASSIFICATION: SOPHOMORES

    Second-level
    classification: Full-time students

                         Part-time students

FIRST-LEVEL
CLASSIFICATION: JUNIORS

    Second-level
    classification: Full-time students

                         Part-time students

FIRST-LEVEL
CLASSIFICATION: SENIORS

    Second-level
    classification: Full-time students

                         Part-time students

As organizing tools, classification and analysis make it easier for the writer to organize a complex body of material, thus making it easier for the reader to process the material.

3. *Comparison and contrast* is a way of organizing information on two or more items or subjects. There are essentially three different ways of comparing and contrasting. In the following outlines, we show how two items can be compared and contrasted, but the outlines can be easily expanded to include more than two items.

    a. *Item-by-item* organization is a method of comparison and contrast that looks at each item separately. It is especially useful when the items being compared and contrasted do not have clear-cut features that they share.

        Item A
            Feature 1
            Feature 2
        Item B
            Feature 1
            Feature 2
            Feature 3

    b. *Feature-by-feature* organization is a method of comparison and contrast that looks at the features shared by the items, and examines how the items are alike or different in these features. This method is especially useful when you want to give the reader a detailed look at these shared features.

> Feature 1
>> Item A
>> Item B
> Feature 2
>> Item A
>> Item B
> Feature 3
>> Item A
>> Item B

c. *Similarity-and-difference* organization is a method of comparing and contrasting that emphasizes the ways in which the items are like and unlike. Either the similarities or the differences may be presented first. It is especially appropriate when you want to call attention to either the similarities or the differences, or both.

> Similarities between Item A and Item B
>> Feature 1
>> Feature 2
>> Feature 3
> Differences between Item A and Item B
>> Feature 1
>> Feature 2
>> Feature 3

4. *Definition* as a conceptual order may employ potentially all of the organizing strategies discussed thus far. Because words can sometimes have different meanings for different readers, you need to define key terms or concepts that may potentially confuse readers. In many cases, merely looking up the word in a dictionary will provide enough information for you to clarify your meaning. You might, for example, add a more familiar word or a clarifying phrase, or perhaps a more formal sentence definition. At other times, however, when a word or concept that needs defining is central to the argument in your piece of writing, you may need to extend your definition beyond a single sentence to one or more paragraphs. In fact, in some situations, a writer may devote the entirety of a piece of writing to a definition. In discussions of very complex issues like pornography and abortion, for example, often the focus is on the interpretation of key terms like *obscenity* and *life*. These longer, more detailed definitions, called extended definitions, usually encompass more than one ordering strategy.

Defining a word is limiting or restricting the meaning of that word; *definition* comes from the Latin word *definire*, meaning "to limit" or "to set boundaries." When a key term in your piece of writing is ambiguous or confusing, it is your responsibility to define its meaning so that your readers can more easily follow your discussion. Whenever you define a term, you are giving your readers a rule, so to speak, that they must observe to understand the message you are attempting to communicate. It is as though you are saying to the reader, "This word is important to my discussion, and when you see it in my paper, this is what it means. If you assume other meanings not specified here, you may mistake my meaning and misread my paper."

Traditionally, definitions follow a very formulaic pattern, consisting of the word to be defined, its genus or class, and specific differences that set the word apart from other members of the class. By studying this pattern, you can learn to write good sentence definitions and, when necessary, to develop extended definitions that help you fulfill your purpose in writing.

When you write a formal definition, you first place the word to be defined into a larger class (i.e., you *classify* it) and then distinguish it from other members of that class (i.e., you *contrast* it). In his essay about the CD player (sample 1C), for example, Michael defines a CD player as "a unit that plays back pre-recorded music by lasers." He first places the word to be defined into a larger class—"a unit"—and then adds characteristics that distinguish it from other members of its class—"that plays back pre-recorded music by laser." The CD player is thus distinguished from other "units" such as turntables and tape players, neither of which use lasers as a means of producing sound.

In some situations, you may not agree with the "limits" or "boundaries" of a dictionary definition, and you may want to stipulate either a narrower or broader definition—one that better suits your purpose in a piece of writing. This often happens with words that are abstract. You may want to stipulate a definition that you believe is more accurate or perhaps more sensible than the standard definition. Such definitions usually require more detail and hence more time.

For example, suppose you want to argue that television programs like "Sesame Street" and "Electric Company" are not learning experiences for children. They entertain, you say, but they do not educate. Before you advance the argument of your paper, you will need to define what you mean by "learning experiences," for your readers may interpret a "learning experience" in a way that is not consistent with your own interpretation. To you, a "learning experience" may require sustained attention, whereas someone else may place a higher value on creativity. The success of your argument would depend, in part, on whether you could convince your readers that your definition is sound and credible.

So you would need to develop a definition that goes beyond a sentence definition. That is because your definition of "learning experiences" will play a much more significant role in your piece of writing than Michael's definition of a CD player. In developing your extended definition, you would be using definition as a major conceptual order, with other ordering strategies—both imitative and conceptual—as a means of building your definition. The following exemplifies the variety of ways that a definition of "learning" could be developed using the imitative and conceptual orders we have been discussing:

CLASSIFICATION:	Learning is an active *process* consisting of *three* stages.
ANALYSIS:	Learning involves reading, writing, listening, and speaking.
CAUSE:	Learning requires readiness, study, and experience.
EFFECT:	Learning leads to awareness, understanding, and self-actualization.
COMPARISON:	Learning is like an underwater exploration.
CONTRAST:	Learning is not memorizing.
TIME:	Learning begins at a very early age, with visual and auditory stimuli.
SPACE:	Learning occurs most often in the home and classroom, but it really has no spatial boundaries.

As you can see, some or all of these orders may be used to develop a definition of learning. Notice how Mortimer Adler uses definition as a conceptual order in the opening paragraphs from a chapter in his book *How to Speak How to Listen* (New York: Macmillan, 1983, p. 85):

> The ears have nothing comparable to eyelids, but they can be as effectively sealed as eyelids can be closed. Sometimes both close at the same time, but it is often the case that the ear is turned off while the eyes are open. That matters little if, in either case, the mind's attention is turned to other matters than what is being heard or seen. What the senses register are then sounds and sights that lack significance.
>
> Listening, like reading, is primarily an activity of the mind, not of the ear or the eye. When the mind is not actively involved in the process, it should be called hearing, not listening; seeing, not reading.

If Adler had relied only on a sentence definition derived from a dictionary, he would have written that listening means "making a conscious effort to hear." To achieve his purpose, however, he needed to define *listening* in a special way. In these opening paragraphs, Adler begins to define what he means by *listening*. As the writer, he chooses to focus on listening as an *active* rather than a *passive* activity, and he contrasts the words *listen* and *hear* to clarify his meaning. Because much of his book is about listening, definition is the means he uses to convey his perspective.

Persuasive Organization. When your purpose is to persuade your readers, to convince them of the validity of your particular viewpoint, there are two special organizational patterns you can use: direct and indirect.

1. *Direct* persuasion order dates from ancient Greece and is based on the assumption that your reader is a reasonable person who will be persuaded by good reasons. In direct persuasion, you simply state your position—an assertion you make about your topic—and then list reasons for it. Kathy's autobiographical essay to the nursing school for admission into the program (sample 3A) is organized in this way: she first states what she believes are the primary influences on her decision to pursue a degree in nursing, and then sets out to demonstrate the truth of what she says, to persuade her readers that these influences are in fact significant.

If you have written school papers that were based on a thesis statement, then you have used direct persuasion in writing. A thesis statement, you recall, is a statement of a position, an assertion you make early in your paper and then support with reasons in the rest of your paper. The second paragraph of Constance's autobiographical essay (sample 3C) ends with a thesis statement, which the rest of her essay supports:

> Each [of her three brothers] has exposed me to various facets of life, facets that I, alone, would never have realized existed.

Of course, by virtue of the fact that you are writing to *persuade* readers, some readers may not share your particular views, at least not at the start. In direct persuasion, a clear and orderly discussion of your reasons supporting your view will contribute significantly to the persuasiveness of your piece of writing. How fully you develop your reasons will also be an important factor. But, in some cases, it may be to your advantage to address any opposing views, especially the more significant ones that compete with your own view.

To do this, first you present an opposing view fairly and objectively, and then you say why you think it is inadequate or illogical. By dispensing with the key opposing views, you place your readers in a position to listen more carefully to your own views on the subject. Also, once you deal with the opposing views, the way is clear for you to advance your own reasons for believing as you do.

2. *Indirect* persuasion is also ancient in its use but has not often been formally taught until recently. It is based on the assumption that your reader has an opposing position that he or she may not easily give up. Efforts to confront such a reader directly may lead not to successful persuasion but to a

hardening of the reader's original position. So your attempt at direct persuasion may in fact be counterproductive. Therefore, indirect persuasion attempts to persuade the reader by creating an atmosphere of cooperation and mutual understanding.

To persuade indirectly, begin by stating the problem objectively and, especially, by stating the *opposing* position accurately. By doing so, you demonstrate that you are a fair person who can see things through your reader's eyes. Having done this, you even go a step further, stating the circumstances in which your opponents' position is, in fact, the right one.

At this point, your relationship with your reader should be firmly established, so you can safely proceed to state *your* position and the circumstances in which *it* is the correct one. Notice that you have not threatened or alienated your reader by opposing his or her position; instead, you have agreed with it, at least in certain circumstances. All you have done is shown that circumstances *also* exist in which your position is right.

With this balance established between the two positions, you can go ahead to tip the scale your way, by showing that the circumstances in which your position is the right one are the circumstances that exist now. Better still, you can sometimes present your position as simply a desirable modification of the opposing one, or you can suggest a combination of both positions as the best solution.

Exercises

A. Choose two of the following sample papers and discuss their organizing systems and how they could be improved. Notice that some pieces of writing have a combination of the systems listed earlier.

1. Christina's instructions for job hunting (sample 1B).
2. Mandy's description of Rome (sample 2A).
3. Joe's description of the old barn (sample 2D).
4. Kathy's autobiographical essay (sample 3A).
5. Constance's autobiographical essay (sample 3C).

B. Choose one of the essays you have written, and identify the organizing strategies you have used in presenting the content of your piece of writing.

C. From your own reading, select a piece of writing that has a persuasive purpose. Does the writer use direct or indirect persuasion? In your opinion, what motivated the writer to use one pattern and not the other?

D. Many of the ordering strategies discussed can be used in the beginning of a piece of writing as well as in the middle. Read the following beginnings taken from published works, and discuss their organizational plan. The first excerpt is the opening paragraph of Bruno Latour and Steve Woolgar's *Laboratory Life: The Social Construction of Scientific Facts* (Beverly Hills: Sage, 1979, p. 17); the second excerpt is the opening paragraph in the preface of E. D. Hirsch's *Cultural Literacy: What Every American Needs to Know* (Boston: Houghton Mifflin, p. xiii).

1.   Since the turn of the century, scores of men and women have penetrated deep forests, lived in hostile climates, and weathered hostility, boredom, and disease in order to gather the remnants of so-called primitive societies. By contrast to the frequency of these anthropological excursions, relatively few attempts have been made to penetrate the intimacy of life among tribes which are much nearer at hand. This is perhaps surprising in view of the reception and importance attached to their product in modern civilised societies: we refer, of course, to tribes of scientists and to their production of science. Whereas we now have fairly detailed knowledge of the myths and circumcision rituals of exotic tribes, we remain relatively ignorant of the details of equivalent activity among tribes of scientists, whose work is commonly heralded as having startling or, at least, extremely significant effects on our civilisation.

2.   To be culturally literate is to possess the basic information needed to thrive in the modern world. The breadth of that information is great, extending over the major domains of human activity from sports to science. It is by no means confined to "culture" narrowly understood as an acquaintance with the arts. Nor is it confined to one social class. Quite the contrary. Cultural literacy constitutes the only sure avenue of opportunity for disadvantaged children, the only reliable way of combating the social determinism that now condemns them to remain in the same social and educational condition as their parents. That children from poor and illiterate homes tend to remain poor and illiterate is an unacceptable failure of our schools, one which has occurred not because our teachers are inept but chiefly because they are compelled to teach a fragmented curriculum based on faulty educational theories. Some say that our schools by themselves are powerless to change the cycle of poverty and illiteracy. I do not agree. They *can* break the cycle, but only if they themselves break fundamentally with some of the theories and practices that education professors and school administrators have followed over the past fifty years.

ENDINGS: LEAVING THE READER

Like beginnings, endings are perhaps best thought of not as separate parts of pieces of writing, but rather as activities involving the writing and the reader. The ending is simply the place at which you leave the reader. You therefore need to remember several points in planning endings.

First, the middle of the piece of writing may have left the reader at a relatively minor point in the subject matter: detail 3 of subpoint C of main point IV, for example. Just stopping there would give that minor detail undue emphasis; it would be the last thing on the reader's mind. So you may need to end the paper by returning the reader to a more important topic. For example, Mike's instructions for buying a CD player (sample 1C) would end with the relatively minor point about most players being made in Japan or Korea, if it were not for Mike's more general last paragraph. Similarly, without its last paragraph, Amy's description of Ceralvo would leave the reader's attention focused on the 1937 flood.

Second, the piece of writing may have been long enough that the reader may need to be reminded of its major point. This is probably the case in Constance's autobiographical essay (sample 2C); readers may have become so interested in the stories of Constance's brothers that they will have forgotten why she is telling the stories. Her last paragraph provides the reminder.

Third, you may have a particular closing message you want to get across, perhaps a particular action you want your reader to take. Ending with that message will help give it emphasis. For example, Michael's letter to his landlord (sample 4C) ends with his offer to help achieve a solution.

Exercises

A. Choose three of the following sample papers and evaluate their endings. In what ways are they effective? In what ways could they be improved?

1. Amy's instructions on applying for FHA office (sample 1A).
2. Christina's process essay about the campus employment service (sample 1B).
3. Mandy's description of Rome (sample 2A).
4. Michael's description of the Berlin Wall (sample 2E).
5. Kathy's autobiographical essay for admission to nursing school (sample 3A).
6. John's autobiographical essay for a scholarship (sample 3D).

B. Rewrite the ending of one of the papers just listed, to make it more effective. Be prepared to discuss the reasons for the changes you have made.

C. Choose two samples of writing from your own reading that illustrate different ways of ending a piece of writing. Analyze the endings, and then discuss the writers' plans for "leaving" the reader.

Drafting: Following the Organization

When you begin drafting, you should focus your attention on the writing situation and the content of your piece of writing. You should also organize the content to meet the readers' needs and expectations. Working within these guidelines, you should aim to produce a complete draft of your piece of writing so that you can begin revising and editing, in the postdrafting stage. Your ability to sustain a clear focus while you draft will improve as you continue to practice writing for different purposes and situations.

Many of you will find it challenging to keep your attention focused on the variables of the writing situation as you draft the content of your piece of writing. Adding to that an organizational plan may be doubly challenging. As a practicing writer, you might think that working within all of these guidelines at the drafting stage is confusing—perhaps overwhelming. That may very well be the case.

Of course, in our description of the writing process, we are suggesting that the decisions you make in the predrafting stage about the writing situation, the content, and the organization of your piece of writing will save you many steps in the drafting and postdrafting stages, not to mention considerable time. But don't be discouraged if you are unable to make all of the right decisions in advance or if you fall short of your expectations in a draft. The ability to plan a piece of writing and to follow that plan in the drafting stage should be a goal you set for yourself, one you can achieve reasonably well over the course of a semester, rather than an immediate expectation.

Your progress in achieving this goal will depend on the level of your experience as a writer and on your own process of composing. As you experience writing for different purposes and situations, you will develop greater control of your writing and an ability to express your thoughts with more clarity and focus. But none of this will happen unless you develop a healthy self-consciousness about yourself as a writer. What do you do well? What must you improve on? What steps will you take to improve? How will taking these steps alter your composing process? Developing a sensitivity to your own composing process is, in large part, discovering the power of writing. By continually reflecting on your process, you will eventually tailor a process that suits you as a writer and that leads to effective writing.

Your composing process at the present time, in fact, will determine the role organization plays in the drafting stage. Some writers, for example, may begin drafting without much concern for the order of information as it flows onto the page. These writers prefer a more natural composing style, allowing ideas to fall into place as they are written. Such writers tend to focus on organization only after they have something to work with on the page.

This style of composing, to some extent, allows the writer to compose without so many constraints that the writing becomes stilted. By first drafting a piece of writing and then analyzing its organization, the writer may identify inconsistencies in the organizational plan that can then be addressed in the postdrafting stage. If following this process is effective for such writers, they should not try to alter it.

Conversely, some writers work best with their organization plan in front of them as they draft their piece of writing. In this way, they keep their overall organization plan clearly in mind so that they don't veer off course or "get lost" in the details of sentences and words. Perhaps you will want to keep a written outline—even if it is only a very rough sketch—in front of you while you draft. Some professional writers fasten their outlines to the wall as they draft or write them on large blackboards in their work areas.

Remember again that you don't have to draft the paper in the order of its final product. In the drafting stage, you can write your draft "in pieces," in whatever order you find easiest. You'll be able to put the pieces back together at your postdrafting stage.

So whether you choose to write with or without a preplanned sketch of your ideas will depend on your own process. Of course, the more preplanning you can do will save you time; however, you also need to be open to any discoveries you make in the drafting stage. Writing is very much a discovery process, so too much preplanning can be a hindrance, too, if you resist the possibilities that drafting offers you.

Learning as much as you can about your own composing style cannot be overemphasized. Ultimately you should do what works best for you as a writer. If organization is a feature of writing that you consider only after you have produced a draft, then follow this process. If you find that you are taking many more steps than you need to, costing you time and energy, then try gradually to integrate organization into your preplanning. As you experiment with your process of composing, take small steps so that you can recognize your achievements.

Postdrafting: Revising the Organization

Whatever order you have written your draft in, now, at the postdrafting stage, you should read it in the order your reader will see it. Put yourself in your reader's position, and see if the draft "meets" the reader well at the beginning, "leads" the reader in the best possible order through the middle, and "leaves" the reader effectively at the ending. Remember that any decision you make about the organization of your piece of writing must be suited to your writing situation.

In Chapter Two, we introduced three Gricean maxims—relevance, quantity, and quality—and demonstrated their usefulness as guides to revision at the postdrafting stage. We showed how these three maxims can help focus your attention on the content of your piece of writing. A fourth and final maxim, not discussed in the last chapter, is manner—the way you express and present content to your readers. This maxim focuses your attention on form and style, for the way you express and manage ideas is as important to readers as the ideas themselves.

The way you express content—your manner of presentation—involves many choices and conventions, or tools and rules, related not only to the organization of content but also to the clarity and correctness of sentences and to the accuracy of word choice. We will discuss various aspects of form and style throughout the remainder of the book, but here we want to focus on organization as one aspect of manner.

ONE ASPECT OF MANNER: REVISING ORGANIZATION

Organization as an aspect of manner is as important in writing as it is in speaking—probably more so, in fact. It is essential to the clear and effective presentation of information, because without organization your readers would have difficulty processing the content of your piece of writing.

In a speaking situation, you may have relevant and completely developed ideas to contribute, but if they are not presented in an orderly fashion, you will probably not communicate effectively. Of course, if you violate this maxim in a speaking situation, you can usually clarify any confusion on the part of your listeners, provided you take the opportunity. In a writing situation, however, your failure to organize information can create serious problems for your readers, who are not present to voice their confusion.

Writers, therefore, often pretend to be their own readers when they revise in the postdrafting stage; they examine the beginning, middle, and ending of their piece of writing from a reader's perspective. In this way, they anticipate the questions and uncertainties of their readers and then plan their revisions to address these concerns.

When Kathy revised the draft of her autobiography in the postdrafting stage, she saw that her beginning did not reflect the content of her paper; her beginning, in fact, related only to a small part of her paper—the influence of her parents on her decision to pursue a career in nursing. Here is the beginning she wrote in her first draft.

> The two greatest influences in my life have been my parents. Each one is a unique personality with a variety of strengths and beliefs.

Kathy also noted that this beginning left many questions unanswered about the writing situation. In her revisions, she wanted to give her readers a clearer sense of her subject and purpose.

> Some people know from a very early age what they want to accomplish in life. My present desire to become a Registered Nurse has come through a continuous progression of change and growth. The one thing that has remained constant is my desire to work with

people and make a positive difference in their lives. I have been greatly influenced by people and events, and that has led to my goal to become a Registered Nurse. I greatly respect the hard work, dedication and warmth of the nursing profession. It is my wish to be a part of this unique group of people.

This revised beginning captures the writing situation much more effectively than the original.

One way to look critically at the middle of your piece of writing is to ask yourself how you have presented the content to your readers. If you began drafting with an organizational plan, you obviously know the answer to this question; however, if you began drafting without first preplanning the organization, you will have to read over your draft until you can identify the way you have ordered information. With a knowledge of the ordering strategies we have discussed in this chapter, you should be able to identify the predominant order—the one that frames the whole of your piece of writing.

You cannot really determine the effectiveness of your organization unless you've considered other possibilities for ordering the content of your piece of writing. If your piece of writing follows a time order, for example, what other alternatives did you consider? What made you choose time order over another? Kathy's autobiographical essay (sample 3A) follows a time order: she begins by discussing the influence of her parents on her career choice as she was growing up, then she depicts her life after marriage as a young mother and business owner, and finally she details her later work experience in the medical field. Would a persuasive order have been more effective than a time order? What does the time order contribute to the writing situation? What would a persuasive order contribute? Which is preferable, and why?

These are questions that force you to think about the choices you make as a writer. As in any business situation, when you make a decision, you have to consider the pluses and the minuses; you ask yourself what the tradeoff is when you choose option A over option B. So when you make decisions about content or organization, you have to consider how these decisions—these choices—will impact the variables in the writing situation.

Another question, after you have identified the ordering scheme, is whether you have made this order visible to your readers. If ordering information in your piece of writing is intended to help your readers understand the development of your ideas, the clarity of your thinking, then the ordering scheme must be explicit to your readers. So an important question to ask yourself is: How have I made the organization explicit so that my readers can easily follow the progression of my ideas?

In Kathy's essay, for example, you need only look at the signals she leaves at the beginning of many of her paragraphs to know that her essay follows a time order.

In my sophomore year of high school . . .

Five years later . . .

With the birth of my youngest daughter . . .

The next four months . . .

Through this very difficult time . . .

When my youngest daughter was two . . .

After three years . . .

In the fall of 1989 . . .

Although Kathy might have given more thought to the ordering scheme she used in her essay, she has effectively made the time order visible to her readers. Most of her paragraphs begin with time markers, which enable the reader to follow the progression of her essay.

One point we have made repeatedly throughout this chapter is that our composing processes are uniquely our own. For some writers, it may be difficult to preplan the organization of a piece of writing—to outline the essay in advance of drafting; for other writers, working from an organizational plan may be the only way to compose. If organization is a weakness in your writing, you might try to do more organizational planning at the predrafting stage. In any case, it is never too late at the postdrafting stage to make changes in organization. With a paper copy you can "cut and paste"; on a computer, you can move blocks of text around in your file. Either way, you can always revise to achieve the best possible organization for your writing situation.

Exercise

Using the draft of your next essay, develop a new plan for organizing the content of your piece of writing. For example, if you follow an imitative order in your draft, try following a conceptual order instead. How does this new order affect your subject and purpose?

Assignment 3: Autobiography

Assignment: Write an autobiographical essay, for a specific, non-classroom purpose and audience.

This assignment should also be a fairly simple one, because your subject should be very familiar to you. But the main problem is limiting that subject: nobody's entire life story can be told in a brief essay. At the predrafting stage, you must consider carefully what your purpose is in writing the essay and what information about yourself will best achieve that purpose.

Sample Papers

Sample 3A (Kathy)

[An autobiographical essay for admission to a nursing program]

Some people know from a very early age what they want to accomplish in life. My present desire to become a Registered Nurse has come through a continuous progression of change and growth. The one thing that has remained constant is my desire to work with people and make a positive difference in their lives. I have been greatly influenced by people and events, and that has led to my goal to become a Registered Nurse. I greatly respect the hard work, dedication and warmth of the nursing profession. It is my wish to be a part of this unique group of people.

The two people that have influenced my life the most have been my parents. They have both played an important part in shaping my personality and outlook on life.

From my mother I learned the importance of closeness in a family and the ability to all pull together. Through family squabbles, financial difficulties, and the daily problems that occur in raising a family, my mother remained patient and strong. She managed with little money to make our childhood happy and interesting. We spent many days at the beach, cooking together, or dancing to rock-and-roll music on the radio. She also managed to spend time alone with each of her four children. It is a tradition that I have tried to carry on with my own children.

I learned different lessons from my father. He was a very hard working and dedicated man. While my mother influenced the way I would raise my children, my father influenced my decision to become involved in the retail grocery field. I knew from an early age that I wanted to combine a family and a career, so working with my father was very important to me. He was manager of several Standard Grocery Stores while I was growing up. But it was his dream to one day purchase his own grocery. When I was about eleven years old he had finally saved enough money to put a down payment on one. Our whole family had to pull together to make the new business work. Although I had thoughts of going into Social Work my freshman year of high school, I discovered I had a good business instinct. Managing money and stock purchase came easily to me. I especially enjoyed the customer contact. By working with my father I also learned a great deal about organizing my time and about sacrifices. I worked three days after school and on weekends. By managing my time wisely, I could work, keep my grades up, and still participate in school activities.

In my sophomore year of high school I continued working for my father and enrolled in business courses. I also hoped to be the owner of a retail grocery someday. I had met my husband Bernie the previous year, whose father also owned and operated a family business where Bernie worked. When we married four years later, we began working towards our goal of owning our own business.

Five years later with the help of my family, we started a small grocery on the southwest side of Indianapolis. We put in long hours and money was very tight. But it finally began to prosper. By now our two children had made a happy and demanding difference in our lives. I was able to schedule my hours around their needs and continue to work. I had reached my goal of combining family and work. But in the back of my mind was always the desire to return to school and earn a degree in Social Work. With two small children and a demanding business, it seemed very unlikely that I would get the opportunity to do so.

With the birth of my youngest daughter my whole outlook on life changed. She was born four months prematurely and weighed one pound and five ounces. We were told that there was very little if any chance for her survival. The doctors left the decision to my husband and me whether to try any means of life support. With only a few minutes to decide we asked that she be placed on a respirator.

The next four months were an emotional rollercoaster. Our tiny daughter had amazed the physicians by surviving, but there were many obstacles to overcome. She came close to death many times. We were told of the possibilities of blindness and brain damage due to the high amounts of oxygen used. But through the expert love and care she received in the Intensive Care Nursery, our fragile daughter began to thrive. Two weeks after her original due date she was released from the hospital. Although she had to be released on an apnea and bradycardia monitor, she was basically healthy. We were overjoyed.

Through this very difficult time something became very clear to me. The professional care, love and support given to my baby and the rest of my family had been overwhelming. The medical field which I had always considered clinical and somewhat cold had a very different side to it. I decided that I wanted to belong to this very special group of people. Someday I would return to school and become a part of the medical field.

When my youngest daughter was two and her health had stabilized, my husband went to work at Roadway Express, as a Dock Clerk. The hours were varied, but he was home more now. I decided it was time for me to return to school. I enrolled at Aristotle College in their Medical Assistant Program. It was difficult trying to study with three active children, but the discipline I had gained working with my father while attending high school gave me an edge. I knew how to sacrifice to gain something important. My mother was very supportive and helped a great deal with the children. My husband was both encouraging and proud. I graduated a year later with an A average.

I began work immediately. My first position was in a physician's office. The doctor I worked for was an Osteopath as well as a family practitioner. I received a wide range of experiences. I was responsible for all lab procedures such as venipunctures, microscopic urinalysis, and sedimentation rates. I also performed electrocardiograms, ultra-sounds, and assisted with minor surgeries. It was a very challenging and satisfying position. After three years the opportunity to head the small Lab Department in a Nursing Home became available. I interviewed and received the job. This is where my position in the medical field became very clear to me.

I felt immediately at home. I enjoyed talking with and helping the elderly residents. My duties in the Lab included venipuncture, maintaining a lab log, and scheduling appointments for the residents; I was also responsible for performing electrocardiograms and scheduling yearly physicals. I had never been in an environment where I felt so needed. I found myself wanting to make a positive difference in their lives. The only thing that was missing, however, was adequate patient contact. Since I was in the Lab, my contact with the residents was limited. I knew I wanted to be more directly involved with their day-to-day care. Three years later I resigned my position and made the decision to return to college.

In the fall of 1989 I enrolled at IUPUI to begin work towards an Associate Degree in Nursing. My goal is to work in geriatrics. I hope to use my knowledge and experience in order to improve the lives of the elderly who reside in long-term care facilities. I know it will not be easy working as a Registered Nurse. The hours are unpredictable and long, and the work is often stressful. But it will also be very rewarding. I look forward with great anticipation to the time when I will begin my career as a Registered Nurse.

Sample 3B (Amy)

[Part of a scholarship application]

Events in one's life can heavily influence the career goals one may set. Negative situations can either greatly reduce or highly increase one's will to achieve those goals. An unhappy period in my life could have, in fact, kept me from planning for my future. Luckily, however, those events supplied the basis for my decision to become a genetic engineer and they have inspired me to strive towards reaching my goal.

My father was diagnosed as having lymphoma, or cancer of the lymph system, in June of 1985. His illness raised many questions and problems not answered or dealt with by hospitals and doctors. Medical professionals could neither find the cause of the disease, nor provide a cure for it. Chemotherapy treatments slowed the progression of the cancer for a time. However, complications such as an intestinal blockage and pneumonia eventually led to my father's death.

During my father's illness, I read many articles about lymphoma and other types of cancer. I noticed growing numbers of reports dealing with genetic causes of cancer. Through genetic research scientists had found that genes which were deformed in some way were often the origins of many types of cancer. I had been interested in genetics before my father became ill; therefore, I was strongly motivated to use these interests in the future to find answers for the problems we as a family have faced.

My father's illness and death are the main reasons I have decided to become a genetic engineer. I realize that finding the causes and hopefully the cures for cancer will be difficult, if not impossible. Yet nothing that I am aware of will keep me from heeding my inner calling and trying to reach this goal.

My research may someday save the lives of others who suffer with the dreaded disease called cancer. It is my deepest desire that I will be able to turn my negative situations into a finding that will help mankind.

Sample 3C (Constance)

[Part of an application for admission to honors program;
the program asked for "an autobiographical essay on a cultural
or intellectual experience"]

It was a terrifying experience, blindfolded, tied up, and placed in a bathtub. I hear the door lock and feel the darkness. At the age of five, I am alone and frightened. The cruel captors are outside the door laughing and whispering. I suppose they are making plans, more plans for punishment. The door unlocks; I am lifted from the tub; a feeling of dread washes over me. What now? Once again my three brothers have taken advantage of being left to babysit me, their "baby sister."

Perhaps I should make an introduction? Before my illustrious entrance into this world my parents had three boys: Don, Jeff, and Chris. Each in his own way has had an awesome impact upon me. Each has exposed me to various facets of life, facets that I, alone, would never have realized existed.

In his thirty years Don has passed through three phases: hippie, preppie, and now the healthy, young and beautiful yuppie. Donnie at the age of sixteen graduated ninth in a class of six hundred. Gradually through college he acquired the knowledge and cunning attitude to manipulate and eventually have whatever he so desired. First it was a Trans-Am, then a Corvette, and eventually his true love, a Porsche. All was bought and paid for through personal drive. Not only did he have the car, the job (executive), and the degree (engineer), but he had much more, a soft spot for his sister. Surrounding me with his vast knowledge, he has exposed me to art, theatre, quantum theories, wealth, and the good things in life. He has inspired and infuriated me.

Were it not for Don my aspirations would not be as high. Don has dared to dream and dreamed to dare. I too have set goals and work hard to fulfill them. I may not always win but losers are sometimes winners. There are points in my life when I want to have all that Don has, but most of the time I want more. I want to be better than the best. Impossible? No, Don has taught me that all things are not impossible. I strive to prove myself in a field of just one competitor—Don. It is a tough goal but maybe one day I'll be happy just to achieve one half of what my brother has accomplished. Then again—I believe that to be satisfied I must prove myself worthy of his praise.

Every family has its black sheep, but God gave us two. One with the ability to jump over his fence, the other with the clumsiness to trip.

Not only did he jump over his fence, but, Jeff wandered, and wandered, and. . . . In fact, he strayed beyond green fields into a world full of drugs, prostitutes, and death. One mistake and your life. But, I was a little girl and he was my playmate or so I thought.

On my eighth birthday I visited the mental ward. Jeff strung out on quaaludes and alcohol had jumped through a window and running half naked through the neighborhood yelled death to everyone. The ward was stark and Jeff was a shell. That itself has always taught me a lesson, the box wrapped in gold paper and topped with a silver bow may be empty.

I have stared at Jeff from afar. I envy him his intellect and damn him for abusing it. Jeff has tasted the wild life: jails, drugs, promiscuity. I have lived the life of an outlaw through him and in doing so have no desire to do wrong or to "experiment." I would not say that Jeff is a failure. He has companions, happiness, adventure. Still there is much more to desire—security. I long for Jeff's hugs. I miss his games of delight. He has taught me strength and light-heartedness and if nothing else—how to tell tall tales; in his case, those tall tales are quite true.

Speaking of clumsiness and tripping? Yes, Chris at the young age of seventeen tripped. He fell into a car with a nut high on drugs and smashed by alcohol. The addict wrecked. Chris was thrown through a window instantly crushing his skull. For three days I prayed that he would not die. It was hard for me at twelve to face the fact that Chris might die. He pulled through. Still he had been permanently affected. After six months of therapy for multiple injuries, both mental and physical, he decided to never take a chance. At twenty-five he still lives at home. There are times when he is insane, yelling, screaming, chasing me. Then he is crying and begging. Even this year has brought another hole into Chris' path. Ironically, he was stabbed by another insane person. This time I did not pray.

Though Chris is much older than me, I think of him as my "baby brother." There have been many nights when I have stayed up with Chris through feigned threats of suicide. I was never quite sure if he had the guts to take his own life. He gave me the ability to comfort and tolerate even those who cannot be easily comforted or tolerated. Many times Chris was looked down upon. I know not to look down on others because they may be looking up at you pleading for acceptance. Chris has shown me what defeat is. I will never be defeated; I have the ability to sneak around it. And if I did not pray it was because I was taking care of him. One cannot always wait for prayers to be answered.

My brothers were not always gentle teachers and certainly I was not the attentive pupil, yet, I did learn. I may resent them for hard knocks and cruel jokes but not for valuable lessons.

Sample 3D (John)

[Part of a scholarship application]

As I look back at my years in high school, junior high, and

elementary school, I realize that education has played an important role in my life. I have always been encouraged to be the best that I could be. This encouragement led me to set personal goals and to strive to achieve these goals.

Before I even started school, I can remember being encouraged to learn the ABC's. I also remember being urged to learn words and eventually to make sentences. My father would sit with me for hours playing with magnetic letters and a magnetic board. Then, when I started school, I was encouraged to do the best that I could and make good grades. I was never told that I had to make all A's, but I was told to do the best that I could do. For me, this meant making all A's. I was never satisfied with anything less. My parents were, of course, delighted that I desired A's and rewarded my efforts. This early support formed a foundation upon which all my education has been built.

After my first year in elementary school, my parents divorced. I moved with my mother and stepfather to Corbin, about 20 miles away from my hometown—and my father. Although I saw my father a couple weekends a month and in the summers, I never quite got over the divorce. My father always stressed to me the importance of getting an education. One reason I feel that I have done well in school is his advice. Somehow I thought that doing well in school would bring him closer to me when we couldn't be together.

Ironically, a failing test grade also contributed to my success. In the middle of my fourth grade year, my parents decided that the education I was receiving was not adequate. Upon reaching this decision, they enrolled me in another elementary school. At my former school I had been at the top of the class. After about a week of classes at Central, my school, we were given a timed multiplication test—my first timed test. And I was behind in multiplication tables when I changed schools.

I failed that test with a fifty-six percent. I hated the feeling of being a failure. I wanted to go back to my old school, but my parents would not let me. Instead, they encouraged me and offered support. Through hard work and extra homework, I caught up with the class and even struggled to get back at the top. On the next test, I made an A. I feel that this experience sparked a desire within me to be the best. I have never quit trying.

Making an A on that math test was probably one of the first goals that I set for myself. Since then I have set many goals and worked hard to reach each one. One of the most important was becoming valedictorian of my graduating class. I realized near the end of my sophomore year that I was in the top of the class. The desire to become valedictorian grew from that realization. Achieving this goal required a great deal of work, but I made some sacrifices and eventually reached this goal. Another goal that I set was becoming a Governor's Scholar. By getting teacher recommendations and filling out applications, this too became a reality. But I have not quit setting goals. As soon as I attain one goal, another bigger goal awaits me.

As you can see, I have learned more in school than just subject matter. Education has taught me to want more—to be the best. I have learned the importance of setting goals and working to reach them. And I have accomplished many of these; I have been the best. However, there are always new goals to be set. This summer, for example, I was participating in a program for pre-med students. There were about thirty-six participants, divided into four groups by math placement scores. I placed in the second group. I was upset at first, and did not know if I could handle not being the best. At the awards banquet at the end of the program, I was presented the math award. I decided that I wanted to be at the top of the class, and through hard work I achieved this goal. I have not stopped yet. Facing me now is the desire to become a doctor. "The road goes ever on."

Discussion Questions

1. What information in these four papers could have been left out? What information *not* in these papers should have been?

2. Which of these four writers do you feel you know best as a result of reading their essays? Which do you feel you know least? If you were on the scholarship or admissions committee, what would be your opinions of these writers?

CHAPTER FOUR

The Process of Writing Paragraphs

This chapter probably should not have "Paragraphs" in its title at all. Many writers have already heard so much confusing advice about paragraphs that any new advice may just add to the confusion. Instead, this chapter should perhaps be called "Writing Sentence Groups," or "Sentence Clusters," or "Sentence Chunks"; that way, the chapter could start fresh, without the confusion caused by earlier learning. But any alternative titles would be awfully clumsy—so "Writing Paragraphs" it is.

Still, you should keep in mind that this chapter is not mostly about paragraphs as such. Instead, it is about everything in a piece of writing that is larger than individual sentences but smaller than the whole product. It is, in fact, about writing "sentence groups," "sentence clusters," or "sentence chunks." Some of these groups or clusters or chunks may be set off as one or more paragraphs; some may not be.

One of the pieces of confusing advice you may have learned is that a paragraph is "a unit of thought." Although that definition is usually true, it is not very useful: words, sentences, and whole books are also "units of thought." A paragraph is simply a unit of thought that is visually marked in a certain way.

You have also probably heard the dictum that a paragraph begins with a topic sentence, expressing a main idea or "topic" that is then developed in succeeding sentences. It is true that many paragraphs have topic sentences, but not all paragraphs *begin* with a topic sentence. As we will illustrate later, some paragraphs have their topic sentences in the middle or at the end, some may not state a topic at all but merely imply one, and some may not have a topic.

To say, then, that a paragraph begins with a topic sentence is really to define only one kind of paragraph. This particular definition is a popular one in writing classes because it describes a model that students can use to practice writing neatly structured and well-formed paragraphs. However, while such models are often useful as learning aids, they do not tell the whole story about paragraphs. In fact, it is doubtful that a single model—or even a set of models—could adequately describe the composition of *all* paragraphs. The reason is that a paragraph is not an autonomous unit: its substance and shape depend on what precedes it and on what follows it in a piece of writing.

Perhaps the best way to learn about paragraphs and all their variations is to examine them in your own reading—in newspapers, textbooks, novels, academic articles, and personal letters. Of course, what you will read and learn about paragraphs in this chapter will provide a solid foundation on which to build your knowledge of paragraphs. You will find it helpful to use some of the models we describe as you practice writing paragraphs, but do so with the understanding that paragraphs vary considerably in form and style. Learning to shape effective paragraphs that fit the writing situation is an important step on the way to developing your power as a writer.

So, as you have probably surmised, trying to formulate a definition that can account for *all* paragraphs is problematic. Given the wide range or variety of paragraphs possible in a piece of writing, it is perhaps best to say only that a paragraph is one or more sentences separated from surrounding sentences with extra spacing or indentation or both.

Why are some sentences separated from others in this way? One reason is purely visual. Modern readers need frequent breaks in long passages of writing; a page of prose without paragraph breaks will be difficult to read no matter how well written it is. So most modern writers supply a paragraph break every one to three inches down a page, often varying the lengths for purposes of readability. (As a result, newspaper paragraphs, in their narrow columns, tend to have fewer sentences than book or magazine paragraphs. The physical dimensions of a published piece of writing, in other words, can determine the frequency of indentations.)

Another reason for paragraphs is to provide emphasis. A single sentence, even a single word, may be given a paragraph of its own just to draw attention to it. One way to emphasize an important point in a piece of writing is to set it off in a paragraph by itself. For example, the last paragraph of Alan's essay on computer evolution (sample 4C) has only two simple sentences: any more would probably be unnecessary.

Man has created the computer in his own image, mirroring the evolution process in its development. Perhaps man's creation will someday be better than he is.

Naturally, if one- or two-sentence paragraphs are used too often, they lose their impact on readers.

A third reason for paragraphs is probably the most familiar one for you. Sentences are grouped into paragraphs to show the reader that they have a closer relationship to each other than they do to the surrounding sentences. Such paragraphs organize information into meaningful chunks, often providing readers with a visual sense of the logic and development of ideas in a piece of writing. Looked at in this way, a paragraph *is* a unit of thought—a unit usually larger than the individual sentence but smaller than the whole piece of writing. A paragraph, seen in this way, is the smallest subdivision of a piece of writing above the sentence level.

Predrafting: Planning Topics for Paragraphs

As Figure 1 indicates, concern with paragraphs may usefully start at the predrafting stage. From the predrafting strategies you use to generate ideas and to define the scope of your subject, you will probably end up with a list of ideas—or topics—that you want to cover in your piece of writing. As you formulate these topics at the predrafting stage, you may well be planning the general topics for your paragraphs. For example, at the predrafting stage of writing her essay about the abortion controversy (sample 4B), Janice wrote the following informal outline:

Freedom to choose/controversy

Teen years

Personal experience

Long-term effects/emotional

Effects on personal life if child kept

In the final version of Janice's essay, she follows the order of these topics and includes paragraphs on freedom of choice (paragraphs 1–2), her teen years (paragraphs 3–4), her personal experience at an abortion clinic (paragraphs 5–6), the emotional effects of that experience (paragraphs 7–8), and a reflection on other possible outcomes had she been given a choice (paragraphs 9–10).

Of course, how easily your topics transfer into paragraphs will depend on the extent of your predrafting. If you are the kind of writer who works well in the predrafting stage, sketching and planning ideas in advance, you may find that your topics fall neatly into place as you draft your piece of writing. But if you are like many beginning college writers—and many professional writers, for that matter—you might not be able to produce, in the predrafting stage, a list of topics as clearly defined or as complete as you would like. So you may have to start drafting with a list of ideas, or general topics, that may take shape only after you begin drafting. Some may be topics for single paragraphs, whereas others may be more general topics for clusters of paragraphs. As you draft, you may think of ways to divide your more general topics into specific topics that can be developed in separate paragraphs.

Exercise

In your journal, develop a list of topics for the next essay you write, and then compare it with your draft of the essay. Do your topics fall neatly into separate paragraphs in your draft, or are some more general, dividing into subtopics in the drafting stage? What light does this comparison shed on your composing process?

Drafting: Writing Paragraphs

Most writers probably do not do detailed paragraph planning at the predrafting stage; at that stage, they consider only the general topics of the paragraphs or, perhaps, of groups of paragraphs. The actual organizing of paragraphs usually happens at the drafting stage.

TOPICS AND "TOPIC SENTENCES"

Most paragraphs *do* have a topic—the subject or point that the paragraph develops. But this topic can be stated, or not stated, in a variety of ways.

As we said earlier, some paragraphs state the topic in a single sentence—sometimes called a "topic sentence"—at the beginning of the paragraph, then use the remaining sentences to develop or support the topic. Look, for example, at this paragraph from Alan's essay on computer evolution (sample 4C):

> As each new generation of man hopes to be better than the one before—to know more, to do more, to be more—each "generation" of computers *has been* better. We can classify these generations based on the technological developments that precipitated them. The first generation of computers (1951–1958) were built with vacuum tube technology. Consequently, they were bulky, slow, and unreliable. The second generation of computers (1959–1964) were built from transistors. At this time, the first programming languages were written to make using the computer easier. The third generation of computers (1964–1971) were built from integrated circuits (IC's)—tiny

chips of silicon containing the same circuitry as entire cards of transistors. During this time the input and output (I/O) were also improved. Fourth generation computers (1971–present) utilize large-scale integration (LSI) and very large-scale integration (VLSI). This continuing reduction in size has led to computers one thousand times smaller than their great grandfathers.

The first sentence states the topic of the paragraph, that each generation of computers "has been better" than the preceding one. The second sentence announces the organizational plan for the remainder of the paragraph, which outlines major developments in the history of computers and resulting improvements in the quality and performance of computers.

The second paragraph of Amy's process essay on applying for FHA state office (sample 1A) also begins with a topic sentence:

The first step is to determine whether you are eligible to become an officer candidate. In order to apply, you must have held an office at the chapter and regional levels of FHA, preferably the same one as the state office you wish to hold. Other requirements are that you must have a "B" average in school and you must be willing to attend the National FHA meeting the following summer.

Some paragraphs, however, postpone the topic sentence until the middle or near-middle of the paragraph. In Lisa's description of the Indianapolis Produce Terminal (sample 2B), for example, the topic sentence is not until the third sentence of the paragraph.

Warmed up a bit, I took a walk along the main aisle, dodging busy adults who took no notice of me. I loved to look at each company's display. Always showing their biggest and best produce, they showed my eyes a kaleidoscope of color and a beautiful array of shapes and sizes. Boxes were lined up neatly on a slant, containing bright yellow and orange citrus alternating between various shades of red and green apples. A row of lettuce and other salad vegetables along the top included every tint of green imaginable. Intermittent cases of smaller fruit—deep purple grapes, grass green avocados, hairy little kiwis—made the large fruit look even larger. The display was seasonally framed by bunches of Indiana corn hanging all around and bordered at the bottom by earthen colored squash bulging out the tops of bushel baskets. Indeed the marketplace was a scene to awaken the senses.

Lisa's descriptive essay is set in a narrative context, so before she introduces a new topic for her descriptive detail, she must continue the narrative. Therefore, in the first two sentences, she tells the reader where she is and what she is doing. In the third sentence, she focuses on the topic of the paragraph—the produce displays—which she describes in the remaining sentences. The final sentence rounds off the paragraph by reiterating the topic.

Other paragraphs postpone the topic sentence until the end, giving the supporting sentences first. The seventh paragraph of Constance's autobiographical essay (sample 3B) is an example of this kind of paragraph structure:

> On my eighth birthday I visited the mental ward. Jeff strung out on quaaludes and alcohol had jumped through a window and running half naked through the neighborhood yelled death to everyone. The ward was stark and Jeff was a shell. That itself has always taught me a lesson, the box wrapped in gold paper and topped with a silver bow may be empty.

Here, the point of the paragraph is expressed in the last sentence. The first three sentences of the paragraph "support" this last sentence by describing the writer's personal experience at an impressionable age.

Similarly, the second paragraph of John's essay, written as part of a scholarship application (sample 3D), postpones the topic sentence to the end:

> Before I even started school, I can remember being encouraged to learn the ABC's. I also remember being urged to learn words and eventually to make sentences. My father would sit with me for hours playing with magnetic letters and a magnetic board. Then, when I started school, I was encouraged to do the best that I could and make good grades. I was never told that I had to make all A's, but I was told to do the best that I could do. For me, this meant making all A's. I was never satisfied with anything less. My parents were, of course, delighted that I desired A's and rewarded my efforts. This early support formed a foundation upon which all my education has been built.

Other paragraphs may have a topic, but it may not be stated explicitly; instead, they "spread" the topic over the entire paragraph. Not until after you read the entire paragraph can you infer the topic, or main point. Consider the second paragraph of Michael's description of the Berlin Wall (sample 3B):

> There it stands, a concrete slab that horrified and shocked the world. The physical aspect of the wall is frightening. The part seen by most tourists is a tall cold gray wall with an ominous guard tower standing behind it. Through the darkly tinted windows of the tower a high powered machine gun is unmistakably seen in a small porthole.

> The Wall itself looks as if it has a million stories of struggle to tell; its pock marked, graffiti ridden surface is accented by large red signs telling people to keep behind the metal railing.

In this paragraph, no single sentence states the topic; instead, the message of the paragraph is conveyed almost equally by the five sentences that make it up.

Look also at the third paragraph of Amy's article on the town of Ceralvo (sample 2C):

> During the early part of this century, river travel declined due to the increased popularity of railroads. Because river travel was the life blood of Ceralvo, the city met with hard times. It was at this time that several businesses, such as the dry goods store, moved to the growing city of Owensboro. Families and professional people also moved to more prosperous cities around the state. The final, crippling blow to the city was the flood of 1937, which wiped out most of what remained in Ceralvo.

The overall topic of the paragraph, Ceralvo's decline, is not stated in a single topic sentence; instead it is conveyed by all four sentences working together. In both instances, the topics are implicit rather than explicit.

Finally, many paragraphs do not have a topic sentence at all. Sometimes such paragraphs do not have topics so much as *functions*; they are designed not to make a certain point but rather to take the reader from one place to another. Notice, for example, the fifth paragraph of Constance's autobiographical essay (sample 3C):

> Every family has its black sheep, but God gave us two. One with the ability to jump over his fence, the other with the clumsiness to trip.

The function of this paragraph is to introduce the second and third of Constance's brothers; because it serves as a transition, rather than developing a main point, it does not really have a topic sentence.

Of course, beginnings and endings, which we discussed in the last chapter, are also often expressed in paragraphs that do not develop a topic, or main point. Beginnings function to introduce a subject and to prepare readers for the ensuing discussion, whereas endings often function to reiterate important points. Beginnings direct the reader's attention forward in a piece of writing, whereas endings often direct the reader's attention backward. They are special kinds of paragraphs because they serve a directive function, helping the reader to follow the development of a piece of writing.

Given all of these variations in paragraph structure, you may wonder how a writer decides whether a topic sentence should be placed at the beginning, middle, or end of a paragraph; whether it should be spread over the entire paragraph; or whether a topic sentence is even necessary. Because a paragraph forms an integral part of a much larger piece of writing, the way you structure a paragraph will depend on its relation to other paragraphs. As you draft your piece of writing, the flow of information from paragraph to paragraph should guide your decisions about topic placement. Much will depend on what you have written in preceding paragraphs and what you plan to write in the next one.

Consider, for example, the structure of these paragraphs from Janice's essay about the abortion controversy (sample 4B):

> Within the week, we were on our way to Louisville. I was too far along to have one in Indiana. These were the most terrifying two days of my life. I had no preparation or prior knowledge of what was to take place. I went through several tests and was left in rooms with other girls, as frightened as me, to wonder what was next. Near the end of the first day, I was given something to induce a miscarriage and was allowed to leave for the night with my parents. That night I lay in bed and cried with pain and without so much as a word from my parents in the next bed.
>
> The second day began with an IV given by a woman, who, in my opinion, had never given one before. I was stuck repeatedly in both hands, until she finally got it right. I was later left again, in a room of six or eight other girls. We all had IV's and had robes and gowns on. Waiting to be taken to the operating room, my water broke. I had no idea what had happened and began to cry. My clothes were soaked before a nurse came to help. After awakening from general anesthesia, we were given instructions, a snack, and sent on our way.

In the paragraphs preceding these two paragraphs, Janice writes about her pregnancy as an unwed teenager. Notice that in the first paragraph she continues the narrative, relating what happened to her after she informed her parents. The topic sentence of the paragraph is the third sentence: "These were the most terrifying days of my life." The remaining sentences in the paragraph detail her experience the first day in the doctor's office. At this point, even though her discussion of the topic is incomplete, she decides to begin a new paragraph.

The second paragraph develops the same topic, but the focus is now her experiences on the second day. The paragraph itself does not have a topic, because the topic has already been stated in the first paragraph. Janice probably decided to indent at this juncture to break up the text—to make it more visually welcoming to her readers.

As you draft the paragraphs in your piece of writing, then, you should focus your attention on a topic and let the flow of information help you determine whether a topic sentence is necessary, and if so, where it should appear in your paragraph. If paragraphs were autonomous, self-contained structures, we could simply describe their structure and advise you to adhere to it whenever you write. If the matter were only that simple!

What we have said about paragraphs in this section should help you to begin thinking about paragraphs in your own writing and reading. Your learning does not end here. There is much more to know about paragraphs, and that will come with practice in writing and from your own observations about paragraphs in your general reading.

Exercises

A. Which sentence, if any, in the following paragraphs is the topic sentence? Be prepared to discuss the reasons for your choices.

1. Lastly, you must attend the state meeting, which is held one weekend in early spring. During the first meeting open to the entire state association, you will be asked a question and be graded on the content of your answer and how well you present yourself. Next, you must take a written test covering FHA facts. You must also attend several seminars and luncheons with the present state officers. The final criterion is an interview with the candidate committee. (sample 1A)

2. Feeling the chill of an October morning, I stopped at the coal stove, where a few old white-haired men gathered daily, observing their sons and grandsons handling the business which they had thrived on for years. Sitting in their armchairs, they reminded me of kings on thrones, ruling their kingdoms. I stood silently, remembering conversations that I had overheard between my father and grandfather which gave clear testimony of their great respect for these patriarchs of produce. Warming my backside, I shut my eyes and breathing deeply tried to distinguish all the heavy aromas which pervaded the area. Strongest were the scents of pungent citrus and spicy apples. Also I noticed the unmistakable musk of onion and an occasional waft of rotten potatoes. (sample 2B)

3. After my first year in elementary school, my parents divorced. I moved with my mother and stepfather to Corbin, about 20 miles away from my hometown—and my father. Although I saw my father a couple of weekends a month and in the summers, I never quite got

over the divorce. My father always stressed to me the importance of getting an education. One reason I feel that I have done well in school is his advice. Somehow I thought that doing well in school would bring him closer to me when we couldn't be together. (sample 3D)

4.   As I sat in the surgery waiting room in my back-less hospital gown, I began to feel the Valium that they administered to me take effect. Was this meant to reduce my pain? If so—physical or emotional? Would this drug mend my broken heart and seize my despair? In scrutinizing the room, I noticed the others; all of them young and chatting casually as if it were no big deal. Were they not feeling what I was feeling? I don't think they were, I cried. I was at the lowest level of humiliation. I thought "I'm going to murder my child that I prayed for and was blessed with." Should there be no regard for the ruthlessness of this brutal execution? Would there be no consequences of remorse? Yes, there would be. (sample 4A)

5.   As hideous a thought as it is to take another person's life, I believe it is one of mankind's necessary evils. There are some criminals whose murderous rages are of such a brutal and grotesque nature that death seems to be too trivial a punishment. Any sane person who would deliberately rape and kill a small child should not be allowed the opportunity to commit this same crime with someone else. The example of Ted Bundy illustrates this point very well. At 42 years of age, he was good looking, well educated, and had been raised as a Christian. "Suspected of killing as many as 50 young women. . . ," he was executed "after he was convicted of mutilating and murdering a 12-year-old. . . ." The day before his death he stated: "I deserve, certainly, the most extreme punishment society has, and I think society deserves to be protected from me and others like me" (Nichols 54). (sample 4D)

B. Choose one of the preceding paragraphs that you think could be made more effective by adding a topic sentence, omitting a topic sentence, or changing the position of a topic sentence. Revise the paragraph in one of these ways, making any other changes you wish.

C. Choose one of the sample papers at the end of this chapter, and examine the topic sentences in the paper as a whole. Does each paragraph have a topic? Where does the topic sentence occur in the paragraph? If there is no topic sentence in a paragraph, is the topic implied? Is it stated in a preceding paragraph? In your opinion, has the writer made effective choices?

PARAGRAPH PATTERNS

Wherever the topic sentence is located in a paragraph—or whether or not the paragraph even has a topic sentence—the paragraph needs to be organized. That is, it needs a *pattern* to take the reader easily through its information. This organizational pattern need not be limited to a single paragraph; it may very well link several paragraphs in a piece of writing. As we pointed out in the last chapter, a piece of writing may have several orders operating at different levels. While one order may function to organize the content of a whole piece of writing, another order may function, at a subordinate level, to organize information in one or more paragraphs. As you draft, remember that a paragraph must have a clear pattern, or order, to help the reader follow the flow of information.

Paragraph patterns are very much like organizational patterns for whole pieces of writing. Some paragraphs are organized "imitatively," in time or space order. For example, the following paragraph from the middle of Constance's autobiographical essay (sample 3C) is organized in time order. Writing her essay about the influence of each of her three brothers on her own life, Constance, in the following paragraph, shifts her focus to her third brother, Chris.

> Speaking of clumsiness and tripping? Yes, Chris at the young age of seventeen tripped. He fell into a car with a nut high on drugs and smashed on alcohol. The addict wrecked. Chris was thrown through a window instantly crushing his skull. For three days I prayed that he would not die. It was hard for me at twelve to face the fact that Chris might die. He pulled through. Still he had been permanently affected. After six months of therapy for multiple injuries, both mental and physical, he decided to never take a chance. At twenty-five he still lives at home. There are times when he is insane, yelling, screaming, chasing me. Then he is crying and begging. Even this year has brought another hole into Chris's path. Ironically, he was stabbed by another insane person. This time I did not pray.

Most of the second paragraph of Mandy's paper on Rome (sample 2A) is organized in space order, describing impressions in the order they would be seen as you entered St. Peter's.

> Rome contains art galleries, ancient ruins, and many other tourist sites, but one particular site which impresses tourists is St. Peter's Cathedral. As you walk through the archway into the entrance hall of this incredible structure, you immediately feel as if you have entered another age. It looks quite different from anything found in

America. The huge spacious rooms and high ceilings seem to engulf you. You walk on marble floors worn by thousands of feet. These floors still give vivid impressions of swirling creamy designs combining ivory white with strings of sparkling gold. While you walk, your eyes are finding bold sculptures and immense altars symbolizing sacrifices and images you cannot begin to understand.

Other paragraphs are organized conceptually, showing cause and effect, classification or analysis, comparison or contrast, and definition. For example, the third paragraph of Amy's autobiographical essay (sample 3B) has a cause-and-effect organization:

During my father's illness, I read many articles about lymphoma and other types of cancer. I noticed growing numbers of reports dealing with genetic causes of cancer. Through genetic research scientists had found that genes which were deformed in some way were often the origins of many types of cancer. I had been interested in genetics before my father became ill; therefore, I was strongly motivated to use these interests in the future to find answers for the problems we as a family have faced.

Notice that the first three sentences, as well as the first clause of the fourth sentence, present causes for the effect stated in the second clause of that last sentence.

In the following paragraph, from his essay about computer evolution (sample 4C), Alan uses classification as an ordering scheme. He classifies ways of storing information into three categories to draw a parallel between humankind and the computer.

All organisms on earth store information for survival in one or more of the following manners: genetic—"prewired" information stored in the nervous system; extragenetic—learned information acquired through experience; and extrasomatic—information stored outside of the body. The lowest organisms store information solely through their DNA, while man alone uses all three methods (Sagan 3–4).

The concluding paragraph of Joe's essay on capital punishment (sample 4D) is organized analytically. In presenting his case for supporting the death penalty, Joe considers a piece of evidence that may dissuade some from taking his position on the issue:

Possibly the only major drawback with the death penalty is that it is irrevocable. Once the sentence has been carried out, nothing can change the outcome. The fear of putting an innocent person to death is reason enough to retain the lengthy appeals process. This process guarantees that every death sentence will eventually be heard by the Supreme Court. This lengthy appellate procedure is more than sufficient to protect those that may be innocent.

In addition to presenting his own reasons for supporting the death penalty, Joe saw the need to address this opposing view. But first he had to analyze the issue—to break it down into its parts—to identify the point that he needed to discuss.

The third paragraph of Mike's paper on buying a CD player (sample 1C) has a comparison-contrast organization:

Once you decide the amount of money you are going to spend, you should then look at the different models compact disc players come in. By this I mean that you should decide when you will be listening to your CD player the most, and in turn choose a model that best fits your needs. Say, for example, that you most frequently listen to music while in your car; then you obviously would want one designed to replace your current car stereo. The most popular model, however, is one that hooks up to your home stereo system, assuming your stereo has an auxiliary outlet. There are two reasons this model is the most popular. One is because this model is generally more advanced than the car or portable ones. The other is that the music sounds better being played through powerful speakers rather than headphones or car speakers.

Paragraph patterns may vary widely, as long as they make sense to the reader. When a paragraph does not have a sensible pattern, confusion results. Here, for example, is one paragraph from Joe's first draft of his descriptive essay about the old barn (sample 2C):

A place which returns many memories to my mind is an old barn which stood on the farm where I was born. It was a very large structure with siding which has been worn and cracked by the many years of harsh sunshine and bitter cold winters. A hayloft, which covers most of the upper story, became a large playground in the early spring when most of the hay had been fed to the cattle. A soft mat of loose hay still covered the floor to cushion your falls and bruises. In late spring and summer, fields of hay were cut and baled to refill the loft for the coming winter. Refilling the loft was usually a hot and dirty job.

Although this draft is a good start, with generally well-crafted sentences, the order of the sentences is confusing, especially in the last half of the passage. After briefly describing the old barn's exterior, Joe focuses on one part of the barn—the hayloft—and his recollection of it as an ideal playground in early spring. Then the pattern of the paragraph shifts abruptly, leaving gaps in the flow of information, and we are told what happens to the hayloft in late spring and summer.

In the postdrafting stage, Joe divided some of these sentences into separate paragraphs, adding new sentences to establish a clearer focus and more helpful transitions. Notice the descriptive detail he adds after rethinking the organization of his draft at the postdrafting stage.

A place which returns many memories to my mind is an old barn that stood on the farm where I was born. It was a very large structure with siding that had been weathered and cracked by the many years of harsh summer sunshine, and the bitter cold of winters. Years of rain had rusted many of the nails, leaving dark brown stains, streaked into the grayness of the siding. Some of it had fallen to the ground. Off of one end of the barn, a gently sloped roof extended over an open area. A long corn crib ran parallel to the barn and supported the outer end of this roof. Each wooden shingle of this roof seemed to be trimmed with a soft, green moss.

A grassy mound of soil rose to the second story of this barn. By walking up this hillside, you could reach the upper section of the barn. Opening two large doors reveals to you a large open area. A few tiny holes in the roof let the sunlight pierce the darkness of this hayloft. Allow a few minutes for your eyes to adjust to this darkness and you can see that a massive skeleton of large wooden beams surrounds you. Each beam still carries the axe marks where someone had shaped them by hand. Wooden pegs hold them solidly together. By autumn, bales of hay would occupy much of this space.

This version of the passage is much easier to follow than the first, mostly because of its improved organization. The paragraphs now have a pattern. Although Joe was able to make these changes at the postdrafting stage, he perhaps could have saved time by more careful predrafting of his essay or by considering paragraph organization as he drafted.

Exercises

A. How is each of the following paragraphs or sequences of paragraphs organized? Be prepared to discuss the reasons for your answers.

1. After you finish filling out the application, it goes back to the person at the desk. Now it is time to look for a job.

There is a bulletin board in the hallway outside of the office that lists hundreds of full and part-time positions of every job from general office workers to cashiers. Go out and look on the board for jobs that interest you, but remember, the board only lists the position title and a brief description, so you must copy down the numbers assigned to the jobs you are interested in, and bring them back into the office in order to get a referral slip with more information. (sample 1A)

2.   On the Western side there is an ominous reverence for the Wall. Visitors and tourists speak in hushed voices and toss nervous glances toward the guard tower. Watch the faces of the people looking toward the East. What do you see, sadness?

A man begins waving and shouting in German, "Hallo, Hallo!" On the Eastern side an old man waves back. The old man shouts out something but the other does not hear. A tear runs down the man's cheek as he turns sadly away. Look back over to the East. Soldiers are already forcing the old man to leave. (sample 2E)

3.   The next thing you should look at are the options you want your unit to have. The home unit is really the only one that will have a wide selection of options to choose from. The tracking, or searching, option, which allows you to skip from song to song with the push of a button, comes standard on all home units, so you need not worry about it. A wireless remote control is an important option to consider, simply because it is so convenient. If you look hard enough and are willing to pay a little extra you can even get a remote for the car and portable models. "Programmability" is a must for the serious music listener. This function enables you to program the order in which you wish to listen to the tracks on the disc. "Indexing" actually lets you program what part of each song you wish to hear. Many units offer what is actually called the "shuffle" function. What this does is that it randomly picks a song and acts as though it is track one and goes on from there. The "repeat" button is a rather interesting function. It lets you play a song, or a portion of a song, over and over until you press the button again. The portable and car models don't really come with "options," except for the remote. They will come standard with tracking, forward search, and review, just like the bigger home units. Some of these options are quite extravagant, but the others definitely need to be taken into consideration before you actually purchase a compact disc player. (sample 1C)

4.   The death penalty was used often and quite freely while settling

the old American West. Stealing a horse was often enough reason to lead the thief to the gallows. Gunfights and duels were a common method of settling differences. As towns grew into cities and civilization took a stronger grip on the population, the number of executions began to decline. Unfortunately, during the mid–1960's, nearly all methods of capital punishment came to a complete standstill. This punishment was reinstated to the United States penal code in 1976. Keeping capital punishment for some crimes is favored by 79% of Americans. This has increased from 42% in 1966 (Tooley, 81). These figures run parallel with our neighbors to the north. Canada is trying to reinstate the death penalty to its penal codes. Two of every three Canadians are supporting this measure (Faulkner 400). (sample 4D)

5.   As I sat in the surgery waiting room in my back-less hospital gown, I began to feel the Valium that they administered to me take effect. Was this meant to reduce my pain? If so—physical or emotional? Would this drug mend my broken heart and seize my despair? In scrutinizing the room, I noticed the others; all of them young and chatting casually as if it were no big deal. Were they not feeling what I was feeling? I don't think they were, I cried. I was at the lowest level of humiliation. I thought "I'm going to murder my child that I prayed for and was blessed with." Should there be no regard for the ruthlessness of this brutal execution? Would there be no consequences of remorse? Yes, there would be. (sample 4A)

B. Choose one of the preceding paragraphs and revise it to give it clearer, more effective organization. Be prepared to discuss the reasons for your revisions.

C. In your journal, prepare a list of questions, for your peer critic, about paragraph patterns in one of your own drafts. Your questions should be phrased to elicit substantive responses from your peer, so avoid yes-no questions. Begin your questions with information words like *what, where, when,* or *how.*

Postdrafting: Revising Paragraphs

When you revise your paragraphs at the postdrafting stage, you need to consider the writing situation, the content, and the organization of your piece of writing. In other words, you should try to apply everything you've learned thus far about writing, as both a process and a product, to your revising of paragraphs. As you resee your paragraphs and plan your revisions, then, keep in mind that it's still not too late to clarify any of the variables in the writing situation (writer, reader, subject, and purpose), to supply more content, or to adjust the organizational plan for your piece of writing.

In the postdrafting sections of the last two chapters, we focused our discussion on how to revise the content and the organization of your piece of writing. In that discussion, we introduced Grice's conversational maxims (relevance, quantity, quality, and manner) as aids to revision at the postdrafting stage. These maxims, we said, define and organize the postdrafting process, offering beginning college writers a clearer and more complete understanding of *revision*.

If you have used these maxims to resee or rethink the content and organization of your piece of writing, you know that *revising* is not merely changing a mark of punctuation or correcting a misspelled word. Clearly, the process of revision is much more complex. By continuing to practice revising from a Gricean perspective, you can learn to plan and implement a revising strategy to produce a more effective piece of writing, one that meets the needs and expectations of your readers.

In his conversational model, in addition to describing the four maxims we observe in conversations, Grice emphasized the importance of realizing the goal and purpose of the communication. Without a goal and purpose, the maxims are not very useful; they are effective only if anchored to a particular situation, in speaking or in writing. So when you apply the maxims to your paragraphs at the postdrafting stage, you cannot ignore the writing situation. Just as you cannot determine what is "relevant" attire unless you know something about the occasion you are attending, you cannot effectively apply Grice's maxims unless you know something about the writing situation.

How can Grice's maxims guide your revision of paragraphs? In this section, we will show you how Grice's maxims can help focus your attention on two important qualities of effective paragraphs: coherence and cohesion.

REVISING FOR COHERENCE

Relevance and Quantity. When a paragraph does not make sense to its readers, the problem is often with the content of the paragraph: the *relevance* of the topic (whether stated or implied) to the writing situation, and the *quantity* of supporting information. A paragraph may be well formed, with a clearly expressed topic and sufficient evidence to support it, yet the paragraph may not be *coherent*. Its content may not be appropriate for the writing situation. When a paragraph is *coherent*, it fits the writing situation: its topic sentence—wherever it occurs—is relevant and purposeful, and its supporting content satisfies the purpose of the writer and the expectations of the intended readers.

The maxim of relevance should serve as a reminder that the ideas expressed as topic sentences in a piece of writing must be relevant to the writing situation. At the postdrafting stage, then, you should examine your paragraphs and try to identify the topics you cover and the way you focus these topics to substantiate the larger point in your piece of writing. Remember too that some topics will be developed in single paragraphs, whereas others may require two or more paragraphs. How do these ideas expressed as topic sentences contribute to the focus you established at the beginning of your piece of writing?

Once you have examined the topics, you can then evaluate the supporting information for each topic. Sometimes you may have clearly stated topics in your piece of writing, but the supporting information may not be well suited to the writing situation—to the purpose of the essay and its intended readers. How does the content of the paragraph support the topic sentence? If a sequence of paragraphs develops a single topic, what does each paragraph in the sequence contribute to that topic? Is the content sufficient to support the topic? Is the supporting information you provide more than is necessary, given the assumptions you have made about the knowledge of your readers?

By asking yourself—and your peer editors—these kinds of questions, you will be evaluating the *coherence* of your paragraphs and revising, as needed, to observe the maxims for effective communication. For paragraphs to make sense to readers, they must be coherent. That is, your ideas, expressed as topic sentences and sustained by the content of paragraphs, must be relevant to the writing situation and sufficiently developed to meet the needs of your readers.

Consider this paragraph, for example, from Kathy's first draft of her autobiographical essay (sample 3A) for admission to a nursing program:

> I began work immediately. My first position was in a physician's office working in the lab and assisting with minor surgeries. The job was both satisfying and challenging. After three years the opportunity to head the small Lab Department in a Nursing Home became available. I interviewed and received the job. I immediately felt at home. The elderly residents I worked with were quite a challenge. Each one had a story to tell and were always ready to tell it. Some were cranky, some were happy. But it was a place you felt truly needed and appreciated. The only thing that was missing was adequate patient contact. Since I was in the Lab my contact with the residents was limited. I knew I wanted to be more directly involved with their day to day care. Three years later I resigned my position and made the decision to return to college.

Because Kathy was writing to gain admission into a nursing program, she knew that her work experience would be an important topic to cover. Thus, she assumed that her readers would be interested in her past work experiences and their impact on her decision to pursue a degree in the nursing field. At the postdrafting stage, she analyzed this paragraph for the relevance and quantity of its content.

After rethinking the paragraph and consulting with her peers, Kathy decided to add more information about her first job experience working in the physician's office. In the draft, she wrote that the job was "satisfying and challenging," but she didn't provide the supporting material. She thought she should perhaps let her readers know more about her actual work experiences in the medical field, not simply list them. As you will see in the following passage, she decided to devote a separate paragraph to each of her job experiences, adding new sentences to give the reader a clearer picture of her job responsibilities:

> I began work immediately. My first position was in a physician's office. The doctor I worked for was an Osteopath as well as a family practitioner. I received a wide range of experiences. I was responsible for all lab procedures such as venipuncture, microscopic urinalysis, ultra-sounds, and assisted with minor surgeries. It was a very challenging and satisfying position. After three years the opportunity to head the small Lab Department in a Nursing Home became available. I interviewed and received the job. This is where my position in the medical field became very clear to me.
>
> I felt immediately at home. I enjoyed talking with and helping the elderly residents. My duties in the Lab included venipuncture, maintaining a lab log, and scheduling appointments for the residents; I was also responsible for performing electrocardiograms and scheduling yearly physicals. I had never been in an environment where I felt so needed. I found myself wanting to make a positive difference in their lives. The only thing that was missing, however, was adequate patient contact. Since I was in the Lab, my contact with the residents was limited. I knew I wanted to be more directly involved with their day-to-day care. Three years later I resigned my position and made the decision to return to college.

Quality. When you revise your paragraphs for *quality*, you look at the accuracy and truth, or probability, of the ideas expressed in your topic sentences. A topic sentence is, after all, a generalization you make based on your knowledge of the subject, acquired either through personal experience or through study. Even though you may have determined the *relevancy* of your topic sentences to the focus of your piece of writing, your responsibility as a writer is to ensure that your topics—your generalizations—are based on a careful study of the subject and not on personal bias. We all have our opinions about current issues like abortion, gun control, AIDS prevention, environmental pollution, animal research, and the like. But if we do not attempt to keep informed about the issues, especially when we write about them, we may fall into the trap of arguing opinions that may reflect only how uninformed we really are about the subject. Often, when we delve beneath the surface of an issue, our opinions reflect a greater sensitivity to the issue and the problems it poses.

The same is true when, as writers, we borrow information from published sources to use in a piece of writing. As a writer, you must evaluate the generalizations made by other writers in published sources before you use them. If you are borrowing information and you have questions about its validity, you certainly do not want to perpetuate inaccuracies by including this information to support a point in your own piece of writing. The maxim of quality should remind you that your topic sentences, as well as those in published sources, should be generalizations based on a reasonable investigation of your subject.

REVISING FOR COHESION

Manner. As you may recall from the last chapter, the maxim of manner refers to the way you express your ideas in a piece of writing. When you revise your "manner of expression" in paragraphs, you are revising for *cohesion*. Earlier we discussed some important points about revising for *coherence*. When you revise for coherence, you examine paragraphs in relation to other paragraphs and to the writing situation. In this section, we are concerned not with *coherence* but with *cohesion*. When you revise for *cohesion*, you examine groups of sentences or, if you will, paragraphs. A paragraph is cohesive when its sentences "stick together."

To check the cohesiveness of your paragraphs at the postdrafting stage, you need to examine each paragraph for its "focus words" and "relationship signals."

Focus words. If a paragraph is a group of sentences that have more of a relationship with each other than they do with surrounding sentences, then the sentences in a paragraph need to be cohesive—they need to be linked together. One important way that the sentences in a paragraph are linked together is with *focus words*, words in successive sentences that repeat, or refer to, the topic of the paragraph, and so serve to keep the reader's attention focused on that topic.

For example, consider the second paragraph of Amy's article on Ceralvo (sample 2C).

During the mid–1800's, water travel was the most popular form of transportation; consequently, many cities sprang up along rivers where they would have easy access to water routes. Ceralvo was one of those cities. Ceralvo grew very quickly because the ferry boats that docked there brought new people to the area. The ferry was also responsible for bringing supplies which were stored in several warehouses built along the river. The city had nearly all of the institutions one would expect to find—a post office, two general stores, a dry goods store, a church, and a school. Ceralvo also had a hotel, a drug store, and three tobacco factories where tobacco was stored and traded. The city was home to such professionals as a blacksmith, a cobbler, and two doctors. Ceralvo even had a college, although it consisted of only a handful of students taught by a professor.

The topic of this paragraph is clearly the city of Ceralvo, so, as you would expect, the word *Ceralvo* is repeated several times in the paragraph; this repetition helps tie the paragraph together. If words are repeated too often, however, they can become distracting for the reader, so focus words are often synonyms or pronouns that refer to the paragraph's topic(s). Twice Amy refers to Ceralvo as "the city" to provide the necessary variety.

So focus words may be pronouns that point back to the topic of the paragraph or synonyms that substitute for the topic. When you use synonyms as substitutes for a paragraph topic, however, you should be cognizant of the new meaning carried by the synonym. Consider the focus words, for example, in this paragraph from Alan's essay about the computer evolution (sample 4C):

> We are now on the verge of the 5th generation of computers. The term for this is "Artificial Intelligence" or AI. If computers have achieved a state of artificial intelligence, how far away can "Artificial Consciousness" be? If we can create machines that can learn through experience and do original thinking, how far away is it before we can create a machine that can feel? How long before the machine can evolve autonomously?

The focus words in this paragraph are *computers* and *Artificial Intelligence*. Notice that the pronoun *this* in the second sentence refers to *the 5th generation of computers* in the first sentence, thus linking the two sentences. The third sentence repeats the focus word *computers*, but the fourth and fifth sentences use the synonym *machines* in place of *computers*. Alan uses the synonym *machines* to avoid repeating the same focus word too often. More important, however, he is no doubt sensitive to the new meaning carried by the synonym. By using the synonym *machines*, Alan calls attention to just how far and how rapidly humankind has progressed.

In one of Amy's other papers, she sometimes does not supply enough focus words. Notice the fourth paragraph of her instructions on applying for FHA office (sample 1A):

> If you are accepted as an officer candidate, the next step in the process is planning a tentative program for the annual summer

leadership camp. This is an important step because it displays your creativity and your organizational skills, both of which are essential in holding a state office. Your program must include a theme for the camp; also, it must include what materials will be covered, who the guest speakers will be, and the type of recreation for each meeting.

The topic of this paragraph is the tentative program for the summer leadership camp, but the key words *program* and *camp* appear only once after their first mention. This paragraph would probably be more effective for its readers if it were revised into something like the following:

> If you are accepted as an officer candidate, the next step in the process is planning a tentative program for the annual summer leadership camp. This camp program is an important step because it displays your creativity and your organizational skills, both of which are essential in holding a state office. Your program must include a theme for the camp, as well as a list of materials, guest speakers, and recreational activities for each of the camp's meetings.

Relationship signals. Another way to give a paragraph cohesion is with *relationship signals,* words or phrases that show the relationship of each sentence with a previous one. These words or phrases, as categorized by Ross Winterowd, are like the turn signals on a car; the writer (like a driver) uses them to signal changes in direction. Such signals make it easier for the reader to follow the writer through a paragraph.

One easy way to provide relationship signals is to think of sentences as having only six possible relationships: *and, or, but, so, because,* and *the colon.*

AND. Two sentences have an *and* relationship when the second sentence simply adds more information of the same kind. An *and* relationship is thus like a plus sign in mathematics. Besides the word *and,* this relationship can be signaled with such words and phrases as *also, too, moreover, furthermore, in addition, next, second, third,* and the like. Here are some examples of *and* relationships in the sample papers.

> In order to apply, you must have held an office at the chapter and regional levels of FHA, preferably the same one as the state office you wish to hold. *Also,* you must have completed your state degree. (sample 1A)

> Don has dared to dream and dreamed to dare. I *too* have set goals and work hard to fulfill them. (sample 2C)

> The *next* four months were an emotional rollercoaster. (sample 4A)

Before I even started school, I can remember being encouraged to learn my ABC's. I *also* remember being urged to learn words and eventually to make sentences. (sample 3D)

OR. Two sentences have an *or* relationship when they present alternatives. Besides the word *or*, this relationship can be signaled with the words *alternatively* or *otherwise*.

You could spend a still moment watching purple barn swallows, their tails forking out to a V-shape, as they would dart through an open door or window. *Or* you may sit in the comfort of the loft, with the fresh smell of new mown hay, and watch for the old barn owl to return to its nest that you have discovered. (sample 2D)

You will also need a pair of high quality headphones for the portable model. *Otherwise* the music would be no different than if you were listening to a cassette. (sample 1C)

BUT. Two sentences have a *but* relationship when the second sentence contradicts, partially contradicts, or qualifies, the first. Besides the word *but*, this relationship can be signaled with such words and phrases as *however, nevertheless, nonetheless, conversely,* and *on the other hand*. Notice that relationship signals sometimes allow the two sentences to be combined into one:

One might think that Ceralvo has always been simply a rural residential area; *however,* the buildings there today are actually the remains of a thriving city of another era. (sample 2C)

Indeed, many of man's greatest achievements have been only in the past fifty years.
Another species on our planet, *however,* is evolving much more rapidly. That species is the computer. (sample 4C)

My parents told me that they loved me and nothing would change. *But* things did change. (sample 4B)

SO. Two sentences have a *so* relationship when the second expresses the result or conclusion or effect of the first sentence. Besides the word *so*, this relationship can be signaled with words and phrases like *therefore, thus, for this reason,* and *consequently*:

I had been interested in genetics before my father became ill; *therefore,* I was strongly motivated to use these interests in the future to find answers for the problems we as a family have faced. (sample 2B)

The first generation of computers (1951–1958) were built with vacuum tube technology. *Consequently*, they were bulky, slow, and unreliable. (sample 4C)

BECAUSE. The *because* relationship is the opposite of the *so* relationship: two sentences have a *because* relationship when the second gives the cause or reason for the first. Besides the word *because*, this relationship can be signalled with such words as *since* and *for*.

It is challenging *because* you must meet strict requirements and will be up against the toughest competition in the state. (sample 1A)

One disadvantage of this model is that it can be broken easily, *because* it is portable. (sample 1C)

Sometimes the *because* or *since* sentence (or clause) can even precede the sentence (or clause) that expresses its result or effect:

Since the application determines whether you become an officer candidate, you should put much time and effort into your answers. (sample 1A)

COLON. Two sentences have a *colon* relationship when the second sentence gives a specific case or cases for the generalization made in the first sentence. Beside a colon, this relationship can be signalled with words and phrases like *specifically*, *for example*, and *to illustrate*.

Climb up the small platform overlooking the Wall. What is there to see? An obstacle course of death: barbed wire, deep sand, trenches, landmines, and dog tracks where the Germans run fierce German Shepherds trained to kill. (sample 2E)

Mike is a new student at IUPUI. He just registered for classes and is all set to begin in the fall, but he does have one problem: he needs a job. (sample 1B)

By this I mean that you should decide when you will be listening to your CD player the most, and in turn choose a model that best fits your needs. Say, *for example*, that you most frequently listen to music while in your car; then you obviously would want one designed to replace your current car stereo. (sample 1C)

However, there are always new goals to be set. This summer, *for example,* I was participating in a program for pre-med students. (sample 2D)

Relationship signals can improve the cohesiveness of your paragraphs, but, like anything else, they can be overused. Focus words should perhaps predominate in your writing because they are less obvious than relationship signals. But when you want or need to emphasize a relationship between sentences, a relationship signal makes it easily visible to the reader. Knowing how to achieve such cohesion in your writing is part of discovering your power as a writer.

Exercises

A. Copy the following paragraphs, circling the focus words and underlining the relationship signals. Be prepared to discuss the effectiveness of the paragraphs.

1.   Man, long considered (at least by man) to be the supreme species on our planet, has had an evolutionary process unprecedented in the animal kingdom. While he has gone from little more than an ape to his present sophisticated form in a few million years, man's mental evolution has been much more rapid, apparently only over the last few thousand years. But it has only been in the past century that the development has been most rapid. Indeed, many of man's greatest achievements have been only in the past fifty years. (sample 4C)

2.   My father was diagnosed as having lymphoma, or cancer of the lymph system, in June of 1985. His illness raised many questions and problems not answered or dealt with by hospitals and doctors. Medical professionals could neither find the cause of the disease, nor provide a cure for it. Chemotherapy treatments slowed the progression of the cancer for a time. However, complications such as an intestinal blockage and pneumonia eventually led to my father's death. (sample 3B)

3.   Ironically, a failing test grade also contributed to my success. In the middle of my fourth grade year, my parents decided that the education I was receiving was not adequate. Upon reaching this decision, they enrolled me in another elementary school. At my former school I had been at the top of the class. After about a week of classes at Central, my school, we were given a timed multiplication

test—my first timed test. And I was behind in multiplication tables when I changed schools. I failed that test with a fifty-six percent. I hated the feeling of being a failure. I wanted to go back to my old school, but my parents would not let me. Instead, they encouraged me and offered support. Through hard work and extra homework, I caught up with the class and even struggled to get back at the top. On the next test, I made an A. I feel that this experience sparked a desire within me to be the best. I have never quit trying. (sample 3D)

B. Revise one of the preceding paragraphs to increase its cohesion and effectiveness. Be prepared to discuss the reasons for your revisions.

C. Select a paragraph or a group of paragraphs from an earlier essay or from one you are now drafting, and use Grice's maxims to analyze the coherence and cohesion of your writing. Is the topic of your paragraph(s) relevant to the writing situation? Is the supporting information adequate? How effectively do you use focus words and relationship signals?

Assignment 4: Writing about Ideas

Assignment: The passages reproduced below refer to topics that have been discussed, often debated, in magazines and journals and on news programs. Choose one of the passages, or one from your own reading, and use it as a springboard into an essay of your own. In your essay, you may refer to the passage or, if you like, quote from it, but you need not refer to it at all. The passages are meant only to stimulate your own thinking.

Your essay should express a clear thesis, either explicitly or implicitly, and be supported with information you draw primarily from your own experience. If you choose, you may use information from experts and publications, but it should not substitute for your own thinking.

Imagine that you are writing this paper as a requirement for a college course (one related in subject matter) and that your paper will be kept on file and read by other students who enroll in the course in a future semester.

Selected Passages

1.   In 1963 Betty Friedan, a modern Charlotte Gilman, wrote *The Feminine Mystique*. She described how women's magazines formed the popular conception of the ideal woman. In their attempt to imitate the accepted ideal, women suffered from economic discrimination, male stereotyping, and ultimate dehumanization. . . .

Kate Millet, more militant than Friedan, published *Sexual Politics* in 1970 in which she argued that nothing short of a political, economic, and intellectual revolution would bring women justice. . . . Some publicists suggested that the only real love was that between women and that the time was coming when women would no longer need men to sire children. Women's liberation was raising basic and profound questions about the nature of human society. (From H. L. Ingle and James A. Ward, *American History* [Boston: Little, Brown, 1978], pp. 474–75)

2.   Grades focus our attention. But on what? On the test. Academic success, as everyone knows, is something that we measure not in knowledge but in grade points. What we get on the final is all-important; what we retain after the final is irrelevant. Grades don't make us want to enrich our minds; they make us want to please our teachers (or at least put them on). Grades are a game. When the term is over, you shuffle the deck and begin a new round. (From Jerry Farber, *The Student as Nigger* [New York: Simon and Schuster, 1969], p. 67)

3.   I see in painters prose writers and poets. Rhyme, measure, and the turning of verses, which is indispensable and which gives them so much vigor, are analogous to the hidden symmetry, to the equilibrium at once wise and inspired, which governs the meeting or separation of lines and spaces, the echoes of color, etc. (From the journal of Eugene Delacroix, as reprinted in *Artists on Art*, eds. Robert Goldwater and Marco Treves [New York: Pantheon Books, 1945], p. 227)

4.   In the final years before the millenium there will be a fundamental and revolutionary shift in leisure time and spending priorities. During the 1990's the arts will gradually replace sports as society's primary leisure activity. This extraordinary megatrend is already visible in an explosion in the visual and performing arts that is already underway. (From John Naisbitt and Patricia Aburdene, *Megatrends 2000* [New York: William Morrow, 1990], p. 62)

5.   We make the computer's meaning what we will. If it seems impersonal, overly complicated, unyielding, full of vague dread, as well blame the computer as any other phenomenon. Its sinister nature is immediately apparent: it's just like all the other bad machines, only worse, because it can go beyond brute force and outfox—and humiliate—you. Or alternatively, the computer is amplifier of everything that matters to you. (From Pamela McCorduck, *The Universal Machine: Confessions of a Technological Optimist* [New York: McGraw-Hill, 1985], pp. 112–13)

6.   What you learned about language from your teachers, you learned consciously, and you consciously applied what you had learned. But what you learned was facts and opinions about your language and how to use it effectively, which, compared to the language itself, were quite insignificant. The language itself was something you had already mastered, long before anyone tried to teach it to you. . . . Quite unconsciously, and without any formal training, you had somehow developed a system so complex that linguists have still not figured out just how it works. (From Frank Henry, "Sentence Structure,"

reprinted in *Language*, 4th ed., eds. Virginia P. Clark, et al. [New York: St. Martin's, 1985], p. 295)

7.   It is easy enough to assert that all languages are equal and efficient in their own sphere of use. But most of us do not really believe in this idea, and certainly do not act as if we did. . . . It isn't that we cannot understand each other—Southerners, Northerners, Californians, New Yorkers, blacks, whites, Appalachian folk—with only the slightest effort we can communicate just fine. But because of our history of experiences with each other, or perhaps just out of perversity, we have developed prejudices toward other people's language which sometimes affect our behavior. (From Harvey A. Daniels, "Nine Ideas about Language," reprinted in *Language*, 4th ed., eds. Virginia P. Clark et al. [New York: St. Martin's, 1985], p. 19)

8.   The metaphysical assumptions and moral implications inherent in aspects of evolution theory have been a source of innumerable battles for over a hundred years. PreDarwinian biologists based their science on theological assumptions. Science was rooted in religion: its purpose was to provide the existence of God, using as evidence the design and purpose in nature. Darwin introduced an explanation of biological change that excluded the necessity of supernatural intervention and incorporated elements of chance and indeterminacy. Thus Darwin's *Origin of the Species* was viewed as a revolutionary document in 1859, although its primary contribution was to organize and synthesize a set of ideas that had pervaded the scientific literature for more than fifty years. (From Dorothy Nelkin, *Science Textbook Controversies and the Politics of Time* [Cambridge, MA: MIT Press, 1978], p. 9)

9.   A *Wall Street Journal*/NBC News poll taken a week after the massive prochoice march in Washington indicated an increase in sentiment that the abortion choice should remain with the woman: 71 percent agreed that the woman, not the government, should decide. (From Peggy Simpson, "The Political Arena," *Ms.*, July/August 1989, p. 46)

10.   Driven by a broad upheaval in the American workplace and by their own aspirations and needs, millions of adults are taking undergraduate and postgraduate courses for credit. . . . The number of such students had risen 114 percent since 1970, to 5.1 million—or 42 percent of the nation's 12.2 million college students, according to the Federal Department of Education. . . . By comparison, the enrollment of students under 25 in college has increased only 15 percent since 1970, actually declining since 1980.
     The pattern . . . may be symptomatic of a deeper current, according to some experts, who argue that Americans are yearning for a greater sense of independence and more individualism in their work. (From Lee A. Daniels, "The Baby-Boomers Change Courses," *New York Times*, 3, January 1988, section 12, p. 12)

Sample Papers

Sample 4A (Cathy):

Abortion?

It seems that women's rights, equal rights, constitutional rights, etc., have all evolved to such extremes. I have questions—legitimate questions—about the recent issue of abortion. What will become of this issue? What are the rights of the unborn child? Is this child being discriminated against because of its temporary place of residence? Just because it cannot yet voice an opinion or vote it does not have the same rights to life as we do? An infant cannot do these things either, yet we protect its rights to life and call it "murder" if someone purposely ends that life.

When I look into the eyes of my eight-year-old son, I see the most beautiful miracle that I was blessed with. I might very well have not been able to say this had things gone as planned.

My now-ex-husband and I wanted a child; probably I a little more than he. We were successful in our attempt. Shortly after confirming the good news, my husband, being elated, told his mother of our news. She then persuaded him into believing that this was a terrible mistake (for reasons of her own selfishness) and that abortion was the only way out of this "mess."

The arrangements were made and, of course, this she knew would drive me out of her son's life; and it did—we separated. My husband took me to a clinic to obtain an abortion. In the emotional trauma, I refused to get out of the car at the clinic until we managed to miss our appointment. He rescheduled the appointment and took me back a few days later.

As I sat in the surgery waiting room in my back-less hospital gown, I began to feel the Valium that they administered to me take effect. Was this meant to reduce my pain? If so—physical or emotional? Would this drug mend my broken heart and seize my despair? In scrutinizing the room, I noticed the others; all of them young and chatting casually as if it were no big deal. Were they not feeling what I was feeling? I don't think they were, I cried. I was at the lowest level of humiliation. I thought "I'm going to murder my child that I prayed for and was blessed with." Should there be no regard for the ruthlessness of this brutal execution? Would there be no consequences of remorse? Yes, there would be.

Sitting there reflecting upon my past and contemplating my

moral upbringing as a child, I found myself consumed with contempt. At that moment, I requested the nurse to summon my husband to a place where we could speak privately. Finally, I expressed my disdain and unyielding fury! This child's life would certainly not be ended due to his apprehensions about fatherhood; even if I had to raise it all by myself.

After leaving the clinic that day, everything seemed to fall into place for awhile. We reunited and attempted to contend with my mother-in-law, but eventually failed and divorced.

Consequently, I am overwhelmed at the image of what almost took place that day in May. The remorse felt in the murder of this child would have haunted me forever. My personal opinion is (and was) that if you are old enough to engage in sexual activities—you are then old enough to take on the responsibilities for what might result. According to my religious beliefs, one of those responsibilities is to uphold the trust that has been placed in us to care for this creation of God.

My decision was largely based upon my faith in God. This was a human life and I had no right to destroy it. I decided to turn these monumental obstacles (such as opposition) over to God. This at least took some of the pressure from my shoulders. Although my son, Josh, and I have experienced some trying times, I have never regretted having him. As a matter of fact—he is the most cherished aspect of my life.

What will you decide about the fate of your child?

Sample 4B (Janice):

Freedom to Choose

Today in this country, abortion is a huge moral and political issue. Whatever happened to freedom of choice? Granted freedom of speech is also an issue here, but what gives pro-life activists the right to frighten young women with their horror stories? Just because they believe in something doesn't mean it is right for everyone. How can they judge someone on something they have never experienced, something they have never had to make a choice about? Is expressing your opinion worth all the anger and resentment? Is it worth a trip to jail? You see people on television being bodily carried away by the police. These people aren't helping anyone; they are just making fools of themselves. This isn't success, it's failure. Failure of our rights as American citizens.

I think all women should have a choice, whether a teenager or a grown woman. Every woman knows what is best for her. Teenagers should maybe have some guidance, but they should still have a choice. Having a child is a lot of responsibility, but so is a sexual relationship. Birth control is so important, as well as education. All girls think, "It won't happen to me," but it can, and it does.

When I was a teenager, I became pregnant. Terrified, I waited four months until I broke down and told my mother. She couldn't believe I had "gone all the way" with a boy. This "boy" as it happens was of legal age, and claimed he was sterile.

Before I knew it, I was at the doctor's office, where it was confirmed. Moments later arrangements were made between him and my mother. No one asked me or even thought to ask what I might want or how I felt. Even though I was young shouldn't I have had a choice, or at least an opinion? Now we are on the way home to tell my father. His reaction was less than what I expected. He asked only one question, "Who's the father?" Those were the last words he spoke to me for the next two weeks.

Within the week, we were on our way to Louisville. I was too far along to have one in Indiana. These were the most terrifying two days of my life. I had no preparation or prior knowledge of what was to take place. I went through several tests and was left in rooms with other girls, as frightened as me, to wonder what was next. Near the end of the first day, I was given something to induce a miscarriage and was allowed to leave for the night with my parents. That night I lay in bed and cried with pain and without so much as a word from my parents in the next bed.

The second day began with an IV given by a woman, who, in my opinion, had never given one before. I was stuck repeatedly in both hands, until she finally got it right. I was later left again, in a room of six or eight other girls. We all had IV's and had robes and gowns on. Waiting to be taken to the operating room, my water broke. I had no idea what had happened and began to cry. My clothes were soaked before a nurse came to help. After awakening from general anesthesia, we were given instructions, a snack, and sent on our way.

My brother and sisters were never told, and to this day have no knowledge of my abortion. They were told we were going on a business/pleasure weekend with my father. My parents told me that they loved me, and that nothing would change. But things did change. For the rest of my life at their home, I felt like they were ashamed of me. Like I had let them down. The subject has never been discussed since. It's as if nothing ever happened.

For eight years I never told anyone how I felt, or how much the experience had hurt me. Only two people have ever shared my feelings and cared enough to listen. They have both been through this also. My best friend and my husband. My parents' lack of communication and support has left a scar on me that can never be erased. What a relief it was to share with my husband and my friend all the pain and anger I had carried for so long.

Though my experience was bad and the healing slow, I feel no one should be able to dictate what you can and cannot do with your body and your life. I wasn't given a choice, and if I had been I would probably have a child today. I wonder, would my friends still be my friends? Would I have gone to the prom or to parties and ball games? The most important question of all is, "Would I have my wonderful husband?" He has been such a blessing to me in so many ways. He understands my pain and my sense of emptiness and loss.

Not much time goes by that I don't think of what might have been. I love children, and long for one of my own. I'm older now and more mature. More prepared mentally and financially. Abortion is not for everyone, but God made us free. Free to live our lives. To choose for ourselves what is best. No one should be allowed to tell us what to do. Isn't that what this country is? America the Free.

If you ever decide to have an abortion, ask questions. It's your body. You have a right to know what is happening and know what will take place. You should have the freedom to choose.

Sample 4C (Alan):

The Computer Evolution

Man, long considered (at least by man) to be the supreme species on our planet, has had an evolutionary process unprecedented in the animal kingdom. While he has gone from little more than an ape to his present sophisticated form in a few million years, man's mental evolution has been much more rapid, apparently only over the last few thousand years. But it has only been in the past century that the development has been most rapid. Indeed, many of man's greatest achievements have been only in the past fifty years.

Another species on our planet, however, is evolving much more rapidly. That species is the computer. The evolution of the computer parallels the evolution of man but on a highly compressed time scale. But how can we think of computers as an evolving species?

All organisms on earth store information for survival in one or more of the following manners: genetic—"prewired" information stored in the nervous system; extragenetic—learned information acquired through experience; and extrasomatic—information stored outside of the body. The lowest organisms store information solely through their DNA, while man alone uses all three methods (Sagan 3–4).

The first electronic computers—dinosaurs, if you will—were prewired, as well. The computer's program could only be changed by rewiring it. Later machines utilized programs stored in memory, which could be easily changed or modified through learning. Finally, external storage on magnetic tape and other media was devised (Bailes & Rizer 8).

As each new generation of man hopes to be better than the one before—to know more, to do more, to be more—each "generation" of computers *has been* better. We can classify these generations based on technological developments that precipitated them. The first generation of computers (1951–1958) were built with vacuum tube technology. Consequently, they were bulky, slow, and unreliable. The second generation of computers (1959–1964) were built from transistors. At this time, the first programming languages were written to make using the computer easier. The third generation of computers (1964–1971) were built from integrated circuits (IC's)—tiny chips of silicon containing the same circuitry as entire cards of transistors. During this time the input and output (1/0) were also improved. Fourth generation computers (1971–present) utilize large-scale integration (LSI) and very large-scale integration (VLSI). This continuing reduction in size has led to computers one thousand times smaller than their great grandfathers (Bailes & Rizer 8–11).

We are now on the verge of the 5th generation of computers. The term for this is "Artificial Intelligence" or AI. If computers have achieved a state of artificial intelligence, how far away can "Artificial Consciousness" be? If we can create machines that can learn through experience and do original thinking, how far away is it before we can create a machine that can feel? How long before the machine can evolve autonomously?

Man has created the computer in his own image, mirroring the evolution process in its development. Perhaps man's creation will someday be better than he is.

Works Cited

Bailes, Gordon L., and Robert R. Rizer. *The IBM 370: Computer Organization and Assembly Language.* St. Paul: West, 1987.

Sagan, Carl. *The Dragons of Eden: Speculation on the Evolution of Human Intelligence.* New York: Random House, 1977.

Sample 4D (Joe):

Execution Is the Right Answer

The death penalty was used often and quite freely while settling the old American West. Stealing a horse was often enough reason to lead the thief to the gallows. Gunfights and duels were a common method of settling differences. As towns grew into cities and civilization took a stronger grip on the population, the number of executions began to decline. Unfortunately, during the mid–1960s, nearly all methods of capital punishment came to a complete standstill. This punishment was reinstated to the United States penal code in 1976. Keeping capital punishment for some crimes is favored by 79% of Americans. This has increased from 42% in 1966 (Tooley 81). These figures run parallel with our neighbors to the north. Canada is trying to reinstate the death penalty to its penal codes. Two of every three Canadians are supporting this measure (Faulkner 400).

In this decade that is now drawing to a close, the American judicial system seems to be taking a much stronger view of death as a sentence for certain crimes. If, as a New York prosecutor implies, the penalty of death is kept in the penal codes, a criminal chose to be executed "when he decided to be a criminal . . ." (Jacoby 67). More than 50 criminals have met this fate since reinstating the death penalty (Inciardi 485).

As hideous a thought as it is to take another person's life, I believe it is one of mankind's necessary evils. There are some criminals whose murderous rages are of such a brutal and grotesque nature that death seems to be too trivial a punishment. Any sane person who would deliberately rape and kill a small child should not be allowed the opportunity to commit this same crime with someone else. The example of Ted Bundy illustrates this point very well. At 42 years of age, he was good looking, well educated, and had been raised as a Christian. "Suspected of killing as many as 50 young women . . . ," he was executed "after he was convicted of mutilating and murdering a 12-year-old. . . ." The day before his death he stated: "I deserve, certainly, the most extreme punishment society has, and I think society deserves to be protected from me and others like me" (Nichols 54).

I believe anyone who has the mindset of some of the people that are now serving time on death row deserve to be executed. Why should we as American taxpayers have to house, clothe, feed, and give medical care to a person who would intentionally kill another human for the pure enjoyment of it? People of this caliber deserve nothing more than death from anyone.

Possibly the only major drawback with the death penalty is that it is irrevocable. Once the sentence has been carried out, nothing can change the outcome. The fear of putting an innocent person to death is reason enough to retain the lengthy appeals process. This process guarantees that every death sentence will eventually be heard by the Supreme Court. This lengthy appellate procedure is more than sufficient to protect those that may be innocent.

Works Cited

Tooley, J. Ann. "Taking the Last Mile Slowly." *U.S. News & World Report*, Jan. 30, 1989, 81.

Jacoby, Tamar. "Caught Between Two States." *Newsweek*, May 2, 1988, 67.

Faulkner, T. S. "Restoring Canada's Death Penalty." *The Christian Century*, Apr. 29, 1987, 400.

Nichols, Mark. "A Killer's Final Hour." *Maclean's*, Feb. 6, 1989, 54.

Inciardi, James A. *Criminal Justice*. San Diego: Harcourt Brace Jovanovich, 1987.

Discussion Questions

1. How well do the first two papers, about the abortion issue, fulfill the requirements of the writing assignment? If you were to revise either of these papers, what changes would you make? Be prepared to explain the reasons for your revisions.

2. In the last two papers, the writers incorporate other voices from external sources. After reading these two papers, do you sense that the writers are in control of their source material? If so, how have they achieved this control? If not, what would you do differently?

CHAPTER FIVE

The Process of Writing Sentences

If any feature of the written product deserves to be called a "unit of thought," it is not the paragraph but the sentence. For a sentence is the smallest unit of writing that *says something*. Words just name things; sentences make assertions, give commands, ask questions. Good sentences are the essence of good writing.

But how do we define "good sentences"? One way to define a good sentence is to describe its parts—or its grammar. In grammatical terms, a good sentence is a complete unit of thought composed of a subject and a predicate: the subject tells what the sentence is about, and the predicate says something about the subject. So, *John works at the zoo* is a good sentence because it has both a subject—*John*—and a predicate—*works at the zoo*. But *John working at the zoo* is not a good sentence because it lacks a simple predicate, or verb. (Because the *-ing* word, *working*, is without its helping verb, a form of *be*, it cannot function as a predicate; in fact, no *-ing* word that stands alone can ever function as a predicate.) To make this sentence a complete grammatical sentence, we can add *is, was, will be*, or some other form of *be*, to *working*: for example, *John is working at the zoo*. A "good sentence," then, is one that is grammatically complete. In this chapter, we will discuss some features of sentence grammar that can help you, at the postdrafting stage, to write correct and effective sentences.

Of course, looking only at sentence grammar in your piece of writing is insufficient, unless you treat each sentence in isolation, apart from other sentences. In any piece of writing, when you revise sentences, you look at each sentence in the context of other sentences, so you need to consider not only grammar but also style. Therefore, another way to define a "good sentence" is in terms of its style, or the way a sentence fits cohesively with other sentences to carry the content, or the meaning, of a piece of writing. When you evaluate a sentence, you look at both its grammar and its style.

For example, all of the following sentences are well formed, but only the first one is stylistically effective as an opening sentence in the fifth paragraph of Nancy's essay (sample 5I):

Another memorable match that highlighted my youth was between a tag wrestler, Goliath, and the infamous forehead biter, Freddie Blassie.

My youth was highlighted by another memorable match between a tag wrestler, Goliath, and the infamous forehead biter, Freddie Blassie.

What highlighted my youth was another memorable match between a tag wrestler, Goliath, and the infamous biter, Freddie Blassie.

Goliath, a tag wrestler, and Freddie Blassie, the infamous forehead biter, were another memorable match that highlighted my youth.

A tag wrestler, Goliath, and the infamous forehead biter, Freddie Blassie, were another memorable match that highlighted my youth.

Each sentence begins with a different subject, and the effect is a slightly different sentence focus. Though each is grammatically complete, Nancy chose the first sentence because its subject carried the focus she needed in her paragraph.

When you evaluate your sentences for grammar and style at the postdrafting stage, you might have a sentence that is effective in style but ineffective in grammar. That is, one of your sentences may not be grammatically *complete*, but it may be stylistically effective. In such instances, sentence style may take precedence over sentence grammar.

In his description of the Berlin Wall (sample 2E), for example, Michael deviates from sentence grammar when he answers a question with a grammatically incomplete sentence:

Climb up the small platform overlooking the Wall. What is there to see? An obstacle course of death: barbed wire, deep sand, trenches, land mines, and dog tracks where the Germans run fierce German Shepherds trained to kill.

Michael might just as well have written "You see an obstacle course of death. . ." in place of the third sentence, but by eliminating the subject and simple predicate, he answers his question more directly and forcefully. We can say, then, that Michael deviates from sentence grammar for a particular stylistic effect.

Or consider another example, this one from Constance's autobiographical essay (sample 3C):

> Speaking of clumsiness and tripping? Yes, Chris at the young age of seventeen tripped. He fell into a car with a nut high on drugs and smashed by alcohol. The addict wrecked. Chris was thrown through a window instantly crushing his skull. For three days I prayed that he would not die.

The first sentence in this passage is not grammatically complete, yet it serves as an effective transition sentence. Constance needed a connection, a smooth transition, between one section of her essay, in which she describes her experiences with her brother Jeff, and the paragraph partially quoted previously about another brother Chris. The transition sentence, an incomplete statement followed by a question mark (which tells us to read it with rising intonation at the end), maintains her conversational style of writing in the essay and thus serves a stylistic purpose.

Michael and Constance both deviate from standard sentence grammar to produce a different kind of sentence, unlike most of the other sentences in their pieces of writing. Traditionally, these sentences have been called sentence fragments, or "nonsentences." In your experiences writing in school, you may recall some of your teachers advising you to avoid sentence fragments. Yet, you have probably read many such fragments, and you have probably wondered why professional writers can get away with writing them and you cannot.

One reason is that your teachers wanted to be sure that you got plenty of practice writing grammatical sentences—ones having a subject and a predicate. After all, most sentences are grammatically complete. Moreover, in academic writing, you are expected to express your ideas in complete sentences, with subjects and verbs. By cautioning you to avoid sentence fragments, your teachers were preparing you for writing in academic contexts.

However, you should not think of sentence fragments as wrong or incorrect. They are appropriate and effective in some instances, and inappropriate and ineffective in others. As we mentioned earlier, professional writers use sentence fragments when they want to achieve a particular style or effect in a piece of writing, especially in narrative and descriptive writing. In expository writing and in more formal contexts, however, sentence fragments are used sparingly, if at all.

So if you are writing a formal letter to your teacher to appeal a grade, you should check to be sure that your sentences conform to your reader's expectations. If you do use a sentence that lacks a subject or predicate, it should reflect a conscious choice on your part, and serve a particular purpose in your piece of writing.

Grice says that when we break one of the rules of conversation (relevance, quantity, quality, and manner), we must do so *knowingly*, with the expectation that our listener(s) will reason the meaning we intend. It must be a conscious decision on the part of the speaker. If a student goes to his or her teacher and asks, "Did I miss anything last class," and the teacher responds sarcastically, "Does the sun rise in the east?" the teacher has violated the maxim of relevance. But the teacher expects the student to reason the meaning behind that response. Similarly, in formal writing situations, when you write a sentence that lacks a subject or a predicate, you have to ask yourself if your readers will understand the purpose behind your choice. If you are simply not aware you are using incomplete sentences, your readers will probably judge your writing ineffective.

As you can see, we are operating now with two definitions of a good sentence, one grammatical and one stylistic. Moreover, as we have said, one can potentially cancel out the other: A "good sentence" in style need not be a "good sentence" in grammar. At this point, you can begin to see that a single definition of a "good sentence" may not be so easy to produce. In considering sentence style, we have, in effect, "muddied the waters."

In fact, a sentence is as difficult an entity to define as a paragraph. In the last chapter, you may recall, we said that a paragraph is not easy to define because its structure and style depend so much on the context of the whole piece of writing. We did not say that all paragraphs begin with a topic sentence, for example, because we know that some have their topic sentences in the middle or at the end, and that some may not state a topic sentence at all. These variations in paragraph form and style result from the writer's choices in presenting, developing, and organizing information for readers.

Like paragraphs, sentences also function in the context of other sentences, and to some extent, they too defy definition. They are not autonomous units of meaning, just as paragraphs are not autonomous units of discourse. So when judging the effectiveness of a sentence, you need to consider the content of other sentences that precede and follow it in a piece of writing, and the way they fit together to form a coherent whole.

It is certainly true that most sentences have subjects and predicates; they express complete thoughts. But some sentences may not have subjects and predicates. So when you revise sentences in your piece of writing, considering not just grammar but also style, you may find it more effective, in some writing situations, to use a sentence fragment. If you abandon the idea of thinking of these kinds of sentences as nonsentences or fragments, and instead think of them as sentences—just of a different type—you will see them as possible choices in some writing situations rather than structures to avoid in your writing.

In the end, it is perhaps best to think of sentences, not as complete grammatical units, but as anything in a piece of writing that begins with a capital letter and ends with a terminal mark—a period, question mark, or exclamation point. This definition is rather abstract, but it allows for sentences that may consist of a single word or phrase.

Of course, just because you write a sequence of sentences, each beginning with a capital letter and ending with a period, does not mean you have composed a sequence of "good sentences." A good sentence is one that expresses an idea clearly and coherently and is appropriate in the context of the writing situation.

As with the other features of written products (content, organization, paragraphs), sentences must be examined in relation to the writing situation. This chapter will show you when and how to revise your sentences for both grammar and style.

Predrafting: Capturing Sentences

As Figure 1 indicates, you need not be concerned with sentences at the predrafting stage. Naturally, if a particularly effective sentence occurs to you at this stage, write it down and save it. Or if a kind of informal "sentence outline" helps you plan the organization or logic of the piece of writing, by all means use it. But your concern at the predrafting stage should be for the "big picture," not the wording of individual sentences.

Some writers, however, like to tinker with key sentences while in the process of formulating their ideas for drafting. They may write a sentence, for example, that expresses the main idea of their piece of writing, and they may not begin drafting until it says what they want it to say, even though it may change again in the drafting stage.

So if your attention to writing effective sentences in the predrafting stage is a step toward clarifying some aspect of the writing situation, then it is purposeful, and you should continue doing what works best for you as a writer. However, if you are overly concerned about the correctness of your sentences for no other reason than to get them right, then this concern is premature and potentially inhibiting for you as a writer. Your aim should be to see the whole piece of writing—the larger picture—at the predrafting stage. Otherwise, your attention to detail will interfere with your ability to translate your thoughts into words on the page.

Drafting: Writing Sentences

At the drafting stage, you of course write sentences. But you don't need to worry, at this stage, whether they are grammatically or stylistically effective. Your main concern, even at the drafting stage, should be with the piece of writing as a whole—with making sure that it addresses the situation, that its content is accurate and adequate, and that it is effectively organized. You can be concerned with the wording of individual sentences later.

Some writers like to draft their piece of writing in sections. That is, they draft until they finish a section, and then they review their draft, editing and refining sentences in the process. This particular strategy is purposeful when it allows the writer to clarify his or her thinking, and perhaps even to discover new ideas in the process of drafting a piece of writing. Again, be attentive to your own process of writing. By knowing where you succeed and where you fail in the writing process, you can adjust your process by experimenting with new strategies. By analyzing your process in this way, you will eventually write more efficiently and productively. In short, you will improve your writing performance.

Whether you draft the whole piece of writing or just sections of it, you need to write as quickly as you can to keep your ideas flowing. You don't want to continually interrupt the drafting process to repair faulty sentences, because then you risk losing your thought process. Your ideas will not flow smoothly. Some writers who have felt constrained by the physical act of writing or typing, have experimented with talking their draft, or parts of it, into a tape recorder and then transcribing from the tape. Though this technique may not suit you, you should make an effort to get your ideas on paper as quickly as your thoughts come to you. Any problems with sentence construction can be corrected later in the process.

Postdrafting: Revising Sentences

Only at the postdrafting stage do you need to become really concerned about sentence construction. At this stage, the piece of writing has been written completely through once, so you can now look closely at individual sentences in their larger context. Sentence revision is one aspect of Grice's maxim of manner, the "manner of expression" in a piece of writing. Specifically, when you revise the "manner of expression" in your sentences, you begin to look at two features of sentences: their parts and the order in which those parts are arranged.

SENTENCE PARTS

Though sentences may sometimes be single words and phrases, as we discussed earlier, most sentences in English have two main parts: a subject (which, in the case of some commands, may be unstated) and a predicate. The subject—a noun or pronoun, and its modifiers—tells who or what the sentence is about. The predicate—a verb and its modifiers, complements, and objects—states an assertion, question, or command about the subject. Look, for example, at the first sentence of Amy's instructions on applying for state FHA office (sample 1A):

> Applying for a state office in the Future Homemakers of America is a challenging and rewarding task.

The subject, *Applying for a state office in the Future Homemakers of America,* identifies what the sentence is about. The predicate, *is a challenging and rewarding task,* makes an assertion about the subject.

The following sentence from Michael's process description (sample 1B) has an unstated subject:

> Look past the Wall and barbed wire.

In this sentence, the subject (an implied "you") is unstated because the writer is issuing a command, a type of sentence construction that is common in instructions.

Sometimes it is necessary to distinguish further between subjects and predicates by identifying the simple subjects and simple predicates. A simple subject is the "headword(s)," or noun, without its modifiers, and a simple predicate is the verb(s) without its modifiers, objects, or complements. So in Amy's sentence

> Applying for a state office in the Future Homemakers of America is a challenging and rewarding task.

the simple subject is *Applying,* and the simple predicate, or verb, is *is.* Understanding this distinction will be important when you read about number agreement later in this chapter.

Up to now, we have considered only simple sentences, having one subject and one predicate. Sometimes sentences are combined, and there is more than one subject and predicate in the sentence. For example, in her autobiographical essay (sample 3A), Kathy combines two sentences:

> The hours are unpredictable and long, and the work is often stressful.

Both sentences could be written separately, but here they are combined with the conjunction *and.* The simple subject in the first sentence is *hours,* and the simple predicate, or verb, is *are;* the simple subject in the second sentence is *work,* and the simple predicate, or verb, is *is.* When two sentences are combined in this way to make one, we call it a compound sentence.

Another important distinction to make in a discussion of subjects and predicates is between main clauses and dependent clauses. Both types of clauses have subjects and predicates, but only a main clause, sometimes called an independent clause, can stand alone as a complete sentence; for example, the preceding sample sentence by Kathy consists of two main clauses, each one capable of standing alone. But some clauses cannot stand alone and therefore need to be attached to main clauses. These clauses, called subordinate or dependent clauses, are usually preceded by a subordinate conjunction (e.g., *when, if, though, before, because, after*, etc.). In the following sentence from the same essay, Kathy combines a dependent clause with a main clause:

> When we married four years later, we began working towards our goal of owning our own business.

Each clause has a subject and predicate, but only the main clause can stand alone as a complete sentence: *we began working towards our goal of owning our own business*. The dependent clause, *When we married four years later*, must be attached to the main clauses because, by itself, it is incomplete. The simple subject in the dependent clause is *we*, as it is in the main clause, and the simple predicate in the dependent clause is *married*; in the main clause, it is *began*. When a dependent clause is combined with a main clause, we call this a complex sentence.

As we alluded to in the introductory section of this chapter, writers have both conventions to follow and choices to make about sentences. The major conventions of sentences are called "grammar"; the choices in sentences are called "style."

Sentence Conventions: Grammar. Our language is so natural to us that we often forget how tremendously complex a system of rules we have mastered as native speakers. We spend the largest part of our lives using language in some form, whether it be speaking, listening, writing, or reading. Everyday we speak and write and hear sentences for the first time, yet we have no difficulty understanding their meanings. We possess this ability to use language for our communicative purposes because we have internalized the code called *grammar*.

The word *grammar* is used in several different ways. One way it is used is to refer to the *structure* of a language, known intuitively by everyone who speaks and writes it. This "internal grammar" is extraordinarily complex, yet we all know almost all of it by the time we start school.

We may not know that we know it, however. For example, unless you are a professional linguist, you probably cannot state the rule for the order of adjectives of size and color in English. Yet, if you are a native English speaker, you will intuitively order these words in only one way:

> sign   red   a   large

That is, you will order them in exactly the same way John did in the second paragraph of his description of the Berlin Wall (sample 3B): "a large red sign." The rule for ordering adjectives of size and color, like thousands of other grammar rules, is part of your "internal grammar" even if you do not know it consciously.

Another way the word *grammar* is used is to refer to a *description* of the internal grammar. "Descriptive grammars" are systematic efforts to describe the structure of a language. Unraveling the complexities of our language is the task of linguists, the scientists of language. Some of their descriptive grammars of English run to hundreds of pages, and include rules that govern the order of the words in the preceding example, but no descriptive grammar is complete. The internal grammar of a language has never been described completely.

A third way the word *grammar* is used is to refer to the *etiquette* of language. Someone may say, for example, that the word *ain't* is "bad grammar." Well, use of the word *ain't* has been part of the internal grammar of English, for most speakers, since the eighteenth century, and therefore it is also part of most descriptive grammars. But using *ain't* is considered inappropriate in more formal speaking and writing situations. So the rule against it is part of an "etiquette grammar" of English.

Such "etiquette" rules are established by our society, and if we do not know them, in some situations we may be considered uneducated—a judgment society makes, based on the way we speak or write. In a job interview, for example, we are expected to use appropriate language, just as we are expected to follow the established dress code. In a sense, then, we have "manners" that govern our language use, and we need to know when our "manners" of speech or writing are expected of us.

A fourth use of the word *grammar* is to refer to the particular kind of descriptive grammar that is often taught in schools: "A noun is the name of a person, place, or thing," or "the subject and simple predicate must agree in number." This "school grammar" is a very small subset of a descriptive grammar, covering only a very small proportion of the rules in everyone's internal grammar.

Decades of research show clearly that knowledge of school grammar has no effect on writing ability. They are simply two different skills. People who write effectively and grammatically learned their internal grammar from listening and reading, not from consciously learning school grammar rules. However, research does suggest that a few school grammar rules may be helpful at the postdrafting stage of the writing process, just to alert the writer to some common errors that can be corrected. Two of the most important "grammar" rules worth learning for this purpose are the rules for agreement and parallelism.

1. *Agreement.* In edited written English, subjects and predicates must agree in number. That is, if the subject is singular, the predicate must be singular, and if the subject is plural, the predicate must be plural. In a letter to his state senator (sample 5D), Todd writes

The manufacturers are repeatedly blamed.

The simple subject *manufacturers* is plural, and so is the simple predicate *are blamed*.

When you check the agreement of the subject and predicate, make sure you are not distracted by other words in the sentence. For example, in Mike's instructions on buying a CD player (sample 1C), he writes

> The next thing you should look at are the options you want your unit to have.

The simple predicate *are* should agree with the simple subject *thing*, not the predicate noun, *options*. Therefore, the sentence should be revised to read

> The next thing you should look at is the options you want your unit to have.

If that revision sounds awkward to you, you could revise the subject:

> Next you should look at the options you want your unit to have.

This revision not only eliminates the grammar problem but also results in a more economical and effective sentence.

When you check your sentences for agreement errors, one feature of predicates that may confuse you is the *-s* inflection, or ending, in the third-person singular form of regular verbs. The *-s* added to a noun makes it plural (e.g., *student, students*), but the *-s* inflection on a verb makes it singular, not plural (e.g., That student [singular noun] *reads* well). Because all nouns are either third-person singular or third-person plural, the choice of verb will be either third-person singular or third-person plural. Notice, the *-s* inflection in the third-person singular forms of the verbs in the following conjugation:

	SINGULAR		PLURAL	
FIRST PERSON:	I	vote	We	vote
SECOND PERSON:	You	vote	You	vote
THIRD PERSON:	He	*votes*	They	*vote*
	The man	*votes*	The men	*vote*
	The member	*votes*	The members	*vote*

The only difference in the verb forms is the *-s* added in the third-person singular form. Now consider these sentences from Lucia's letter to the housing office at her university (sample 5B):

The primary reason for these restricted visitation hours seems to be privacy. The people in charge of setting up these hours seem to think that 11:15 P.M. on week nights and Sundays and 2:00 A.M. on Fridays and Saturdays affords a reasonable amount of privacy.

The simple subject in the first sentence is *reason*, a singular noun. Notice that the simple predicate, *seems*, has the -s inflection, indicating that it is also singular. In the second sentence, the simple subject is *people*, a plural noun, and the simple predicate, *seem*, without the -s, is also plural. But look at the subject of the noun clause at the end of the second sentence. The noun clause has a compound subject, *11:15 P.M. . . . and 2:00 A.M.* Because compound subjects are plural (unless they are to be understood as one unit, like *bread and butter*), the simple predicate, or verb, must also be plural to agree in number with the subject. Notice, however, that the verb *affords* has the -s inflection, indicating it is singular. For this verb to agree in number with the compound subject, *affords* would need to be changed to the third-person plural form *afford*.

Be particularly careful about indefinite pronouns used as subjects. In a draft of her autobiographical essay (sample 3C), Constance wrote

Each in his own way have had an awesome impact upon me.
Each have exposed me to various facets of life.

At the postdrafting stage, she realized that the pronoun *each* is singular: it refers to just one of her brothers at a time. She therefore revised the simple predicates to agree with this singular subject.

Each in his own way has had an awesome impact upon me.
Each has exposed me to various facets of life.

The same rule applies to pronouns and the nouns they stand for—their *antecedents*. For example, in her letter to the housing office of her university (sample 4B), Lucia writes

A University of Kentucky residence hall dweller signs a form of lease before they are granted University housing.

The pronoun *they* is plural, of course, but its antecedent, *dweller*, is singular. This error in agreement could be revised as follows:

A University of Kentucky residence hall dweller signs a form of lease before he or she is granted University housing.

or

University of Kentucky residence hall dwellers sign a form of lease before they are granted University housing.

In the first corrected version, the noun *dweller* is kept singular, and the singular pronouns *he* and *she* are used in place of the plural pronoun *they*. Because there is no singular pronoun in the English language we can use when the antecedent can be either male or female, it is necessary to use both male and female pronouns in such cases. If the repetition of *he or she* in successive sentences sounds awkward, an alternative is to make the antecedent plural so that the plural pronoun *they* can be used, as in the second corrected version.

Before the women's movement, it was acceptable to use the generic singular pronouns *he, his,* and *him* when the antecedent could be either masculine or feminine singular. However, women in America, and some men as well, made us conscious of the power of language to influence attitudes about gender and to perpetuate stereotypes. Consequently, it is no longer acceptable, even in formal writing, to use only the masculine pronouns in such situations: it is sexist language.

When you revise sentences with singular pronouns and antecedents that are not gender-specific, you can avoid sexist language in your writing by

1. Using the singular pronouns in pairs, like *he or she, his or hers, him or her*.
2. Making the antecedent plural and using the plural pronoun *they*.
3. Alternating between *he* and *she* (as well as *his* and *hers, his* and *her*) throughout a piece of writing.
4. Recasting the sentence to eliminate the singular pronouns altogether.

Another common agreement error occurs with the pronoun *this* and its plural form *these*. When you revise, you should check the pronouns in your sentences to be sure they refer to single words and not to general ideas. In her response to an editorial urging the legalization of liquor sales in her county (sample 5G), Susan writes

With no present competition, bars, clubs, and liquor stores will be popping up on every street corner. This will cause an increase in traffic, as well as an increase in alcohol-related accidents.

Susan may have used the singular pronoun *this* in the second sentence to refer to *bars, clubs, and liquor stores* in the first sentence. Because the pronoun refers to a compound subject, a plural antecedent, the pronoun would need to be plural to agree in number. So the correct pronoun in the second sentence would be *these*.

With no present competition, bars, clubs, and liquor stores will be popping up on every street corner. These will cause an increase in traffic, as well as an increase in alcohol-related accidents.

But Susan probably used the singular pronoun to refer to the general idea of *bars, clubs, and liquor stores . . . popping up on every street corner.* In informal writing, the use of *this* to refer to a general idea is usually not a matter for concern, but in formal writing, the pronoun should refer to a single word rather than to a general idea. One way to revise this general reference is to add a general word after the pronoun, as follows:

With no present competition, bars, clubs, and liquor stores will be popping up on every street corner. This new development will cause an increase in traffic, as well as an increase in alcohol-related accidents.

Particularly tricky are *collective* nouns, nouns that refer to groups of people. Notice, for example, this sentence from Amy's instructions for applying for FHA state office (sample 1A):

After you have completed the necessary steps in the process of becoming a state officer, the candidate committee makes their evaluations and decides who will compose the next slate of officers.

The simple subject, *committee,* in the main clause is a collective noun, and it can be singular or plural, depending on the emphasis you want to give it. You must, however, be consistent. Amy regards it as singular in choosing her verbs, *makes* and *decides,* but she regards it as plural in choosing the pronoun *their* before the noun *evaluations.* She could correct this problem by making the words that have to agree with *committee* either consistently singular or consistently plural:

. . . the candidate committee makes its evaluations . . .

or

. . . the candidate committee make their evaluations . . .

2. *Parallelism.* In edited written English, words, phrases, or clauses joined by coordinate conjunctions (*and, but, for, nor, or, so,* and *yet*) must be *parallel;* that is, they must have the same grammatical structure. For example, consider another sentence from Amy's instructions (sample 1A):

. . . it must include what materials will be covered, who the guest speakers will be, and the type of recreation for each meeting.

This sentence has three items in a series, joined by the coordinate conjunction *and*. The first two items are expressed as clauses beginning with the relative pronouns *what* and *who*; the third item, however, is a simple phrase, headed by the noun *type*. The series could be made parallel by making all three items clauses

> . . . it must include what materials will be covered, who the guest speakers will be, and what kind of recreation will be available

or by making all three items noun phrases

> . . . it must include descriptions of materials, guest speakers, and recreational activities.

In the following sentence from her essay about Hoosier basketball hysteria (sample 5I), Nancy joins two parallel verb phrases with the conjunction *and*:

> In an unexpected move, Goliath grabbed Freddie Blassie and bit his forehead.

In another sentence from the same paper, Nancy uses a series of parallel prepositional phrases:

> The match was finally called off by the skinny referee who hadn't seen Tanaka throw the salt up in the air, into Morales' face, onto the ring, and even into the faces of a few spectators in the front row.

Similarly, items following pairs of *correlative* conjunctions like *either-or*, *neither-nor*, and *not only-but also* need to have the same structure. An early draft of Mandy's letter to the house council of her dormitory (sample 5A), included this sentence:

> A person either chooses to quit studying or to head to the noisy commons.

The correlative conjunction *either* is followed by the simple predicate *chooses* and the infinitive phrase *to quit studying*; the other correlative conjunction in the pair is followed only by the infinitive phrase *to head to the noisy commons*. So the two items are not parallel. The sentence could be revised either by adding a simple predicate in the second item or by moving the first conjunction to the position after *chooses*.

A person either chooses to quit studying or decides to head to the noisy commons.

or

A person chooses either to quit studying or to head to the noisy commons.

At the postdrafting stage, Mandy actually decided to use two parallel infinitive phrases:

A person has two choices, either to quit studying or head to the noisy commons.

Errors in agreement and parallelism are easy to make at the drafting stage, so many writers look for these errors when they edit their sentences at the postdrafting stage. These, however, are not the only errors possible at the sentence level. As we said earlier, reading a grammar handbook from cover to cover is probably not going to make you a better writer, but you can improve your own editing skills and the quality of your writing by being systematic in the way you deal with sentence errors in your own writing. Throughout this book, we have emphasized the importance of self-assessment—of becoming aware of your own process of writing. Part of that process is becoming your own editor.

As a beginning college writer, you can improve your editing skills by noting the common errors that appear in your writing and by keeping a record of them in your journal. Then you can begin gathering information about these particular errors by talking with your teacher and referring to a grammar handbook. As you learn about the nature of these errors, you can use a part of your journal to write your own grammar book on common errors in your writing. If, for example, you have difficulty with verb forms, such as distinguishing between *choose* and *chose*, use your journal to record information about verb forms including examples that illustrate the error.

Your peer editors and your instructor will help you identify sentence errors in your writing, but at some point you will have to take control of your own editing process. By knowing what specific errors to look for when you revise at the postdrafting stage, you stand a better chance of improving the quality of the final product.

Exercises

A. Revise the following sentences from students' drafts, correcting any errors in agreement or parallelism. (Some have already been corrected or eliminated in final copies of the sample papers; some have not.)

1.   Most of the questions are essay and deal with your experience as an FHA officer and why you feel you are qualified for the position. (sample 1A)

2.   He or she will then give you referral slips, which tell you who the employer is, their address, phone number, and how to apply for the job. (sample 1B)

3.   If a person wishes to truly feel the different culture of Rome, they should interact with the people. (sample 2A)

4.   Unlike most Hoosiers who were weaned on many hours of televised high school basketball games, I grew up in the Northeast, in a home where professional and midget wrestling were watched. (sample 5I)

5.   The purpose of this program would not be to scare the rider, but rather making sure one thinks before doing something foolish on an ATV. (sample 5D)

6.   Each beam still carries the axe marks where someone had shaped them by hand. (sample 2D)

7.   While the hours may be the same in all dormitories, the enforcement of these hours do not correspond with the Tower's and the hours are not fair or just. (sample 5A)

8.   A college student, in most cases, is a mature adult. Therefore they should be able to have guests in their room when they please. . . . (sample 5B)

9.   Anyone wishing to vandalize the park would find a way whether they park a car to do so or not. (sample 5C)

10.   Anytime Congress raises taxes, they always manage to increase spending. (sample 5A)

11.   As I sat in the surgery waiting room in my back-less hospital gown, I began to feel the Valium that they administered to me take effect. (sample 4A)

12.   I believe anyone who has the mindset of some of the people who are now serving time on death row deserve to be executed. (sample 4D)

B. Review the comments and corrections you received on your earlier essays. In your journal, keep a record of the common sentence errors that occur in your writing. Write the sentence containing the error, your revised version of the sentence, and a brief explanation of the error. Review this material in your journal before you revise your next essay.

Sentence Choices: Style. Even with the thousands of rules about sentences in your internal grammar, there are still many choices you can make about sentences. A good sentence, you may recall, is not merely a grammatical sentence; it is one that effectively carries the meaning in a piece of writing as a result of the writer's effective choices. How you make these choices determines the "style" of your sentences. With style, you cannot be right or wrong; you have freedom to create a style of your own. But within that style of your own, you can be effective or ineffective. As you develop your power as a writer, you will learn to style your sentences—to make effective choices—in order to communicate your meaning clearly and coherently.

Here are three sets of tools you can use to write more effective sentences, sentences that take into account the way readers' minds work.

1. *Subjects.* As discussed earlier, the subject of a sentence tells who or what the sentence is about. It therefore serves as the most important link between the writer and the reader, establishing a shared item about which the rest of the sentence will make an assertion, ask a question, or give a command.

Therefore, make sure, when possible, that the grammatical subject of each sentence is also the "real" subject. For example, in his autobiographical essay (sample 3D), John writes

One reason I feel that I have done well in school is his advice.

Here the grammatical subject is *reason*, but if you look at the sentence in context, you will see that *reason* does not express the "real" subject of the sentence.

. . . Although I saw my father a couple of weekends a month and in the summers, I never quite got over the divorce. My father always stressed to me the importance of getting an education. One reason I feel that I have done well in school is his advice. Somehow I thought that doing well in school would bring him closer to me when we couldn't be together.

The sentence in question is not about reasons; it is about John and his father's advice. So why not make one of those the grammatical subject? Possible revisions, in each case, would be

I feel I have done well in school because of his advice.

or

His advice is one reason I have done well in school.

Sometimes the "real" subject may be hidden in a passive sentence construction, where the subject is not the "doer" of the action but the "receiver." For example, in Mandy's response to an editorial supporting a state lottery, she writes

> Much of Kentucky's money is spent on out-of-state lotteries. Why should we support Ohio or Indiana schools when we could support our own?

The subject in the first sentence is *Much of Kentucky's money*, but the "real" subject—the one that identifies who's spending the money—is not expressed in the sentence. The second sentence, however, does include the "real" subject. A possible revision of the first sentence would be

> Kentuckians spend a good deal of money on out-of-state lotteries. Why should we support Ohio or Indiana schools when we could support our own?

Although passive constructions do often hide the "real" subjects of sentences, they are sometimes necessary to maintain focus on the "real" subject. In her essay on Hoosier hysteria (sample 5I), for example, Nancy uses a passive construction to keep the "real" subject in subject position. Notice the passive verb in the third sentence.

> There was the time Professor Toro Tanaka threw salt in Pedro Morales' face. Morales writhed on the canvas for what seemed an eternity. The match was finally called off by the skinny referee who hadn't seen Tanaka throw the salt up in the air, into Morales' face, onto the ring.

In passive constructions, the "doer" of the action is often expressed after the verb, though it may sometimes only be implied. In Nancy's sentence, the "doer" of the action (i.e., the one calling off the match) is stated explicitly after the verb.

2. *Predicates.* Even commoner than hidden subjects are hidden verbs. Our language has a tendency—no, our language *tends*—to "nominalize": to make verbs into nouns, like making the verb *tend* into the noun *tendency*. Once you have made such a change you no longer have a verb to build your predicate around, so you have to insert an "empty," "filler" verb like *has* or *gives* or *makes*. In her autobiographical essay (sample 3A), Kathy writes

> When my youngest daughter was two and her health had stabilized, my husband and I made the decision to sell our grocery.

This is certainly not a bad sentence, but its verb, *made*, carries little meaning. The "real" verb in the sentence is *decide*, nominalized into *decision*. A better sentence might be

> When my youngest daughter was two and her health had stabilized, my husband and I decided to sell our grocery.

Here the verb, *decide*, carries real meaning in the sentence, and the sentence is probably more effective as a result.

In the final sentence of her letter to the housing office of her university (sample 5B), Lucia hides her "real" verb in the noun *consideration*.

> Please take my views into consideration when deliberating this issue.

The verb *take* does not add much meaning to the sentence. Lucia could have written a neater, more economical sentence if she had chosen *consider* as the verb, as in the following revision:

> Please consider my views when deliberating this issue.

So at the postdrafting stage, be alert for hidden verbs and move them "up" to main verb status.

Sometimes, hidden subjects and hidden verbs occur together, particularly in sentences beginning with *It* and *There*. For example, consider this sentence from Nancy's essay (sample 5I):

> It wasn't that I entirely hated gym; it was just that the thought of undressing in front of my better endowed teenage peers horrified me.

The subject in both clauses is *It*, and the verb is *was*. The "real" subject in the first clause is probably *I*, and the "real" verb is probably *hated*; in the second clause, the "real" subject is probably *thought*, and the "real" verb is probably *horrified*. A possible revision would make those words the grammatical subject and verb in each clause:

> I didn't entirely hate gym, but the thought of undressing in front of my better endowed teenage peers horrified me.

In her essay about the city of Ceralvo (sample 2C), Amy writes

> It was at this time that several businesses, such as the dry goods store, moved to the growing city of Owensboro.

The subject of this sentence is *It*, and the verb is *was*; neither carries any real meaning. The "real" subject is probably *businesses*, hidden later in the sentence, and the "real" verb is probably *moved*, also hidden. A possible revision would make those words that carry the meaning the grammatical subject and verb of the sentence.

> At this time several businesses moved to the growing city of Owensboro.

On the one hand, this is a more economical sentence; on the other hand, it changes the emphasis in Amy's actual sentence. When you revise for hidden subjects and verbs, you need to consider the effects of your revision. The *It*, for example, in Amy's sentence functions to give greater emphasis to *at this time*. In the revision, *At this time* is at the beginning of the sentence, but it doesn't receive as much emphasis as it does when it follows *It was*. In this instance, then, we would say that the *It was* at the beginning of the sentence serves a specific purpose.

Of course, in some sentences beginning with *It*, the pronoun *it* has an antecedent in another sentence and so serves as an effective "focus word." In such sentences, the subject is not hidden. For example, in the first paragraph of Amy's instructions (sample 1A), the second and third sentences have the subject *it*, referring to *applying for a state office* in the first sentence.

> Applying for a state office in the Future Homemakers of America is a challenging and rewarding task. It is challenging because you must meet strict requirements and will be up against the toughest competition in the state. It is rewarding because win or lose, you will gain new confidence in yourself as one of FHA's finest members.

Similarly, the pronoun *it* in the following passage from Todd's letter refers to the subject *policy* in the preceding sentence:

> This policy was a dream come true for those who were considering getting out of the dairy business. However, it has done little, if any, to curb milk production.

In another one of her essays, the instructions for applying for an FHA office (sample 1A), Amy writes

> There may also be questions about new ideas you have for FHA activities.

Traditional school grammar usually does not classify *there* as a subject, although some modern descriptive grammars do. Either way, the combination

"There may also be" carries little real meaning. The real subject, *questions*, is hidden later in the sentence, and the real verb, perhaps something like *concern*, is not expressed at all. The sentence might be revised to read

Also, some questions may concern your new ideas for FHA activities.

Not all sentences that begin with *there* or *it* are necessarily wordy or out of focus. In some sentences, *there* may fill the place of the subject for a particular purpose. Because *there* is an empty filler, the "real" subject comes later in the sentence, in the predicate. If the "real" subject has not been discussed previously in a piece of writing, the writer may need *there* in subject position so that the "real" subject can be introduced in the predicate of the sentence, as new information. For example, consider this sentence from Christina's instructions (sample 1B):

There is a bulletin board in the hallway outside the office that lists hundreds of full and part-time positions of every job from general office workers to cashiers.

This is the opening sentence of a new paragraph in Christina's essay. It begins with *There* because Christina has not yet discussed *the bulletin board in the hallway,* and she doesn't want to begin her sentence with information that is new to the reader. So she moves the subject into the predicate and begins the sentence with *There*. However, since she does mention *the office* in previous sentences, she might also have begun her sentence with that information, already known to the reader. Consider this revision:

Outside the office in the hallway is a bulletin board that lists hundreds of full- and part-time positions of every job from general office workers to cashiers.

Later in this chapter, in our discussion of sentence order, we will have more to say about old and new information as a strategy for ordering information effectively for your readers.

Exercises

A. Revise the following sentences to eliminate hidden subjects and hidden verbs:

1.   . . . however, even if you are not elected, the experience will still be very beneficial to you. (sample 1A)

2.   There is a bulletin board in the hallway outside of the office

that lists hundreds of full and part-time positions of every job from general office workers to cashiers. (sample 1B)

3.   There are two reasons this model is the most popular. (sample 1C)

4.   Warmed up a bit, I took a walk along the main aisle, dodging busy adults who took no notice of me. (sample 2B)

5.   It is my deepest desire that I will be able to turn my negative situations into a finding that will help mankind. (sample 3B)

6.   There have been many nights when I have stayed up with Chris through feigned threats of suicide. (sample 2C)

7.   That money could have been put to more efficient use by the U.S. government. (sample 5E)

8.   However, there are such establishments in other dry counties that run successful businesses. (sample 5G)

9.   I suggest that the next time you consider such a controversial issue, you take a look at the entire picture, rather than see only what you want to see. (sample 5G)

10.   In fact, with all the trees and nearby subdivisions, it would be safer to walk than risk the police recognizing the car or getting the license number. (sample 5C)

B. Read the excerpt from Mortimer J. Adler and Charles Van Doren's *How to Read a Book* reprinted in Chapter Two, and pay special attention to the sentences that begin with *there*. Choose a few examples, and then try to determine why Adler and Van Doren used an empty filler to begin the sentences. Be prepared to discuss your reasons.

C. Choose a paper you wrote for an earlier assignment, or a draft you are currently revising, and see if you can find sentences with hidden subjects and hidden verbs. Revise these sentences.

3. *Modifiers.* A sentence needs a minimum of two words to be grammatically complete: It needs a subject and a verb, or simple predicate. *John fell,* for example, is a complete sentence. Some sentences, however, have verbs that require objects or complements for the sentence to be complete. *John is,* for example, is incomplete unless you add a complement, either an adjective that describes *John,* a noun that renames *John,* or an adverb phrase that

identifies his location. Thus, you could write *John is handsome* (adjective), or *John is my brother* (noun), or *John is at the library* (adverb phrase). Similarly, a subject and verb like *The boy teased* is incomplete without an object to follow the verb: *The boy teased his sister.* Once a sentence has these basic parts that make it complete, anything else added to the sentence is a modifier.

Modifiers are words, phrases, or clauses that define or qualify other words, phrases, or clauses in a sentence. They can function either as adjectives, which modify nouns and pronouns, or as adverbs, which modify verbs, adjectives, or other adverbs. Modifiers are important parts of sentences because they add specific meaning that cannot be expressed only in simple subjects and simple predicates. Like an artist who uses paint to add color, dimension, and texture to a painting, a writer uses modifiers to add color, definition, and accuracy to sentences in a piece of writing. Knowing when and how to use modifiers to carry meaning in your sentences is part of developing your power as a writer.

In the following sentence from Michael's description of the Berlin wall (sample 2E), notice the specific meaning expressed in the modifiers (which are italicized):

> *Old* cars and *new military* vehicles *loaded with soldiers carrying AK47s* zip *through the crowded streets.*

All the nouns—except *AK47s*—are limited or described with an adjective modifier, either a single word (*old, crowded*) or a phrase (*loaded with soldiers, carrying AK47s*). The same sentence without its modifiers reads

> Cars and vehicles zip.

Cars and vehicles are the subjects, and *zip* is the verb.

In the following sentence from Lisa's description of the Indianapolis Produce Terminal, two adverb modifiers, one a single word (*knowingly*) and the other a clause (*as he opened the lid . . .*), both modify the verb *watched*:

> I watched knowingly as he opened the lid, stuck his face down on the grapefruit and sniffed.

Adverb modifiers answer the questions *When? Where? Why?* and *How?* In the preceding sample sentence, the single adverb *knowingly* answers the question *How?* and the adverb clause *as he opened the lid . . .* answers the question *When?*

As you can see, you can pack information into your sentences with adjective and adverb modifiers, adding substantially to the length and density of your sentences. But, although modifiers can give freshness and vitality to your sentences, they can also be used excessively and ineffectively. If all of your sentences are loaded with information, for example, your readers may have difficulty focusing on the important details in your sentence. When writers sprinkle modifiers throughout their sentences without a clear purpose for doing so, most readers will think they are overwriting, using words that aren't really needed in the sentence.

At the postdrafting stage, then, you should check your sentences to see that you have used modifiers selectively so that your readers can focus on the important information. You should also check that the modifying information is secondary in importance to the information expressed in the subject and predicate of the main clause.

For example, the most important information in Michael's sentence, cited earlier, is the image of cars and vehicles zipping through the streets. Less important information is expressed in single-word modifiers (e.g., *old cars*) and in phrases (e.g., vehicles *loaded with soldiers*). If Michael wanted to emphasize the soldiers carrying AK47s, he probably would have placed that information in the main clause:

Soldiers carrying AK47s zipped in old cars and new military vehicles.

In the second paragraph of her essay about Hoosier basketball hysteria (sample 5I), Nancy uses an adjective clause to describe the subject, *grandmother*, in the main clause:

Even my grandmother, who watched a *real* sport, baseball, didn't train me to be a proper sports fan.

Nancy wanted to emphasize the fact that her grandmother didn't train her properly, so she expresses this idea in the main clause, leaving the less important information for a modifying clause, *who watched a real sport, baseball.*

In another sentence from the same essay, Nancy uses a modifying adjective phrase instead of a clause:

My grandmother, a petite woman under five feet, loved the game.

The most important information is in the main clause, *My grandmother loved the game.* The less important information, placed next to the word it describes, is in the embedded adjective phrase.

In the next section, on sentence order, we will show you how some of these modifiers can be moved to different positions in a sentence. By shifting the position of your modifiers, you can help the reader to follow more easily the content of your piece of writing.

Exercises

A. In each of the following sentences, underline the basic parts of the information in the main clause, and bracket the information placed in modifiers. Then revise each sentence to change its emphasis.

1. Warming my backside, I shut my eyes and breathing deeply tried to distinguish all the heavy aromas which pervaded the area. (sample 2B)

2. The Berlin Wall was built about three decades ago, separating East and West Berlin. (sample 2E)

3. As you walk through the archway into the entrance hall of this incredible structure, you immediately feel as if you have entered another age. (sample 2A)

4. When I look into the eyes of my eight-year-old son, I see the most beautiful miracle that I was blessed with. (sample 4A)

5. Any sane person who would deliberately rape and kill a small child should not be allowed the opportunity to commit the same crime with someone else. (sample 4D)

B. Choose a paper you wrote for an earlier assignment, or a draft you are currently revising, and check to see if the information you have placed in modifiers is less important than the information you have stated in the basic parts of the main clause.

SENTENCE ORDER

The other feature of sentences to consider besides their individual parts is the order in which those parts occur. To order the parts effectively, you need to place important information at the most emphatic places in your sentence, either at the beginning or at the end of your sentence, leaving the middle for less important details. You also need to consider the order that is easiest for your readers to follow. In most cases, readers like to start with information with which they are already familiar. So you need to begin sentences with pieces of information you assume your readers already know, and end with information that is new to them. These kinds of choices you make in ordering information in a sentence determine the effectiveness and style of your piece of writing.

To revise sentences more effectively, you should first know something about "normal" sentence orders and deviations from those normal orders.

Normal Order in Sentence Types. Normal order depends on the type of sentence you are writing. In English, sentences are classified into four types: statements, commands, questions, and exclamations. Each of these sentence types has its own "normal" order.

Statements make up most of the sentences in English; they begin with the subject and end with the predicate:

> These hours sabotage the independence of the residents and remove their freedom of choice. (sample 5A)

Commands are sentences that usually omit the subject entirely; they begin and end with the predicate:

> Look past the Wall and barbed wire. Look toward the blurred bleakness of the East. (sample 2E)

Questions may be expressed as yes-no questions or information questions. Yes-no questions, which elicit a yes-no answer, begin with an operator, or helping verb, followed by the subject:

> Is it fair that coed dorms and Haggin Hall have endless visiting hours while Blanding Tower has an interrogation unit sitting at the front desk?

Information questions, which elicit substantive responses, also move the operator, or helping verb, before the subject, but unlike yes-no questions, they begin with an interrogative word, such as *who, what, where, when,* and *why*:

> Why are residents of Blanding treated differently than the rest of campus? (sample 5A)

Finally, exclamations are sentences that frequently begin with *what* or *how,* with the subject and operator in normal position:

> What a terrific idea for a paper!
> How rude he can be!

Of these four types of sentences, statements are the most common in English. The other sentence types—commands, questions, and exclamations—occur in special circumstances. Commands, for example, are commonly used in instructions, when you are explaining how to do something; questions are sometimes used to introduce a new topic in a piece of writing, and sometimes merely to achieve a rhetorical or stylistic effect; and exclamations, which occur perhaps least often in academic writing, show the writer's enthusiasm for something.

Given that most sentences in a piece of writing are statements, one way to change the order of your sentences is to use another type of sentence besides statements. In the final paragraph of Nancy's position paper (sample 5I), for example, most of her sentences are statements, beginning with a subject and ending with a predicate. But she intersperses a command and a question, in sentences five and six, so that not all of her sentences begin the same way.

> As you can see, I didn't have a prayer at becoming a basketball fan. I was a victim of my environment. I only ask that Hoosiers be tolerant of me. I promise that as long as I live in Indiana, I'll pretend to like basketball. Give me some time and I'll weave "hook shot, guard, free throws, and rebounds" into my daily conversations. Who knows? Maybe someday I'll recite the high school regional scores like a native, or at least come close.

Of course, you don't want to overuse commands, questions, and exclamations in your writing. Instead, you should consider other ways of changing the order of your statements so that you begin with something other than the subject. The first and last sentence in the paragraph from Nancy's essay, for example, begin with something other than the subject, though the sentences are still statements. You will learn more about these variations in the next section.

Other Sentence Orders. If you begin all your sentences with the subject, you will probably have difficulty keeping your sentences focused clearly for your readers. You may also have difficulty holding your reader's attention and interest, for who enjoys reading sentences that all begin the same way? But there are ways to vary your sentences so that they don't all begin with a subject.

When writers revise their sentences at the postdrafting stage, they don't revise simply to add variety to their sentences. In most cases, they look at the order of information in a sentence, and they ask themselves if that order is effective; that is, they evaluate the sentence in the context of other sentences. When they revise a sentence, then, they change the ordering of information so that the sentence expresses their meaning clearly and effectively for readers. These revisions usually result not only in clear, coherent sentences but also in varied sentences. So revising sentences for variety is not simply done for its own sake; it results from the writer's attempts to make each sentence communicate meaning effectively and coherently in a piece of writing.

Of course, to order information effectively, you need to know some basic principles about sentences. In particular, you need to remember these two points when you revise for sentence order:

1. The beginning of a sentence is important because that's the starting point for the reader. Whatever the reader needs in order to follow the meaning in the rest of the sentence should be stated at the beginning.

2. The end of your sentence is also important because that's where your reader ends up. The most important information in your sentence should therefore come near the end.

You can change the normal order of sentences so that not all sentences begin with the subject. For example, you can move other elements in the sentence, such as the verb or object, to the beginning. This shift in order, however, should not be done simply for variety; it must give your sentence the emphasis you think your readers will need to follow more easily the flow of information in your sentences. In the opening sentence of his description of the Berlin Wall, for example, Michael inverts the normal order of his sentence by moving the verb and its modifier to the front of the sentence. Notice that both now precede the subject:

> At the end of Seventeenth of June Street, Strasse des 19 zu Juni, lies a fourteen foot wall, the Berlin Wall.

Michael could have written this sentence in normal order:

> A fourteen foot wall, the Berlin Wall, lies at the end of Seventeenth of June Street, Strasse des 19 zu Juni.

However, he chose to invert the subject-verb order because he wanted to put the most important information, the topic of his descriptive essay, near the end rather than at the beginning. That is, he wanted his readers to focus not on the location of the Berlin Wall but on *the Berlin Wall* itself, the topic of his essay.

Similarly, Lisa inverts the subject-verb-complement order in this sentence from her description of the Indianapolis Produce Terminal (sample 2B):

> Hustling and bustling down the aisles were produce buyers of various descriptions, vying for the attention of dark complected salesmen wearing fedoras and smoking cigars.

The sentence that immediately precedes this sentence in her essay happens to be the first sentence in her paragraph: *At nearly 6:00 A.M., the marketplace was a flurry of activity.* Because she ends this sentence with *a flurry of activity*, she begins the next sentence, the one cited previously, not with *the produce buyers of various descriptions*, the subject, but with the verbs, *Hustling and bustling*, which characterize the *flurry of activity.* Interestingly, she also ends the sentence with descriptive detail about the activity at the marketplace. So she begins and ends her sentence with information that is most important to the meaning she is attempting to convey.

These kinds of inversions can pose some difficulties for your reader if they occur too frequently in a piece of writing. Occasionally, you can change the basic order of the main clause to keep your reader focused on the important information. In doing so, you are also beginning your sentence with something other than the subject. But too many inversions of this type can make reading somewhat difficult for your readers, so you need to consider still other ways you can change the order of your sentences so that they begin with something besides the subject (or at least a different subject than the one in your draft).

To increase paragraph coherence, as discussed in Chapter Four, some sentences need to begin with relationship signals:

> Therefore, they should be able to have guests in their room whenever they please—if not to socialize, then to study. (sample 5B)

Sentences sometimes need to begin with a modifying phrase or clause, moved from a later position between the subject and main verb. Consider this sentence from an early draft of Nancy's essay (sample 5I):

> Students sitting on the scooters had to propel themselves forward by first extending their legs and then bending their knees as they pulled their bodies forward.

The definite article *the* before the noun *scooters* tells us that Nancy has already referred to *scooters* in earlier sentences. And if you check her essay, you will see that the two preceding sentences are actually about scooters. At the postdrafting stage, Nancy therefore moved the modifying phrase to the beginning of her sentence:

> Sitting on the scooters, students had to propel themselves forward by first extending their legs and then bending their knees as they pulled their bodies forward.

Whenever you begin a sentence with a modifying phrase like the preceding one, ask yourself if the subject is doing the action described in the modifier; otherwise, the modifier will "dangle"—it will not be modifying the right noun. For example, suppose Nancy had written her sentence this way:

By extending their legs and then bending their knees, the scooters were used by the students to propel themselves forward.

Is the subject, *scooters*, doing the action described in the modifying phrase? We know the scooters are not the ones *extending their legs and then bending their knees*. In this sentence, then, the modifier is dangling.

Sometimes, when many words separate the subject and verb in a sentence, you can move the words to the front of the sentence, making it less difficult for your readers. Consider this sentence from an early draft of Kathy's autobiographical essay (sample 3A):

But our fragile daughter through the expert love and care she received in the Intensive Care Unit began to thrive.

When we read, we temporarily store words in what is called "short-term memory" until we are able to combine them into understandable phrases and sentences. Short-term memory is quite small, with a usual capacity of only about seven words. When more than that many words separate the subject and verb (as they do in Kathy's sentence, between the subject, *daughter*, and the verb, *began*), the capacity of short-term memory is exceeded, and the reading mind cannot hold the subject until the verb is reached. At this point, the reader usually has to read the sentence again to make sense of it. So be very careful about separating the subject and verb by more than seven words or so. At the postdrafting stage, Kathy revised her sentence by moving the modifier to the beginning:

Through the expert love and care she received in the Intensive Care Unit, our fragile daughter began to thrive.

You can also begin sentences with information taken from the predicate of your sentence. Each of the following sentences, for example, begins with either an adverb phrase or an adverb clause that, in normal sentence position, would be in the predicate:

On those days, Grandma would get so mad she could hardly speak. (sample 5I)

Since the middle of 1986 the U.S. government has been purchasing dairy cattle from farmers. (sample 5E)

Upon receiving a passing grade, the operator would receive a license to purchase and operate an ATV. (sample 5D)

When I lived at home, I had a weekday curfew of 12:00 A.M. and a weekend curfew of 2:00 A.M. (sample 5B)

If these sentences were written in normal order, the beginning adverb phrases and clauses would follow the verb. The last sentence in the list, for example, would read *I had weekday curfew of 12:00 A.M. and a weekend curfew of 2:00 A.M. when I lived at home.*

Lucia, however, did not want to place the adverb clause at the end because she needed to distinguish between her curfews at school and her curfews at home. Because her letter is about her objections to the curfew imposed on university housing residents, she wanted her readers to know that, in the sentence quoted previously, she was writing about her curfew at home, not at school. Thus, she moves the adverb clause to the beginning of her sentence.

Old and New Information. The old-new principle of order is another tool that can help you check the order of information in your sentences. To help the reader more easily follow the content of your piece of writing, you should generally begin sentences with "old" information, with something the reader already knows. Information is *old* when it has already appeared in previous sentences or when it can be inferred from the context, or from the general topic under discussion; information is *new* when it is unexpected or when the reader needs to be reminded of certain information in order to follow the progression of ideas in a piece of writing.

For example, consider the opening paragraph of Carlotta's letter to the mayor of her town (sample 5C):

> The recent curfew of midnight placed on Miller Park is ineffective and unjust. This curfew, a result of vandalism, is not the solution to our problem.

Carlotta begins her sentence with information about a recent curfew at Miller Park: it is old information because she can assume her reader, the mayor, is no doubt aware of the curfew. She is saying, in essence, "I'm going to tell you something about the midnight curfew at Miller Park." In the rest of her sentence, Carlotta asserts that the curfew *is ineffective and unjust.* This is the new information—an assertion about the subject—that Carlotta wants to communicate to her reader. The second sentence begins again with old information (*This curfew*), retrievable from the first sentence; that the curfew is *a result of vandalism* is also old information, for surely the major knows what caused the city to impose a curfew. The rest of the second sentence, in the predicate, is new information: the curfew *is no solution to the problem.*

The new information in this opening paragraph, then, asserts something about the curfew: it is ineffective, unjust, and no solution to the problem it supposedly addresses. The old information helps orient the reader, gives the reader time to sink his or her heels into the ground, and prepares the reader for the new information that the paragraph contributes.

By beginning your sentences with old information, you control the rate of new information in successive sentence. If you dispense too little old information, the rate of new information increases and overburdens your reader; if you dispense old information at the end of your sentence rather than at the beginning, your reader will probably have difficulty following the line of argument in your piece of writing. For example, read the third paragraph of Michael's essay about buying a CD player (sample 1C):

> Once you decide the amount of money you are going to spend, you should then look at the different models compact disc players come in. By this I mean that you should decide when you will be listening to your CD player the most, and in turn choose a model that best fits your needs. Say, for example, that you most frequently listen to music while in your car; then you obviously would want one designed to replace your current car stereo. The most popular model, however, is one that hooks up to your stereo system, assuming your stereo has an auxiliary outlet. There are two reasons this model is the most popular. One is because this model is generally more advanced than the car or portable ones. The other is that the music sounds better being played through powerful speakers rather than headphones or car speakers.

This is certainly not a bad paragraph, but some sentences, especially in the latter half of the paragraph, begin with new information rather than old. In these sentences, by not dispensing old information effectively, Michael forces the reader to work unnecessarily hard. Here is a revision that *does* begin sentences with "old" information; note that we have eliminated the repetition in Michael's second sentence, adding some of its information to the first sentence. See if you find this paragraph easier to read:

> Once you decide the amount of money you are going to spend, you should then look at the different models of compact disc players and choose one that best fits your needs. Say, for example, that you most frequently listen to music in your car; then you obviously would want one designed to replace your current car stereo. Most people, however, prefer the model that hooks up to their home stereo system, which must be equipped with an auxiliary outlet. This model is the most popular for two reasons. It is generally more advanced than the car or portable ones, and it produces a better quality sound because it is played through powerful speakers rather than headphones or car speakers.

Just as sentences should generally begin with old information, they should generally end with new information. In this way, a piece of writing constantly leads readers from what they already know to what they do not. Read this brief passage by Constance (sample 2C):

> Chris was thrown through a window instantly crushing his skull. For three days I prayed that he would not die. It was hard for me to face the fact that Chris might die.

For many readers, some of the impact of this moving passage will be lost by the awkward repetition of the word *die* at the ends of the second and third sentences. The repetition seems awkward because we expect sentences to end with new information, not repeated information. Here is a possible revision:

> For three days I prayed that he would not die. It was hard for me to face the fact that he might.

Here is another, perhaps even better, since it saves the powerful word *die* for the end of the passage.

> For three days I prayed that he would live. It was hard for me to face the fact that he might die.

As you add new information in each of your sentences, you must also keep your readers continually apprised of the topic you are discussing. You do this by beginning your sentences with previously known information. This ebbing of old and new information in the sentences of your piece of writing makes it easier for readers to follow the content, while assuring the writer that the information is reaching its audience.

Exercises

A. The following paragraphs are taken from some of the sample student papers appearing at the ends of Chapters Two to Five. In each paragraph, one sentence (and sometimes two) is disassembled and reduced to "kernel" sentences, which are in brackets. First read the sentences before and after the bracketed kernel sentences, and then combine the kernels into one or two sentences that cohere with the other sentences in the paragraph. Copy the paragraph, with your sentence(s) added, on a separate sheet of paper. When you finish, compare your sentence(s) with the student writer's by referring to the sample paper, and discuss any variations between your combined sentence(s) and the student writer's. Which version is better, and why?

1.   Another memorable match that highlighted my youth was between a tag wrestler, Goliath, and the infamous forehead biter, Freddie Blassie. [*Combine*:

Goliath bit the forehead of Freddie Blassie.

It was an unexpected move.

Blassie had platinum blonde hair.

Blassie bled profusely.

Blassie had to be carted away by stretcher.]

But that wasn't enough for Goliath. He kicked Blassie out of the stretcher several times as the audience screamed. This was convincing enough for my father, who searched the evening news for reports of Blassie's condition. "Man, they gotta put that on the news! That guy was really hurt," he insisted. (sample 51)

2.   Feeling the chill of an October morning, I stopped at the coal stove, where a few old white-headed men gathered daily, observing their sons and grandsons handling the business which they had strived on for years. Sitting in their armchairs, they reminded me of kings on thrones, ruling their kingdoms. [*Combine*:

I stood silently.

I was remembering conversations.

They were ones I had overheard.

They were between my father and grandfather.

These conversations gave clear testimony of their great respect for these patriarchs of produce.]

Warming my backside, I shut my eyes and breathing deeply tried to distinguish all the heavy aromas which pervaded the area. Strongest were the scents of pungent citrus and spicy apples. Also I noticed the unmistakable musk of onion and an occasional waft of rotten potatoes. (sample 2B)

3.   A place which returns many memories to my mind is an old barn that stood on the farm where I was born. It was a very large structure with siding that had been weathered and cracked by the many years of harsh summer sunshine, and the bitter cold of winters. Years of rain had rusted many of the nails, leaving dark brown stains, streaked into the grayness of the siding. Some of it had fallen to the ground. Off of one end of the barn, a gently sloped roof extended over an open area. [*Combine*:

A corn crib ran parallel to the barn.

The corn crib was long.

The corn crib supported the outer end of this roof.]

Each wooden shingle of this roof seemed to be trimmed with a soft, green moss. (sample 2D)

4.   During my father's illness, I read many articles about lymphoma and other types of cancer. I noticed growing numbers of reports dealing with genetic causes of cancer. [*Combine*:

> Scientists had found that genes were often the origins of cancer.
>
> The cancer could be of many types.
>
> The genes were deformed in some way.
>
> These scientists were involved in genetic research.]

I had been interested in genetics before my father became ill; therefore, I was strongly motivated to use these interests in the future to find answers for the problems we as a family faced. (sample 3B)

B. Revise the following passages from the sample papers, to give their sentences more effective orders:

1.   The next thing you should look at are the options you want your unit to have. The home unit is really the only one that you will have a wide selection of options to choose from. (sample 1C)

2.   Descending the ladder leads to the lower portion of the barn. It is divided into many stalls. Planks of wood, some of them two feet wide, were used to make the walls of these pens. This lower section of the barn is where the cows were milked, and where other animals could be kept separate. (sample 2D)

3.   With the birth of my youngest daughter my whole outlook on life changed. She was born four months prematurely and weighed one pound and five ounces. We were told that there was very little if any chance for her survival. The doctors left the decision to my husband and me whether to try any means of life support. With only a few minutes to decide we asked that she be placed on a respirator. (sample 3A)

4.   The primary reason for these restricted visitation hours seems to be privacy. The people in charge of setting up these hours seem to think that 11:15 P.M. on week nights and Sundays and 2:00 A.M. on Fridays and Saturdays affords a reasonable amount of privacy. (sample 5B)

5.   The manufacturers are repeatedly blamed. Here is where my concern lies. Why should the manufacturers be blamed for the

irresponsibility of the dealership and chiefly the riders? Basic training at the dealership, in the controls of the particular model, would curb the accident rates. More important is the responsibility and simple common sense of the rider. After all, many accidents occur while trying to do something that the ATV was not designed for. (sample 5D)

C. Choose another passage from one of the sample papers and revise it to improve sentence order. Be prepared to discuss the reasons for your revisions.

Assignment 5: I. Position Letter for a Public Official or II. Response to an Editorial

These assignments ask you to write about a specific issue, either for a public official or for an editor of a newspaper. These assignments differ from the last one because they ask you to take a stand on an issue, saying whether you agree or disagree with the issue as it is presented. To do so effectively, you must define the issue fairly and objectively, and give your reader evidence to support your position.

You may choose to write either a position letter for a public official *or* a response to an editorial, both of which are described below.

I. Position Letter for a Public Official

Assignment: Because public officials often review policy and act on matters that affect the lives of other people, they need to know the views of those people in order to make informed decisions. Write a letter for a public official, stating your position on an issue of importance to you.

Sample Papers

Sample 5A (Mandy)

[A letter to the House Council of her dormitory]

Members of House Council:
As a resident of Blanding Tower, I am concerned with the visitation hours established for my dormitory. While the hours may be the same in all dormitories, the enforcement of these hours does not

correspond with the Tower's, and the hours are not fair or just. These hours sabotage the independence of the residents and remove their freedom of choice.

My first point is concerning fairness. Is it fair that coed dorms and Haggin Hall have endless visiting hours while Blanding Tower has an interrogation unit sitting at the front desk? Why is no I.D. needed when entering Kirwan Tower yet is needed in Blanding Tower? Why are residents of Blanding treated differently than the rest of campus? Blanding Tower is the strictest dorm on campus. Aren't the freshman girls mature enough to decide when visitors are appropriate and when visitors are not? I think we deserve more privileges and more credit than we are receiving.

An example of when personal decision would be better than rules, is when a resident wishes to study with a male classmate. During the week when most studying occurs, visitation ends at 11:15. Very few people I know finish studying before 11:15, so what happens when the guy has to leave? A person has two choices, either to quit studying or head to the noisy commons. If one chooses either of these, good luck! I personally study best in my dorm room, and I think that I should be able to study there with a friend as late as I feel. After all I paid for it.

I remember one specific statement made at Freshman Orientation. An upperclassman stated, "You are on your own now. You must make your own decisions; no one will make them for you." If this statement is true, why then is a stranger deciding when I can have visitors? Isn't my room my private place?

I realize that the policy may be set for my own protection, but other choices exist. One suggestion which works on other campuses is having the second set of doors locked and giving each girl a key. With this method only "wanted visitors" are allowed in.

Maybe this suggestion is not a workable one for this campus but there must be other choices. Visitation must be changed; the rights of Blanding Tower residents must be considered.

Blanding residents should have just as many rights as anyone else on this campus. Sex or status should not make a difference.

Sincerely,

Sample 5B (Lucia)

[A letter to the housing office of her university]

Dear Sirs,

One of the most talked about subjects on campus is that of

dormitory visitation hours. I believe that the majority of students on a college campus are mature adults and should be awarded the privileges of an adult. Because of this, visitation hours should be lengthened.

The primary reason for these restricted visitation hours seems to be privacy. The people in charge of setting up these hours seem to think that 11:15 P.M. on week nights and Sundays and 2:00 A.M. on Fridays and Saturdays affords a reasonable amount of privacy. However, many times I, my roommate, and various other persons on my floor do not even begin to get ready for bed until 2:00 A.M. or even 3:00 A.M. occasionally. We feel no need for privacy until this time. Many others feel the same.

When I lived at home, I had a weekday curfew of 12:00 A.M. and a weekend curfew of 2:00 A.M. Then, when I got to college, I found that my "curfew" on week nights had been set back 45 minutes. This is not what I pictured college life as being.

The primary complaint I have heard about visitation hours concerns studying. Many persons study with members of the opposite sex, and since they cannot be in each other's room after 11:15 P.M., they do not get to study very much. They are forced to go to the library, which closes at midnight, or to one of the 24-hour study rooms on campus. I, personally, find it very hard to study in a room with 20 other people.

University of Kentucky residence hall dwellers sign a form of lease before they are granted University housing. This is similar to the lease on an apartment building, yet in an apartment building a person's guests are not asked to leave at a certain time. It seems only fair that residence hall dwellers be afforded this same privilege.

College students, in most cases, are mature adults. Therefore, they should be able to have guests in their room whenever they please—if not to socialize, then to study. Please take my views into consideration when deliberating this issue.

Yours truly,

Sample 5C (Carlotta)

[A letter to the mayor of her town]

Dear Mayor M————,

The recent curfew of midnight placed on Miller Park is ineffective and unjust. This curfew, a result of vandalism, is not the solution to our problem.

The first obvious question about a curfew to stop vandals is, why midnight? What is so magic about 12:00 that a curfew beyond that will stop vandals? Anyone wanting to cause damage or stir up trouble could do so at 11:30, for example, as easily as after midnight.

Furthermore, the rule states that no one can park after midnight. Who says one has to be in a car to be a vandal? Anyone wishing to vandalize the park would find a way whether they park a car to do so or not. In fact, with all the trees and nearby subdivisions, it would be safer to walk than risk the police recognizing the car or getting the license number.

Also, the curfew directly contradicts the main use of the park. Miller Park has always been the playing site of Campbellsville's Little League baseball games, which sometimes last beyond midnight. According to this curfew, the games will have to be stopped at the bewitching hour. Otherwise, the park would be open past 12:00 for baseball games but for no one else.

The greatest injustice to this curfew, however, is the punishment of innocent people. There are legitimate reasons for being at Miller Park after midnight. Two reasons, playing horseshoe and tennis, have become a tradition for a certain group of citizens who work at one of the local factories. With a work schedule of 7:00 P.M.–11 P.M., these people barely get to the park by 11:30, thus eliminating their time for harmless entertainment.

An alternative to the midnight curfew might be to install better lighting throughout the park. Better lighting is a successful and fair means to stop the vandals while maintaining full use of the park.

Another possible solution would be to remove some of the policemen from duty on Main Street and have them patrol the park. The policemen in Campbellsville tend to go to Main Street, where everyone cruises, to wait for something to happen. While these policemen are waiting for something to happen on Main Street, something is happening at Miller Park. The police are at the wrong place at the wrong time.

This curfew is a black spot on an otherwise honorable administration. It is an irritant and an insult to the fine, innocent citizens of Campbellsville. Hopefully this problem can be remedied. Thank you.

                              Sincerely yours,

Sample 5D (Todd)

                    [A letter to his state senator]

Dear Senator,

Since 1980, the press have given all-terrain vehicles, ATV's, a bad name. To some extent this bad name is deserved. All too often

ATV's are sold, taken home, ridden, and then wrecked. As sales and popularity grew, so did accidents, injury, and the concern over the ATV safety issue. The question frequently arises of who is to blame.

The manufacturers are repeatedly blamed. Here is where my concern lies. Why should the manufacturers be blamed for the irresponsibility of the dealership and chiefly the riders? Basic training at the dealership, in the controls of the particular model, would curb the accident rates. More important is the responsibility and simple common sense of the rider. After all, many accidents occur while trying to do something that the ATV was not designed for.

I suggest that in order to buy an ATV, one must go through a short-term, two-or-three day, training program, possibly similar to the ones that DUI offenders have to attend. The purpose of this program would not be to scare the rider, but rather to make one think twice before doing something foolish on an ATV. During this time the riders would be taught basic safety and the limitations of the ATV. At the end of the program the operator would take a test. Upon receiving a passing grade the operator would receive a license to purchase and operate an ATV. This procedure may be expensive and troublesome but is well worth it. ATV's are useful utility and sport vehicles if treated with respect. It would be a shame to take them away from everyone because of a few irresponsible individuals.

Sincerely,

Sample 5E (Todd)

[A letter to one of his senators in Congress]

Dear Senator:

Since the middle of 1986 the U.S. government has been purchasing dairy cattle from farmers. In my opinion, the whole-herd dairy buy-out program, as it is called, was a mistake.

The eighteen-month program, which is being concluded, was aimed at reducing milk surpluses by providing subsidies to participants in return for them staying out of dairy farming for at least five years. According to *Time* (April 1986), about 1.6 million dairy cows, heifers, and calves were scheduled to be sent to market. These cattle had to be slaughtered or sent overseas in order for the conditions of the program to be met.

This policy was a dream come true for those who were considering getting out of the dairy business. However, it has done little, if any, to curb milk production. Many of the farmers that choose not to sell out have in fact increased their herd size. They are anticipating a larger demand in the future due to the decrease in the number of producers. Consequently we are right back where we started from.

If the government had kept their nose out of dairy farming, they would have seen that eventually the problem would have cured itself due to the basic principle of supply and demand. Weaker farmers would have been forced out of business because of lower prices. The April 1986 *Time* article states that 1.8 billion dollars was to be spent on the dairy buy-out program. That money could have been put to a more efficient use by the U.S. government.

Sincerely,

Discussion Questions

1. Which of these five letters are most persuasive for you? Which are least persuasive? What differences in the use of evidence create this effect?

2. How are Mandy's and Lucia's letters on dormitory visitation hours alike? How are they different? If you were writing a composite letter from the two writers, which features of each original letter would you include?

II. Response to an Editorial

Assignment: Write a letter or essay in response to a newspaper editorial.

The editorial page of many newspapers is an important forum for public discussion of community and national issues. The editorial board of the newspaper enters that discussion by writing and publishing editorials; the readers enter the discussion by submitting letters-to-the-editor and guest essays. As a writer of responses to editorials, you are obliged to be accurate and fair, furthering the discussion rather than just covering old, familiar ground.

Sample Papers

Sample 5F (Kris)

[A response to an editorial criticizing President Reagan
for refusing to deal with the federal budget deficit;
the editorial argued for increases in taxes and decreases
in defense spending, in order to lower the deficit]

Recently you ran an editorial about the budget deficit problem that we face. I am writing in response to that editorial, which blames President Reagan for failure to tackle this problem. You stated that Reagan should agree to demands by Congress to increase taxes to balance the budget.

It is my opinion that the correct way to balance the budget is to cut spending as much as necessary and not to raise taxes. Congress and your editors want to raise taxes, which will result in an increase of unemployment and a decrease of total revenues. Any time Congress raises taxes, they always manage to increase spending. Until Congress is serious about cutting the budget both in defense and non-defense spending, we will continue to have this deficit problem.

In the future, I would suggest that when you discuss balancing the budget, you use basic economic principles to form your conclusion. Congress has failed to cut the budget because it is politically easier not to. Therefore, let's lay the blame where it belongs, on Congress and not on President Reagan.

Sincerely,

Sample 5G (Susan)

[A response to an editorial urging the legalization
of liquor sales in a county, in order to promote
the county's economic development]

To the editor:
In your editorial concerning "the possibilities of what Oldham County could become," you suggested changing the county from "dry" to "wet" in order to attract new businesses. In your opinion, popular businesses that serve alcoholic beverages will be attracted to the county if alcohol sales are legalized. Unfortunately, you did not consider the consequences that legal alcohol sales could hold for the community.

You stated that establishments such as Mr. Gatti's are unlikely to set up operations in a county where alcohol is not served. However, there are such establishments in other dry counties that run successful businesses. The lack of alcohol is not going to stop a business from opening if it desires to come into our county. Perhaps if the community approached such a business and expressed the wish to open a franchise in the county, the business would respond favorably.

The editorial also stated that legalized alcohol sales would be an asset "as long as the bars stay out of . . . Oldham County." How can you stop these places from opening if you legalize the sale of alcohol? With no present competition, bars, clubs, and liquor stores will be popping up on every street corner. This will cause an increase in traffic, as well as an increase in alcohol-related accidents. This is an asset we certainly do not need.

Hopefully, your readers are intelligent enough to realize the consequences of introducing alcohol into the county. They should not be deceived into believing that legal alcohol sales are necessary in order to bring growth and prosperity to the county. I suggest that the next time you consider such a controversial issue, you take a look at the entire picture, rather than see only what you want to see.

Sincerely,

Sample 5H (Mandy)

[A response to an editorial supporting a state lottery]

A waitress from Chicago, Illinois, rushes home to her six children, two million richer and five times happier. She can at last give her children the care they deserve. Another lottery winner helps fund a food and clothing drive for the poor in America. How can actions like these, true stories taken from a lottery article in *Newsweek*, bring damage to the poverty stricken in Kentucky when the lottery may be providing their children's education?

The lottery craze in running rampant in America today. According to a May 1984 *Time*, sixteen states have adopted lotteries since New Hampshire started its lottery in 1963. Recently the states of Iowa, Maine, and Vermont have kicked off new lotteries, and in the House of Representatives there are three bills proposed pushing the idea of a national lottery. Now, Kentucky wants its own lottery and the advantages it can bring.

A state lottery can mean extra bucks for Kentucky's school system. Yes, it is true that earnings each year may fluctuate, but citizens will not settle for increased taxes. As *Time* states, "The games seem to have something for everyone: jackpots for the winners, commissions for the ticket sellers, and a politically safe way for legislators to raise revenues without raising taxes."

Much of Kentucky's money is spent on out-of-state lotteries. Why should we support Ohio or Indiana schools when we could support our own? It's lost money.

Large profits can be made through state lotteries. Figures found in *Time* state that in 1983, Ohio made 145 million in profits,

Pennsylvania 355 million, and next year New York plans to gather in 500 million to be used for education.

Kentucky could easily put this money to use in their schools, and in addition make at least one happy millionaire a day.

As also stated in *Newsweek*, the lottery is a unique way of drawing money from citizens, "for it lays taxes only on the willing." Thousands of people play the lottery everyday, but no one walks them to the line or forces them to stand and buy a ticket. It is their own choice, which brings up the discussion on the lower class.

Poverty-stricken people do tend to play the lottery frequently, but they do realize how slim their chances are. They just desperately want to leave their meager states. Who are we to take the chance away?

Freedom of choice abounds as a major right in America. The poor have this right as well. If the poor will waste money on the lottery, doesn't it seem true that they will waste it elsewhere if the lottery doesn't exist? We might as well get the money for schools.

As citizens of Kentucky, we must look for the most beneficial programs and utilize them. According to *Newsweek*, "Lotteries were launched to support Colonial soldiers, build Harvard, Princeton and Yale—and even secure the roof under which the first regular U.S. Congress held its sessions." As a University of Kentucky student facing a tuition increase, I think it consequential that Kentucky install the lottery and aid the institution of education.

Sample 51 (Nancy)

[An essay on Hoosier basketball mania,
for the editorial page of a local newspaper]

Why I Am Not a Hoosier Basketball Fan:
An Explanation of a Misspent Youth

It doesn't matter how long I've lived in Indiana, or how much of its hard water I drink. I'll never become a true Hoosier and love basketball. Why? It was my poor upbringing.

Unlike most Hoosiers who were weaned on many hours of televised high school basketball games, I grew up in the Northeast, in a home where professional and midget wrestling were watched. My father believed that wrestlers like Professor Toro, Bruno Sanmartino, Pedro Morales, and Lou Albana really fought each other.

Every Saturday afternoon, instead of watching tall, lanky men bounce a ball up and down a court, our family watched sweaty, fat men "half nelson" each other all over the ring. No one could convince my Dad that it was all an act, because the fights would get gruesome at times.

There was the time Professor Toro Tanaka threw salt in Pedro Morales' face. Morales writhed on the canvas for what seemed an eternity. The match was finally called off by the skinny referee who hadn't seen Tanaka throw the salt up in the air, into Morales' face, onto the ring, and even into the faces of a few spectators in the front row. My father still believes that referee was on the take, and will often state this. "How's the weather in New Jersey, Dad?" "You remember that dirty referee in the Morales and Tanaka fight?"

Another memorable match that highlighted my youth was between a tag wrestler, Goliath, and the infamous forehead biter, Freddie Blassie. In an unexpected move, Goliath grabbed Freddie Blassie and bit his forehead. Blassie, who had platinum blonde hair, bled profusely and had to be carted away by stretcher. But that wasn't enough for Goliath. He kicked Blassie out of the stretcher several times as the audience screamed. This was convincing enough for my father, who searched the evening news for reports of Blassie's condition. "Man, they gotta put that on the news! That guy was really hurt," he insisted.

Even my grandmother, who watched a *real* sport, baseball, didn't train me to be a proper sports fan. My grandmother, a petite woman under five feet, loved the game. Her favorite team was the New York Yankees in the days before George Steinbrenner. She would listen to the Yankees games on her blue transmitter radio, which she held closely to her ear. As a child, it always amazed me to hear my grandmother, ordinarily a solemn woman, yell at plays not to her liking. My brothers and I loved to watch her as she listened to the games on Sunday afternoons. Whenever the Yankees made a bad play, she would curse them in her foreign language and then quickly cross herself, remembering she had been to Mass that morning.

No one liked visiting her if the Yankees had lost. On those days, Grandma would get so mad she could barely speak. I remember once approaching her in the kitchen to ask when dinner would be ready. (The adults put me up to this.) I was within five feet of her when she put out her hand abruptly and said, "Leave me alone! I'm so mad at those *stoopid* Yankees!" Of course, the Yankees were the cause of our eating Grandma's many burnt meals, and for our subsequent heartburns.

As a teenager, I was even less inclined towards sports. My classmates respected me for my artistry at avoiding gym class. It wasn't that I entirely hated gym; it was just that the thought of undressing in front of my better endowed teenage peers horrified me. So I invented any story to avoid that emotional trauma. My old gym teacher still reminds me of an excuse I once gave him.

One day in gym we had to sit on these "handleless scooters," and race against other teams. The scooters were really pieces of ten inch square blocks with four wheels on them. Sitting on the scooters, students had to propel themselves forward by first extending their legs and then bending their knees as they pulled their bodies forward. Hands had to stay on hips throughout the race. The gym was very large, and crowded with students. All I needed to see were my girlfriends in those horrible polyester-knit gym suits, struggling to stay on those scooters. I looked at Mr. Werner straight in the eye and said, "I can't sit on those things. I have hemorrhoids!" I was excused, and spent the rest of the gym period in study hall. Until this day when he sees me, Mr. Werner asks if my hemorrhoids are acting up.

As you can see, I didn't have a prayer at becoming a basketball fan. I was a victim of my environment. I only ask that Hoosiers be tolerant of me. I promise that as long as I live in Indiana, I'll pretend to like basketball. Give me some time and I'll weave "hook shot, guard, free throws, and rebounds" into my daily conversations. Who knows? Maybe someday I'll recite the high school regional scores like a native, or at least come close.

Discussion Questions

1. Which of these four responses do you find most persuasive? Which do you find least persuasive? What features contribute to that effect?

2. What parts of these four responses seem genuinely to advance the discussion of these issues? What parts seem simply to repeat conventional arguments?

CHAPTER SIX

The Process of Writing Words

Words are symbols of language that we use to represent the reality, or meaning, we communicate to others when we speak or write. As native speakers of English, we are rather adept at choosing words to fit particular speech situations, such as when we interact with a child, rouse the opposing team at a football game, or voice an opinion in a class discussion. We choose words that are appropriate to the situation and that express our meaning clearly. When we write for different writing situations, we make the same kinds of word choices.

As writers, however, we must often pay closer attention to our written words. We all have more experience *speaking* words than *writing* them, so naturally we need to be more attentive when we write. As beginning college writers, you need to choose words that communicate your meaning effectively. When you revise your piece of writing at the postdrafting stage, choosing the right words must be a conscious, deliberate choice. And writing, unlike speaking, allows you ample time to choose words carefully in order to express your meaning clearly and effectively.

In most speaking situations, if you misuse a word, or make an inappropriate choice, you can usually correct yourself and go on speaking. Of course, you cannot actually take back your words; you can only add more words to correct, qualify, or extend your meaning. Moreover, as you speak, you gauge the effectiveness of your words and the clarity of your meaning by observing your listeners' reactions. If your words do not communicate clearly, your listeners are physically present to express their confusion, either through their facial expressions or simply by asking questions.

In a writing situation, however, you do not have an opportunity to get it right a second time. If you make ineffective word choices in a piece of writing, your readers cannot ask you to explain your meaning. That is why writing is so much more complex than speaking, and why revising at the postdrafting stage is so important for writers. You have to make each word count; each word must contribute to the meaning you are expressing. In writing, you have ample opportunity to change words as often as you like without your readers ever knowing. By choosing your words carefully at the postdrafting stage, you can communicate your meaning precisely and effectively for your readers.

After carefully analyzing your writing situation, gathering and organizing the content of your piece of writing, and considering other aspects of your "manner" of expression, you are ready to make decisions, or choices, about words. In this chapter, we discuss word *conventions* and word *choices* to help you think about your words and their effects on your readers. Careful attention to words can give your piece of writing the clarity, accuracy, and style that distinguish effective writing from ineffective writing.

Predrafting: Discovering Words

As Figure 1 suggests, individual words should probably not be much of a concern at the predrafting stage of your writing. There are some exceptions, however. As you gather content for your writing, be careful to record the exact words of quotations, proper names, titles of books and articles, and the like. Postponing close attention to wording does not mean being careless about specific words that matter.

Let's suppose you composed a clear and coherent letter to a potential employer, but misspelled the company name or—worse yet—the name of the person to whom you wrote the letter. Despite the quality of your writing, you probably would not make a lasting impression on your reader. In fact, such careless letters (as many personnel directors have commented) are usually bound for the wastebasket. Remember that your attention to details may reflect your work habits.

As you define the writing situation, gather content, and organize, feel free to jot down particularly appropriate words that occur to you. Often such key words can help you shape the content and organization of the piece of writing. At the predrafting stage, for example, Alan brainstormed a list of ideas for his movie review (sample 6A), and many of the words he used in his list turned out to be good choices. Here is part of his brainstorming list:

Bond is back—but not the same

Dalton less suave, more serious than Bond

departure from campiness of Roger Moore

Bond not on a mission but out for revenge—a personal vendetta.

opening pre-credit action sequence

only two lovers—neither of whom gets killed

most intense Bond film with the most graphic violence

music like *Goldfinger* theme at first

action confined to Key West, Florida, and the fictitious Isthmus city

If you compare Alan's predrafting with his review at the end of this chapter, you will see that many of the same words and phrases found their way into his review. So even at the predrafting stage, you should make a note of key words or phrases that you think might be useful to you later in the writing process.

Drafting: Writing Words

As you draft, you are of course choosing words from which to construct sentences, paragraphs, and the whole written product. If you have pre-drafted well, with most of your content gathered and a clear organizational plan made, the words should come fairly easily, with little interference from your internal editor. At times, however, all writers are brought to a stop by not knowing what word to write next. At such times, be careful not to let your internal editor's concern for that one word keep your internal writer from maintaining the continuity of the draft.

Your internal editor may try to distract you, so be prepared. A good tool might be "When you draw a blank, draw a blank"; that is, draw a blank space to indicate the missing word, and keep going. If you cannot decide between two possible words, write them both (perhaps with a slash between them). Jacques Barzun, in "A Writer's Discipline," tells an anecdote about a "schoolboy who chewed a pencil to splinters and failed the examination because he sought a word halfway between mickle and muckle" (Reprinted in *The Little, Brown Reader*, 2nd ed., eds. Marcia Stubbs and Sylvan Barnet [Boston: Little, Brown, and Co., 1980], p. 296). So get your ideas on paper, ignore your internal editor's anxiousness about details, and keep writing! Your writing process will be more efficient, your written product will have greater continuity, and your word choices (when you come back to them, at the postdrafting stage) will be informed by a better overall sense of the work as a whole.

Postdrafting: Revising Words

When you reach the postdrafting stage and have that sense of the written product as a whole, look carefully at the words you have used in your draft and ask two questions about them: Do they follow word *conventions*, and are they the most effective *choices*?

WORD CONVENTIONS: DENOTATIONS

As the chart in Figure 1 suggests, there are many more conventions than choices about words. Words have specific meanings, called *denotations*, that make communication possible. A denotation is an explicit meaning, exact, complete, and impersonal. *Notorious*, for example, denotes someone who is widely but unfavorably known, whereas *notable* denotes someone who is worthy of attention and respect. When words are not used accurately, with the right denotations, then writers and readers have difficulty communicating.

For example, Janice, in a draft of her essay about abortion (sample 4B), wrote this sentence: "That night I laid in bed and cried with pain and without so much as a word from my parents in the next bed." At the postdrafting stage, Janice looked again at that sentence; something seemed wrong to her. It occurred to her that *laid* is the verb meaning "to place" and not the one meaning "to recline." The word Janice had been looking for was not *laid* but *lay*, the past tense of *lie*, and she revised accordingly. *Lay* had the right denotation.

In her autobiographical essay (sample 3C), Constance wrote this sentence:

> There have been many nights when I have stayed up with Chris
> through feigned threats of suicide.

If Constance had looked carefully at this sentence at the postdrafting stage, she would have noticed that *feigned* and *threats* both have denotations that, when combined, result in a distorted meaning. One can *threaten* suicide (express the intention to commit suicide), and one can *feign* suicide (pretend as though one has committed suicide). But what does *feigned threats of suicide* communicate? She might have revised her sentence in this way:

> Many nights I stayed up with Chris when he threatened suicide.

If the conventions of meaning are not followed by the writer, then communication eventually breaks down. As Grice would say, when writers unknowingly violate the maxim of manner by misusing words and their meanings, they pose a serious threat to the cooperative agreement that exists between writers and readers. By following word conventions, writers can assure themselves and their readers that the lines of communication are open.

Dictionaries. The main source of information on word conventions is, of course, a dictionary, and a good dictionary is a writer's most important tool. Finding a good dictionary can be difficult, however, because so many unsatisfactory ones exist. Good dictionaries are extremely expensive books to publish, since they involve years of research, writing, and editing (predrafting, drafting, and postdrafting) by many specialists; bad dictionaries, conversely, are extremely inexpensive books to publish since they involve only the reprinting of out-of-date dictionaries. Furthermore, the fact that the term *Webster's* is not a company name or trademark makes it difficult for the consumer to tell good dictionaries from bad.

For college writing purposes, you should generally avoid paperback dictionaries: however good they may be for checking spelling, most simply do not give enough information on word meanings. Also avoid dictionaries that do not include recent additions to the language. Although no dictionary can be expected to include last month's slang expressions, any dictionary can be expected to include the last decade's technological developments. You have a right to expect a dictionary to include the word *laser*, for example, although some dictionaries currently on sale do not.

Four hardcover "desk" dictionaries are widely regarded as excellent; you can't go wrong with the latest editions of any of them:

The American Heritage Dictionary of the English Language

The Random House College Dictionary

Webster's New Collegiate Dictionary (published by the Merriam-Webster Company)

Webster's New World Dictionary of the American Language

These are all "desk" dictionaries, in the sense that they are not easily stuffed and carried in a book bag. You might consider purchasing a second dictionary—perhaps a pocket dictionary—that travels more easily. But if you do, remember to purchase it *in addition to*, not *instead of*, the larger, more complete dictionary.

As you begin to use your dictionary, take time to look over its table of contents and introductory materials to find what kinds of information are included. As with any reference book, the introductory material will explain what the book contains, how it displays information, and what special symbols or notations it uses. Some dictionaries, for example, list definitions in historical order, with the most recent definition last; other dictionaries reverse this order and list the most recent definition first. So if you don't familiarize yourself with the introductory material, you may end up using words whose meanings are out-of-date and probably obscure to the contemporary reader.

Many words whose meanings you understand when you read are not words you commonly use when you speak or write. In other words, your reading vocabulary is much more extensive than your speaking and writing vocabulary. So you may inadvertently misuse words that you may use for the first time in your writing. As you postdraft your writing, consult the dictionary regularly for the meanings of the words you have used, especially those words not part of your everyday speaking vocabulary.

Of course, you will also encounter many unfamiliar words in your college courses. In many of these courses, you will often be expected to use these new words as you write about the subject matter. Words make it possible for us to express our thinking, and without the right words, we are obviously limited in the expression of our meaning. As you encounter these new words, especially ones in your major, it may be a good idea to write them in your notebook or journal with their definitions. Like anything else, you won't *learn* them if you don't *use* them. Keep in mind, however, that long words are no better than short ones, unless they convey a precise meaning that you know your readers will understand. In a later section on word choices, we will discuss in more detail the levels of word usage and the appropriateness of words with special meanings.

Common Problems. Several fairly common words are often used erroneously by inexperienced writers. Many of these are pairs of words pronounced similarly but spelled differently, so the differences between them don't matter much in speech, only in writing. At the postdrafting stage, be especially careful to check that you have used the following sets of words to convey the meanings you want. To emphasize the differences between these words, only approximate meanings are given here; for detailed definitions, consult a good dictionary.

ACCEPT and EXCEPT

Accept means "to receive or agree to." *Except*, as a verb, is used much less often; it means "to exclude." As a preposition, meaning "excluding," it is much more common.

She *accepted* the contract, *except* for its last paragraph.

ADAPT and ADOPT

Adapt means "to change"; *adopt* means "to take as one's own."

He *adopted* the old verse form but *adapted* it to fit his subject matter.

AFFECT and EFFECT

Affect is most often used as a verb, meaning "to influence"; it is rarely used as a noun, with a specialized psychological meaning. *Effect* is most often used as a noun, meaning "result"; as a verb, meaning "to bring about," it is less common.

> Our accountant reported on the *effect* of the new tax law; she determined that it would greatly *affect* our profits unless we *effect* a reorganization of our inventory procedures.

A LOT and ALLOT

A lot means "a large amount or number"; it is always written as two words (the same as *a little*). *Allot* is a verb meaning "to distribute." (*Alot* is a misspelling.)

> *A lot* of food was *allotted* to the refugees.

ALL RIGHT, ALL READY, and ALREADY

All right and *all ready* are two-word expressions (pronoun plus adjective) meaning "all correct or acceptable" and "all prepared," respectively. They should not be written as single words: in particular, the very informal word *alright* should be avoided in formal writing. *Already*, however, is a common adverb meaning "by that time" or "by this time."

> She had *already* left, but that was *all right* with me because she was *all ready* to go.

COMPLEMENT and COMPLIMENT

Complement is a verb meaning "to complete or enhance"; *compliment* is also a verb meaning "to give praise." Both words can also be used as nouns, their meanings distinguished as earlier.

> He *complimented* the decorator on the way the carpet *complements* the wall colors. The decorator appreciated his *compliment*.

DISINTERESTED and UNINTERESTED

Disinterested means "neutral"; *uninterested* means "not interested."

> We thought she would serve well as a *disinterested* mediator, but she was *uninterested* in the job.

IMPLY and INFER

Imply means "to suggest"; it is done by a speaker or writer. *Infer* means "to read between the lines"; it is done by a listener or reader.

>   The article *implied* that a breakthrough is near; at least that's what I *inferred* from it.

IT'S and ITS

It's is a contraction of "it is" (the apostrophe replaces the missing letter *i* in *is*). *Its* is a possessive pronoun; like other possessive pronouns (his, hers, ours, theirs) it has no apostrophe.

>   *It's* important to return the instrument to *its* case.

LAY and LIE

Lay is a "transitive" verb, always taking an object; its past tense and past participle are both *laid*. *Lie* is an "intransitive" verb, never taking an object; its past tense, however, is *lay* and its past participle is *lain*.

>   Someone *laid* the atlas on the wrong shelf; it *lay* there all last week and will *lie* there forever unless someone *lays* it where it goes.

LEAD and LED

Lead as a noun rhymes with *head*. *Lead* as a verb rhymes with *bead*; its past tense is *led*.

>   The guide *led* us to the old *lead* mine.

LESS and FEWER / AMOUNT and NUMBER

These words are used to show quantity or number. To use them correctly, you should first determine whether the nouns they quantify are count nouns (countable objects) or non-count nouns (items that cannot be counted individually). When you are referring to separate items that can be counted, use *fewer* and *number*.

>   She met *fewer* American tourists on her European excursion this year, but the *number* didn't surprise her.

When you are referring to items that cannot be counted individually, use *less* and *amount*.

> The *amount* of gold she won in the lottery was not reported, but it was *less* than she expected.

SET and SIT

Set, like *lay*, is transitive, taking an object; its past and past participle forms are also *set*. *Sit*, like *lie*, is intransitive, never taking an object; its past and past participle forms are *sat*.

> The engineer *set* up the new antenna dish just south of where the old one had *sat*.

THEY'RE, THEIR, THERE

They're is a contraction of "they are" (the apostrophe replaces the missing letter *a* in *are*). *Their* is a possessive pronoun, showing ownership. *There* is an adverb of location, showing the place of something or someone; it may also be an introductory word (*There* is / are . . .).

> *They're* collaborating on a special project that will be announced at our national convention in Boston. *Their* work will be recognized *there* by some of the leading scholars in the field.

General and Specific Words. Besides choosing words with the right denotations, writers use both general and specific words to make their pieces of writing interesting and substantive for readers. As you may recall in our discussion of paragraphs in Chapter Four, we said that a topic sentence often expresses the general meaning of a paragraph or group of paragraphs, whereas other related sentences provide more specific meanings to substantiate the topic. Of course, paragraphs and sentences are made up of words, and some words are general and some specific. Remember, however, that words are only general and specific in relation to each other; that is, the same word may be more general in relation to one word and more specific in relation to another.

For example, consider the following words arranged in the order of increasing specificity:

> Education . . . college . . . liberal arts . . . English . . . writing . . . business writing . . . the memorandum . . . John's memorandum . . .

In this list, *business writing* is more specific than *college* but more general than *the memorandum*, which itself is more general than *John's memorandum*. The specificity of a word is therefore relative to other words in a piece of writing. The words that make up a topic sentence in a paragraph will be more general than the words that make up other sentences in the paragraph, but more specific than the words in the thesis statement. So, to communicate meaning in a piece of writing, writers have to use both general and specific words, first introducing an idea and then saying something about it in more specific terms.

One way to visualize the interplay of general and specific words in a piece of writing is to imagine a word ladder with the top rungs representing the most general words and the bottom rungs representing the most specific words. The rungs in between represent words less specific than the words on the top rungs and more general than the words on the bottom rungs. When you write, you are continually moving up and down the word ladder, moving up to introduce new ideas and moving down to say something specific about those ideas. If you write with too many general words, your readers will not have a specific understanding of your meaning; they will need—or expect—more specific content. On the other hand, if you write with too many specific words, your reader may lose sense of the general idea of your piece of writing. So it's important to learn how to move up and down the word ladder so that you succeed in communicating your meaning clearly to your readers.

Consider the following paragraph from Alan's review of a James Bond movie (sample 6A):

> Yes, Bond *is* back, but this is not the same Bond we have gotten to know over the years. We see this immediately in the opening shot of *License to Kill*, when 007 walks into the familiar camera shutter. This Bond is different, even in his walk. Timothy Dalton, who debuted as Bond in the somewhat disappointing *The Living Daylights* (1987), portrays a less promiscuous, but a more serious and concerned Bond. He may not be as suave as Sean Connery or as flippant and campy as Roger Moore, but he is much more likable. He seems more like a real person.

In the first sentence, Alan is high on the word ladder: he uses general words to tell us that something is different about Bond. In the second sentence, he comes down a few rungs on the word ladder by using more specific words, such as "the opening shot" (movie lingo), "*License to Kill*" (the movie title), "007" (Bond's code name), and the image of Bond walking "into the familiar camera shutter" (a trademark of Bond movies). He might have written, "We see these differences at the very beginning of the movie," in which case he would not have used as many specific words.

In the remaining sentences in the paragraph, he gives more specific information about his topic by describing some of the differences in the Bond character: Bond is "less promiscuous" and "more serious and concerned," not as "suave as Sean Connery or as flippant and campy as Roger Moore but . . . more likable." In these sentences, he comes further down the word ladder to describe Bond's character in specific terms. But notice how he moves back up the ladder in the final sentence, though not as high up as in the first sentence. At this point, having already provided his readers with specifics, Alan can assume his readers know what he means when he describes Bond as "more like a real person."

General and specific words sometimes have a more restricted meaning and, as such, are distinguished as *abstract* and *concrete* words. Abstract words are general words referring to concepts, qualities, and emotions like *democracy, honor, happiness, gentleness,* and *love.* These are the words writers use to get started—to introduce topics for discussion. *Concrete* words, on the other hand, carry more specific meanings, often referring to objects or experiences that can be perceived through the senses. They involve readers in ways that abstract words cannot. Here, for example, is a sentence from Lisa's essay about the Indianapolis Produce Terminal (sample 2B):

> Our bodies rocked from side to side on the squeaky truck seat, as we bounced and bumped along the rough stone driveway leading to the Terminal gate.

Lisa could have written, "We drove to the Terminal in an old truck," but she wanted her reader to experience this event as *she* did in her childhood. So she uses concrete words and images so that her readers can participate vicariously in the experience. Some of these concrete words appeal to our sense of sight (as most concrete words do), but others in her sentence are words we can hear, like *squeaky,* and words we can feel, like *rough.* While abstract words often *tell* readers about an event, concrete words *show* readers by appealing to their senses. In the following list, you can see how concrete words relate to the five senses; many of them are taken from Lisa's essay:

Sight. red, large, rectangular, tattered, dark, bounce, bump.

Hearing. loud, soft, squeaky, noisy, rumble, whisper, shout.

Taste. bitter, sweet, juicy, dry, ripe.

Smell. foul, sour, moldy, rotten, burnt, pungent, spicy.

Touch. rough, smooth, silky, hard, soft, course.

In any piece of writing, abstract and concrete words work together to communicate the writer's meaning, just as general and specific words do. At the postdrafting stage, then, it is important that you consider the balance of general and specific words, as well as abstract and concrete words. An effective balance of these words can add interest, color, and texture to your piece of writing.

Exercises

A. Correct any errors in word denotation in the following sentences from drafts of the sample papers. Some sentences have been corrected in the final copies, some have not, and some are already correct.

1.   If you are excepted as an officer candidate, the next step in the process is planning a tentative program for the annual summer leadership camp. (sample 1A)

2.   Soldiers are already forcing the old man to leave. (sample 2E)

3.   However, complications such as an intestinal blockage and pneumonia eventually led to my father's death. (sample 3B)

4.   First it was a Trans-Am, then a Corvette, and eventually at a standstill, a Porsche. (sample 3C)

5.   Still he had been personally effected. (sample 3C)

6.   Mara is where my concern lays. (sample 5D)

7.   Dairy farmers would have been alright if the government would have just left them alone. (sample 5E)

8.   Although Waters contributed alot to Pink Floyd, he had gotten too big for his pants. (sample 6C)

9.   According to a May 1984 *Time*, sixteen states have adopted lotteries since New Hampshire started its lottery in 1963. (sample 5H)

10.   This movie shows dramatically the ill affects of an extramarital affair. (sample 6B)

B. Choose one of your earlier papers, or a draft of one you are currently revising, and produce a more effective balance of words, whether general and specific, abstract and concrete, or both.

C. In your journal, keep a list of the words you frequently misuse when you write. Beside each word, write the correct denotation, and include a few examples of the word in use. When you revise your next paper, refer to your journal for a quick review of the words you tend to misuse.

WORD CHOICES: CONNOTATIONS

Despite the large number of conventions that must be followed in choosing and using words, many choices are possible. The English language, more than any other, has numerous synonyms, words with similar meanings. So at many points throughout each piece of writing, the writer must choose between pairs or sets of words with approximately the same denotation.

Yet even if denotative meanings are the same, *connotations*, shades of meaning, can vary. For example, the words *inform* and *tell* have the same denotation, but slightly different connotations: some readers might regard it as more polite to be "informed" than to be "told." And in thousands of cases, the differences in connotation are even greater: think of *pass away, die*, and *croak*, for example, or *slender, slim, thin, skinny*, and *bony*. As these examples illustrate, words are often emotionally charged with positive or negative connotations. You would probably agree, for example, that *bony* has a negative connotation and *slender* a positive one.

One of us is reminded of a conversation he overheard between two five-year-old boys. One boy began to tell about an unfortunate accident involving his cat. "My cat was run over by a car last night," he said. "It died." The other five year old asked, "Where did you find it?" and the boy, his eyes to the ground, answered, "Under the car in the driveway." The boy hearing this news was genuinely sad. The other boy, after telling his story, hopped back on his bicycle and uttered what he must have thought was an appropriate ending to a sad story. "It was *dead meat*," he said, and off he rode.

In this situation, the young boy chose the right denotation but the wrong connotation. He made an inappropriate choice, not in using a slang expression but in overlooking the negative connotation of *dead meat*.

You can see, then, how the words you choose in a piece of writing can influence the emotional responses of your readers. By choosing words with the right connotative values, you can exercise your power as a writer to affect the feelings and attitudes of your readers.

Of course, at the drafting stage of the writing process, you should not be too concerned about connotation; such concern will only distract you. But at the postdrafting stage, when you can look at the piece of writing as a whole, you should review your word choices carefully to see that you have communicated not only the desired denotation but the most effective connotation.

Dictionaries and Thesauruses. As with denotation, dictionaries are the most important source of help with connotation. Good dictionaries, including those listed earlier in this chapter, include hundreds of discussions of the differences in connotation among groups of synonyms and near synonyms. For example, under its entry for *hinder, The American Heritage Dictionary* discusses the distinctive connotations of *hinder, hamper, impede, retard, encumber, obstruct, block, dam, bar*, and *balk*.

Because of these discussions, or "word stories," good dictionaries are more helpful with word choices than are most thesauruses. An ordinary thesaurus, providing only a list of synonyms, is useful for helping writers recall words that have slipped their minds. Such a thesaurus, however, is not very useful for helping writers learn new words or choose among synonyms, and many inexperienced writers actually make their writing *less* successful by relying on a thesaurus to find unfamiliar words with the intended denotation but with a totally inappropriate connotation.

Figurative Words. Sometimes the words you choose create pictures, or images, in the minds of your readers. When you use words in this way, you need to be sure that the picture(s) you create communicates a clear meaning. For example, in a draft of her autobiographical essay (sample 3C), Constance wrote the following sentences about one of her brothers:

> Jeff wandered, and wandered, and. . . . In fact, he strayed into the dark side.

For most readers, the words of that unfinished first sentence, although denoting activity outside social norms, carries a connotation of sheep straying; in fact the preceding paragraph in Constance's essay compares her brother directly to a "black sheep." The last words of the second sentence, however, probably convey to most contemporary readers a connotation of the "Star Wars" films, in which the heroes must continually battle the "dark side" of "the Force." The question Constance had to ask herself, at the postdrafting stage, was whether these two connotations—sheep and Star Wars—worked well together. She decided that they did not. As she herself put it, "I had to look at my writing as if I were another person."

As you can see from the previous example, some words suggest comparisons. When Constance uses the words *the dark side*, she is implicitly introducing a comparison for her readers to consider. When words are used in this nonliteral sense, we call such words *figurative words*. If you write, for example, "The teacher growled," you don't expect your readers to interpret your meaning literally—that your teacher made the sounds of a bear, lion, or vicious dog. Rather, you merely imply a comparison so that your readers get a clearer sense of your teacher's manner of response. By evoking the image of a bear, a lion, or a vicious dog, and the sounds they make, you suggest to your readers that your teacher was irritable and unpleasant.

Writers use words figuratively to make what is unfamiliar more familiar to their readers. Two of the most common ways that writers use words in a nonliteral sense is the *metaphor* and the *simile*. These are forms of figurative language that writers use to clarify and illuminate their meaning, but never merely to decorate their piece of writing.

A simile is an explicit comparison between two people, places, or things, using the words *like* or *as*. In the following sentence, notice how Lisa (sample 2B) uses a *simile* to help her readers visualize the flues of the coal stoves on the docks of the Indianapolis Produce Terminal:

> Their long, open fronts were punctuated by coal stoves and flues, rising from floor to ceiling like black columns.

A metaphor, on the other hand, is an implicit comparison, without the connectives *like* or *as*.

In the following sentence, Amy uses a metaphor to convey the impact of the flood of 1937 on the city of Ceralvo (sample 2C):

> The final, crippling blow to the city was the flood of 1937, which wiped out most of what remained in Ceralvo. (sample 2C)

Describing the flood as a "crippling blow," Amy suggests a comparison, perhaps, to a boxing match, in which one fighter delivers a knock-out punch to the other. Even the words "wiped out" are used metaphorically to suggest the disastrous effects of the flood.

Levels of Usage. Another choice available to writers is the level of usage of the words they use. Words are like clothes; different words, like different clothing styles, will be appropriate for specific situations. A suit, for example, will be more appropriate for most job interviews than blue jeans and a sweatshirt, but less appropriate for a softball game. In the same way, some words will be more appropriate for job application letters; others will be more appropriate for letters to friends.

Dictionaries and word usage manuals sometimes classify words by their level of formality. The *American Heritage Dictionary*, for example, labels some of its entries and definitions as "informal." The managing editor of the dictionary explains that "there are always two levels of language, the language of formal discourse and the language of conversation. The great mass of words are the same in both, but there are many words perfectly acceptable in conversation that would not be suitable in formal writing. . . . Informal terms may, of course, appear also in writing when the flavor of speech is being sought" (xlvi).

Not all linguists would agree that there are only two levels of formality; there seems, instead, to be an unbroken continuum of formality from the very informal to the very formal. For example, you might find that the following words, all of which have the denotation of "mother," all have slightly different levels of usage:

> old lady   mom   mother   ma   mater

For most of the writing you will be doing in college and in your professional careers, you will perhaps write in a "middle" style somewhere between the very informal and the very formal. We can define this style more clearly by first discussing some characteristic features of very informal and very formal styles of writing.

Very informal language—what we might call "colloquial"—is the language of everyday speech. It is typically characterized by its use of slang words and expressions (*nerd, rip off, radical, awesome*), clichés (*work like a dog, hear a pin drop, busy as a bee*), contractions (*we're, you're*), nonstandard grammar, fragments of speech, abbreviated words (*narc, T.V., fridge*), and first- and second-person pronouns (referring to persons). The following passage, for example, illustrates very informal language usage:

> I can't stomach some of the trash on T.V. Last night I decided to take a break from studying, turned on the tube about elevenish, and couldn't believe my eyes. Outrageous horror! Blood, guts, and all the rest. How can people stand all that violence? If I catch ten seconds of it by accident, I can't sleep a wink. Know what I mean?

Although this level of style may be appropriate for some kinds of writing, such as personal letters and journal writing, it is usually avoided in college writing assignments.

Very formal usage, at the other end of the continuum, is found typically in writing addressed to educated readers, like the writing in many scholarly journals. It is characterized by the use of "learned" words, jargon (professional terminology), standard grammar, long and difficult sentences, third-person pronouns (referring to objects), and, in some instances, a high percentage of passive constructions. Consider, for example, these opening sentences from an article published in a scholarly journal in the field of rhetoric and composition:

> The general ambition of reader-response criticism has been to argue that affective response, so long maligned as a critical "fallacy," is, in fact, a legitimate point of departure in criticism. This redefinition of critical practice, to include a focus on the reader's interpretive activities, sets the reader-response movement apart from formalism, which emphasizes textual autonomy and internal formal unity as critical norms, and from more recent critical movements such as structuralism, semiotics, and deconstruction, which attribute the construction of meaning to the ultimate authority of textual features. [From Nan Johnson, "Reader-Response and the *Pathos* Principle," *Rhetoric Review* 6.2 (Spring 1988): 152.]

This formal style of writing is what some beginning college writers try to model when they write. They want their writing to sound impressive and important, so they try to imitate a style of writing that sounds "academic" and official. When students adopt this style of writing, however, they usually end up sounding pompous, for a couple of reasons. First, they adopt this style for writing situations in which it does not seem appropriate, and second, they often cannot maintain a formal style with consistency. They start by writing at a very formal level, but eventually they lose control and end up shifting styles.

To the reader, these sudden shifts in style are disconcerting. Imagine listening to a soft, melodious piece by Chopin and then suddenly having the music shift to acid rock and then back again to Chopin. The effects of these sudden changes in musical style on the listener are analogous to the effects of sudden stylistic changes in prose style on the reader. Only very seasoned writers can effectively write at a very formal level when the situation warrants such a style.

In college writing, a "middle" style is usually appropriate for most writing situations. In this middle style, it is sometimes acceptable to use contractions (as we often do in this book), but you should usually avoid slang expressions and clichés. Slang lacks precision, and it changes frequently; clichés, or overused expressions, lack vigor and originality. Because slang and clichés are so commonly used in speech, they can easily find their way into your writing. You also want to avoid jargon when you are writing for readers who will not be familiar with your terms; however, if you are writing for readers who *are* familiar with the professional language, it is often effective and desirable to use it.

Perhaps the best advice is to write in a style that is comfortable and honest. All of the sample papers in this book represent a middle level of style.

So at the postdrafting stage of your writing, check your draft to see that the level of usage of your words, as well as the style they produce, is appropriate for the writing situation and consistent throughout your work. The next section on simple, direct words will discuss an important feature of the middle style appropriate for college writing.

Exercises

A. Choose three of the following paragraphs and revise them to make the connotations of words more effective. Be prepared to discuss the reasons for your revisions.

1.   After you have completed the necessary steps in the process of becoming a state officer, the candidate committee makes their evaluations and decides who will compose the next slate of officers. The committee then reports their decisions at the next open meeting. The new state officers must then prepare for an exciting period of maturation and growth. Not everyone gets to be a state officer; however, even if you are not elected, the experience will still be very beneficial to you. (sample 1A)

2.   Rome contains art galleries, ancient ruins, and many other tourist sites, but one particular site which impresses tourists is St.

Peter's Cathedral. As you walk through the archway into the entrance hall of this incredible structure, you immediately feel as if you have entered another age. It looks quite different from anything found in America. The huge spacious rooms and high ceilings seem to engulf you. You walk on marble floors worn by thousands of feet. These floors still give vivid impressions of swirling creamy designs combining ivory white with strings of sparkling gold. While you walk, your eyes are finding bold sculptures and immense altars symbolizing sacrifices and images you cannot begin to understand. (sample 2A)

3.   There it stands, a concrete slab that horrified and shocked the world. The physical aspect of the wall is frightening. The part seen by most tourists is a tall cold gray wall with an ominous guard tower standing behind it. Through the darkly tinted windows of the tower a high powered machine gun is unmistakably seen in a small porthole. The Wall itself looks as if it has a million stories of struggle to tell; its pock marked, graffiti ridden surface is accented by large red signs telling people to keep behind the metal railing. (sample 2E)

4.   Were it not for Don my aspirations would not be as high. Don has dared to dream and dreamed to dare. I too have set goals and work hard to fulfill them. I may not always win but losers are sometimes winners. There are points in my life when I want to have all that Don has, but most of the time I want more. I want to be better than the best. Impossible? No, Don has taught me that all things are not impossible. I strive to prove myself in a field of just one competitor—Don. It is a tough goal but maybe one day I'll be happy just to achieve one half of what my brother has accomplished. Then again—I believe that to be satisfied I must prove myself worthy of his praise. (sample 3C)

5.   A visitor happening to travel down the winding gravel road that leads to Ceralvo, a tiny community nestled on the banks of the Green River, would find only a few houses and a church that holds services once a year. One might think that Ceralvo has always been simply a rural residential area; however, the buildings there today are actually the remains of a thriving city of another era. (sample 3C)

6.   As you can see, I have learned more in school than just subject matter. Education has taught me to want more—to be the best. I have learned the importance of setting goals and working to reach them. And I have accomplished many of these; I have been the best. However, there are always new goals to be set. This summer, for example, I was participating in a program for pre-med students.

There were about thirty-six participants, divided into four groups by math placement scores. I placed in the second group. I was upset at first, and did not know if I could handle not being the best. At the awards banquet at the end of the program, I was presented the math award. I decided that I wanted to be at the top of the class, and through hard work I achieved this goal. I have not stopped yet.
Facing me now is the desire to become a doctor. "The road goes ever on." (sample 3D)

B. Analyze the following passage from Ethel Paquin's "From Creepers to High-tops" to determine its level of language usage (very formal, middle-high/middle/middle-low, or very informal). Identify particular features of its style to support your conclusion.

By the seventies the canvas shoe market had exploded and hundreds of companies world-wide were producing them. Before you knew it, if you wore shoes at all you probably wore sneakers at least part of the day.

No article of personal wear, with the possible exception of jeans, has ever engendered the kind of love and devotion sneakers have. People feel about them the same way they feel about a close friend. They wear them until they are threadbare. They wear them until their soles have departed their bodies and then they tie strings around them and wear them some more.

They've come a long way from King Henry's day, those little rubber-soled devils. They've sneakered their way into every phase of our lives. Babies wear them, octogenarians wear them, as does every age in between. They've been immortalized in pen, and paint, clay and cloth. What would we do without them? [*Lands' End* 267 (June 1990): 64.]

C. Read the first four paragraphs in the overview chapter of this book, and select three examples of figurative words. What comparisons do the figurative words in your examples suggest? How do these comparisons clarify or illuminate the writers' meaning?

Using Simple, Direct Words. Consider these excerpts from the instructions for the federal income tax forms for 1976 and 1977:

The Privacy Act of 1974 provides that each Federal Agency inform individuals, whom it asks to supply information, of the authority for the solicitation of the information and whether disclosure of such information is mandatory; the principal

The Privacy Act of 1974 says that each Federal Agency that asks you for information must tell you the following:

1. Its legal right to ask for the information and whether the law says you must give it.

purpose or purposes for which the information is to be used; the routine uses which may be made of the information; and the effects on the individual of not providing the requested information. This notification applies to the U.S. Individual Income Tax Returns, to declarations of estimated tax, to U.S. Gift Tax returns, and to any other tax return required to be filed by an individual, and to schedules, statements, or other documents related to the returns, and any subsequent inquiries necessary to complete, correct, and process the returns of taxpayers, to determine the correct tax liability and to collect any unpaid tax, interest, or penalty. . . .

The completion of all appropriate items requested by the return forms and related data is mandatory except for the Presidential Election Campaign Fund designation on the U.S. Individual Income Tax Returns, which is voluntary. . . .

Please retain this notification with your tax records and refer to it any time you are requested to furnish additional information.

2. What purpose the agency has in asking for it, and the use to which it will be put.

3. What could happen if you do not give it.

For the Internal Revenue Service, the law covers the following:

1. Tax returns and any papers you file with them.

2. Any questions we need to ask you so we can—

(a) complete, correct, or process your returns,

(b) figure your tax, and

(c) collect tax, interest, or penalties. . . .

You must fill in all parts of the tax form that apply to you. But you do not have to check the boxes for the Presidential Election Campaign Fund. You can skip that if you wish. . . .

Please keep this notice with your records. It may help you if we ask you for other information.

These two pieces of writing, the 1976 original and its 1977 revision, have the same denotation: by law, they must say essentially the same thing. But you have probably found the 1977 version to be much more readable and understandable. Perhaps the most obvious reasons for this increased readability are at the paragraph and sentence levels, as discussed in earlier chapters: relationships have been more clearly signaled, "hidden" verbs have been eliminated, and sentences have been restructured to avoid overtaxing the reader's short-term memory. But the most important revisions may be less obvious, occurring at the level of individual words. Notice the following changes:

1976	**1977**
provides	says
inform	tell
individuals	you
authority	right
solicit	ask
provide	give
effects	what could happen
inquire	ask
complete	fill in
voluntary	you can skip
retain	keep
request	ask
additional	other

To understand the nature of these revisions, it may help to look briefly at the history of our language. The most important date in that history is 1066, when a French duke named William invaded England in what has become known as the Norman Conquest. The inhabitants of England before that invasion were largely of German origin, and they spoke a Germanic language we now call Old English. But William and his conquering forces spoke a Latinate language, an early form of French, and so as he set up a new government over the conquered English, he imposed a new language on the country.

For the next couple of centuries, both languages existed in England: Norman French as the official language of government and business, and the Old English as the everyday language of most common people. Gradually, however, the languages merged into what we now call Middle English, a language that drew its vocabulary from both Germanic and Latinate sources. Soon, it was enriched by even more Latinate words as the Renaissance spread from southern Europe into England, and modern English was born. This new language, essentially the language we speak and write today, thus derives from two major language families and so has the largest vocabulary of any language in the world.

In activities like farming that were largely untouched by either the Norman Conquest or the Renaissance, today's English words remain largely Germanic in their origin. In other activities, like the performing arts, that were heavily influenced by the Latin countries, our words are largely Latinate in origin. John Brunner, in his science fiction novel *The Shockwave Rider*, demonstrates this difference:

This is a basic place, a farm. Listen to it.
Land. House. Barn. Sun. Rain. Snow. Field. Fence. Pond. Corn. Wheat. Hay. Plow. Sow. Reap. Horse. Pig. Cow.

This is an abstract place, a concert hall. Listen to it.
Conductor. Orchestra. Audience. Overture. Concerto. Symphony. Podium. Harmony. Instrument. Oratorio. Variations. Arrangement. Violin. Clarinet. Piccolo. Tympani. Pianoforte. Auditorium (New York: Ballantine Books, 1975, p. 197).

As Brunner points out, you can "listen" to the difference between the two sets of words. The words in the "farm" list sound plainer; the words in the "concert hall" list sound fancier. Those in the first list are of Germanic origin: forms of these words were used by English farmers before and after the Norman Conquest. Those in the second list are Latinate, brought in, as needed, to a society that had no native words for most of the things they describe.

Many concepts, of course, were part of the language of both Old English and Norman French speakers; these include many common nouns, adjectives, adverbs, and (especially) verbs. As a result, Modern English has a very large number of synonyms from Latinate and Germanic sources. Here are some examples:

LATINATE	GERMANIC
converse	talk
frequently	often
attempt	try
require	need
initial	first
alter	change
confident	sure
discover	find

A surprising fact, when you think about it, is that more than nine-hundred years after the Norman Conquest, these two lists of words still carry a class difference. The Latinate words still seem to us fancier and more "educated," just as the French-speaking officials must have seemed in the eleventh and twelfth centuries. The Germanic words still seem to us plainer and less "educated," just as the Old English-speaking peasants must have seemed then. Perhaps as a result of this difference in perception of the two lists of words, the Latinate words tend to find their way into business, governmental, and academic writing. For example, it was perhaps because of a desire to sound "official" that the writer of the 1976 tax instructions used so many Latinate words in that document; in fact, the "1976" word list is made up entirely of Latinate words.

That would not be a problem except for one important fact: writing made up heavily of Latinate words is more difficult to read. The longer, Latinate words slow down reading and lead to less understanding, even for well-educated readers. Germanic words, on the other hand, make writing more readable. Even educated readers find these shorter, plainer words generally more effective. The revised "1977" list is made up entirely of words of Germanic origin.

The reason for the difference in readability does not lie so much in the history of our language as in the personal history of each individual reader. The Germanic synonyms are, in most cases, the ones we all learn first as children, and they are the ones we hear and read most throughout our lives. No matter how much schooling we eventually get, the Germanic words remain more familiar, more easily accessible, to our reading minds. A passage, like the 1977 tax instructions, made up of these simpler words, will be read more easily and will communicate its content more effectively.

So a useful tool for revising the words in your drafts is this: unless you have a good reason otherwise, substitute simpler Germanic words for fancier Latinate words. Note, however, that you don't need to look up word origins to apply this tool. Just substitute words that a child can understand, and your writing will be more readable for adult readers as well.

Notice, however, that the tool carries the qualification "unless you have a good reason otherwise." Many fancier Latinate words are necessary for their denotation: as the "concert hall" list showed, there are plenty of meanings for which no simple, Germanic words exist. Other Latinate words are useful for their *connotation*: the Latinate word *manufacture*, for example, once meant the same thing as the Germanic word *make*, but over the years, *manufacture* has taken on connotations of large-scale, mechanized "making" that give it a place of its own in our language. Sometimes, too, you will want to choose a Latinate word for variety: if you have used *get* several times in a passage, you may want to substitute *obtain* or *secure* or *acquire* for some occurrences of it. Finally, you may want to choose a Latinate word for reasons of courtesy (a Latinate word itself, derived from the word for the king's court): you may sometimes find it more polite, for example, to *inform* than to *tell*. But in general, your writing will be more readable, and thus more effective, if at the postdrafting stage you substitute plainer words for fancier ones.

As an example, here is a draft of Amy's autobiographical essay (sample 3B), written as part of an application for a scholarship:

> Occurrences in one's life can heavily influence the career goals one creates. Negative circumstances can either vastly diminish or greatly intensify one's determination to accomplish those goals. The events of one unfortunate period in my life could have, in fact, kept

me from planning for my future. Fortunately, those events provided the basis for my decision to become a genetic engineer and they have inspired me to strive towards reaching my goal.

My father was diagnosed as having lymphoma, or cancer of the lymph system, in June of 1985. His illness raised many questions and problems not answered or dealt with by hospitals and doctors. Medical professionals could neither determine the reason for the disease, nor provide a cure for it. Chemotherapy treatments slowed the progression of the cancer for a time. However, complications such as an intestinal blockage and pneumonia eventually led to my father's death. I had read many articles pertaining to cancer, specifically lymphoma, and I had noticed increasing numbers of publications dealing with genetic causes of cancer. Through genetic research scientists discovered that genes which were deformed in some way were frequently the origins of various types of cancer. I had previously had an interest in genetics; consequently, I was strongly motivated to use these interests in the future to find solutions for the problems we as a family have faced.

I realize that researching the causes and hopefully the cures for cancer will not be a simple task. Yet nothing foreseen will be able to dissuade me from heeding my inner calling and striving towards this goal. My research may someday save the lives of others who suffer with this dreaded disease—cancer. It is my sincerest desire that I will be able to turn my negative situation into an advancement that will benefit mankind.

Amy is a fluent writer and clear thinker, but the words she chooses sometimes get in the way of conveying her thoughts clearly to her readers. Naturally, in discussing her father's disease and her resulting academic interest, she has to use technical terms like *lymphoma* and *genetics*; these words cause no particular problem. But even in its first and third paragraphs, this draft tends to include "fancy," Latinate words (like *occurrences*) instead of their more familiar synonyms. When such choices are made too often, writing becomes more difficult to read (even for the relatively well-educated members of a scholarship committee) and portrays the writer as "stuffy" or "pedantic."

At the postdrafting stage, Amy made several word substitutions, such as the following in the first paragraph alone:

DRAFTING	POSTDRAFTING
occurrences	events
vastly	greatly
diminish	reduce

intensify	increase
accomplish	achieve
unfortunate	unhappy
fortunately	luckily

As a result of such revisions, in the direction of simpler language, Amy's essay became much more successful, as this new version of her last sentences should show. The passage can still, of course, be improved (Can you suggest some ways?), but it is certainly more effective than the last paragraph of the draft:

> I realize that finding the causes and hopefully the cures for cancer will be difficult, if not impossible. Yet nothing that I am aware of will keep me from heeding my inner calling and trying to reach this goal. My research may someday save the lives of others who suffer with the dreaded disease called cancer. It is my deepest desire that I will be able to turn my bad situations into a finding that will help mankind.

Exercise

Choose three of the following paragraphs from the sample papers. Revise them to increase readability, paying particular attention to the possibility of substituting simpler synonyms.

1. As I sat in the surgery waiting room in my back-less hospital gown, I began to feel the Valium that they administered to me take effect. Was this meant to reduce my pain? If so—physical or emotional? Would this drug mend my broken heart and seize my despair? In scrutinizing the room, I noticed the others; all of them young and chatting as if it were no big deal. Were they not feeling what I was feeling? I don't think they were, I cried. I was at the lowest level of humiliation. I thought "I'm going to murder my child that I prayed for and was blessed with." Should there be no regard for the ruthlessness of this brutal execution? Would there be no consequences of remorse? *Yes*, there would be. (sample 4A)

2. My first point is concerning fairness. Is it fair that coed dorms and Haggin Hall have endless visiting hours while Blanding Tower has an interrogation unit sitting at the front desk? Why is no I.D. needed when entering Kirwan Tower yet is needed in Blanding Tower? Why are residents of Blanding treated differently than the

rest of campus? Blanding Tower is the strictest dorm on campus. Aren't the freshman girls mature enough to decide when visitors are appropriate and when visitors are not? I think we deserve more privileges and more credit than we are receiving. (sample 5A)

3.   University of Kentucky residence hall dwellers sign a form of lease before they are granted University housing. This is similar to the lease on an apartment building, yet in an apartment building a person's guests are not asked to leave at a certain time. It seems only fair that residence hall dwellers be afforded this same privilege. (sample 5B)

4.   The greatest injustice to this curfew, however, is the punishment of innocent people. There are legitimate reasons for being at Miller Park after midnight. Two reasons, playing horseshoes and tennis, have become a tradition for a certain group of citizens who work at one of the local factories. With a work schedule of 7:00 P.M.–11 P.M., these people barely get to the park by 11:30, thus eliminating their time for harmless entertainment. (sample 5C)

5.   Since 1980, the press have given all-terrain vehicles, ATVs, a bad name. To some extent this bad name is deserved. All too often ATVs are sold, taken home, ridden, and then wrecked. As sales and popularity grew, so did accidents, injury, and the concern over the ATV safety issue. The question frequently arises of who is to blame. (sample 5D)

6.   When Pink Floyd first announced their coming visit to Lexington, fans dashed out to buy tickets and the concert was soon sold out. However, this was a new Pink Floyd, one consisting of just three members, David Gilmour, Nick Mason, and Richard Wright. Roger Waters, the largest force behind the group, had quit. Many speculated about whether or not Pink Floyd would be the same without Waters—they were, in fact, superb. Although Waters contributed a lot to Pink Floyd, he had gotten too big for his pants. Pink Floyd indeed adjusted well to this loss. (sample 6C)

7.   Although the songs were done extremely well, the most memorable aspect of the concert was the light show and special effects. Pink Floyd certainly took advantage of modern technology and put it to work in a truly awesome laser display. During nearly each song of the concert lasers were fired from all directions and reflected off mirrors, creating a virtual "laser web" over the audience.

The web did not remain the same, however, but changed in shape quite frequently. (sample 6D)

8.   Although Douglas and Close are considered co-stars, Close steals the show with her transition from previous good-girl parts to the psychotic villainess that the audience comes to hate. Faced with a very different role, she portrays Alex with a passion that is evident on the screen. She combines violent gestures with an eerie calmness that really haunts the audience. Because Alex is so complex, Close must, in a sense, play two characters. At times Alex appears vulnerable and fragile. Yet, for the most part she is the psycho, obsessed with Gallagher and willing to do anything to get him. Close is not alone, however, in the portrayal of the opposite sides of Alex. Lyne, director, works with the costumers to make the side of Alex being portrayed obvious. For example, when she is the invincible psycho, she has blood-red fingernails, an untamed curly mane, and a rough sallow complexion. In contrast, the unguarded vulnerable Alex dresses perfectly and has a well-groomed hairstyle and flawless makeup. (sample 6B)

9.   It is my opinion that the correct way to balance the budget is to cut spending as much as necessary and not to raise taxes. Congress and your editors want to raise taxes, which will result in an increase of unemployment and a decrease of total revenues. Any time Congress raises taxes, they always manage to increase spending. Until Congress is serious about cutting the budget both in defense and non-defense spending, we will continue to have this deficit problem. (sample 5F)

10.   Hopefully, your readers are intelligent enough to realize the consequences of introducing alcohol into the county. They should not be deceived into believing that legal alcohol sales are necessary in order to bring growth and prosperity to the county. I suggest that the next time you consider such a controversial issue, you take a look at the entire picture, rather than see only what you want to see. (sample 5G)

Checking Readability: The Fog Index. One way to measure, roughly, the readability of your drafts is the Gunning-Mueller "fog index," a formula for computing the approximate number of years of education needed to read a piece of writing. To compute the fog index of a draft

1. Compute the average sentence length, in words.

2. Compute the percentage (as an integer from 0 to 100) of "big" words (words of three or more syllables, not counting capitalized words, easy compounds, and three-syllable verbs ending in -es or -ed).

3. Add these two figures together and multiply the total by 0.4.

As an example, the average sentence length of the last paragraphs of Amy's draft, shown above, is 19 words. She uses 8 "big" words out of a total of 75 words, for a percentage of 11. Her fog index is thus 30 times 0.4, or 12. This is a bit high; even though Amy's intended readers will have had more than twelve years of education, there is no point in building unnecessary barriers to readability. The *Wall Street Journal*, for example, claims a Gunning-Mueller fog index of 11.

Amy's revised paragraph still has an average sentence length of 19, but she has lowered her "big"-word percentage to 6, giving the passage a fog index of 10. Though not all of her changes in the directions of plainer words may be equally effective (for example, *finding*, in the last sentence, may not be as good a choice as *discovery*), she is clearly moving in the right direction as a writer.

Exercises

A. Compute the fog indexes of the excerpts from the 1976 and 1977 tax instructions.

B. Choose one of the sample papers you find fairly hard to read and one you find fairly easy to read. Compute the fog indexes of a paragraph or two from each. Be prepared to discuss your results.

C. Compute the fog index of one of your drafts. Compare it with a revision.

D. Compute the fog index of a passage from this textbook. Find ways to improve the readability of the passage you choose.

Checking Readability: The Cloze Test. A more accurate, if somewhat more cumbersome, way to evaluate the readability of your draft is to use a "cloze test." This test, developed by Wilson L. Taylor, involves deleting certain words from a piece of writing and asking readers to "guess" what the missing words are. The percentage of correct guesses can be used as a measure of the readability of the writing.

To run a cloze test on a draft, count back a hundred words or so from the end (to give your readers a "running start") and underline every fifth word. (This number doesn't matter; you can underline every sixth, or seventh, or tenth word as long as you do so consistently.) Then recopy the passage, replacing the underlined words with numbered blanks; make all the blanks the same length to keep from giving away the length of the word. Now, fold the original passage under, and give your draft and the recopied ending to a reader. That person should read your draft down to the fold, then read the recopied ending, listing his or her guesses for the missing words.

When you get the list back from the reader, compare it with the words you actually used in the draft, and calculate the percentage of "hits," words guessed *exactly* right. (Better still, find *three* readers and score a hit when at least two guess a word correctly.) In general, consider your draft fairly readable if you get 60 percent hits; if the percentage drops much below 60, you may want to give special attention to revising the draft.

The cloze test works because all readers, all the time, make subconscious predictions about upcoming words. If these expectations are usually fulfilled, the reading comes easily; if not, the passage is difficult and seems to lack "flow." Readers, then, are always making hits and misses. The cloze test, by sampling certain words for explicit prediction, simply makes us aware of that fact.

More important, however, than your percentage score is what the cloze test can teach you about the specific words you have used in your draft. Most hits signal a well-chosen word; they let you know that you have fulfilled the reader's expectation and thus made that segment of your draft easier to read. For example, consider the following passage from a student's cloze test:

People who live in the past lose the present because _____ are unable to . . .

All three readers of that student's cloze test correctly guessed the word *they*. The writer therefore knew that she had constructed a readable sentence in which the subject of the main clause was repeated, in pronoun form, as the subject of a dependent clause.

Some hits, however, can be negative:

You can't please _____ of the people all of the time.

This writer got a hit from all three of his readers, but largely because he had used a cliché, a phrase that, because of its extreme familiarity, has lost much of its power to communicate.

Misses are usually much more useful than hits for the writer. Most misses signal places where the draft might be revised to better fulfill readers' expectations. For example, one student had the following passage in her draft:

> The majority of voters can't participate because candidates won't let them. This will continue to alienate _____ until politicians show . . .

Did you guess *voters* or *people*, perhaps? The writer's word was *us*; because it shifted the subject from third person to first person, none of her readers was able to guess it, and she realized that she needed to revise the word. Another student, after reporting on the seriousness of an energy crisis, began her conclusion as follows:

> The crisis will be _____ worse in years to come, so we need to . . .

Most readers guessed *even*. The writer was able to use this word, in her final product, as a better transition than her original word, *much*.

Misses also reveal other kinds of weaknesses in word choice. One student's draft included these sentences:

> America's economic situation is partly caused by people still believing in the myth of unlimited natural resources that we have had in the past instead of facing the reality of present shortages. These _____ show how we must focus on the present if we wish to remain in control of ourselves.

The writer had written *things*; her readers guessed *shortages*, *problems*, and *examples*—all more precise terms. Another student wrote, in a draft,

> A warm glow is felt by those who _____ the challenge of Sky-Bridge.

He had written *completed*; his classmates guessed *accepted* and *survived*. In subsequent discussion, they pointed out that in English, a challenge can be accepted, or survived, or met, but not really "completed."

Occasionally, of course, misses are unavoidable or even desirable, as when a piece of brand-new information happens to fall at a blank, or when the writer provides a pleasantly unexpected word. But such misses are rare; most suggest room for improvement.

Exercises

A. Choose a sample paper from this book that you find fairly hard to read and one you find fairly easy to read. Conduct cloze tests on both. Be prepared to discuss the results and to suggest revisions that would increase the cloze score.

B. Conduct a cloze test on a passage from this book. Suggest revisions that would increase its readability.

C. Exchange drafts of a paper with another student, and conduct a cloze test, following the procedure described in the previous section. Compare your word selections with those of the writer, and after calculating the number of "hits" and "misses," suggest possible revisions to improve the paper's readability.

Assignment 6: Review

Assignment: Write a review, for a newspaper, of a book, theatrical performance, film, or concert.

To write an effective review, you must evaluate your subject, and you must persuade your reader that your evaluation is fair. At the predrafting stage, consider what criteria you are using in your evaluation and how you can gain your reader's trust. Think about what *you* like when you read a book, see a movie, or attend a theatrical performance or concert.

If you have not read many reviews, one of the best ways to prepare to write one is to read two or three, and ask yourself what is common in each of the reviews you read. What do readers expect in a review?

Sample Papers

Sample 6A (Alan)

A Coast Guard helicopter swoops down on a small single-engine plane piloted by Carlos Sanchez, notorious Central American cocaine kingpin and wanted murderer. A handsome, tuxedo-clad man climbs down a steel cable dangling from the helicopter, ties the cable around the plane's tail, and signals to another man, similarly attired above. The chopper pilot pulls up quickly, stalling the plane's engine and leaving it hanging nose downward, while the two tuxedoed men parachute down into the crowd of wedding guests. One man is Felix Lighter, CIA agent and bridegroom, and the other is "Bond, James Bond," British Secret Service Agent 007 and best man.

These exciting scenes in the pre-credit introduction, a trademark of the James Bond films, are just a preview of the action-packed adventure to follow in the new movie, *License to Kill*. Although this already sounds like the typical 007 epic, it is, apart from some superficial ingredients, not your typical James Bond movie.

Yes, Bond *is* back, but this is not the same Bond we have gotten to know over the years. We see this immediately in the opening shot of *License to Kill*, when 007 walks into the familiar camera shutter. This Bond is different, even in his walk. Timothy Dalton, who debuted as Bond in the somewhat disappointing *The Living Daylights* (1987), portrays a less promiscuous, but a more serious and concerned Bond. He may not be as suave as Sean Connery or as flippant and campy as Roger Moore, but he is much more likable. He seems more like a real person.

The content of this movie also makes several departures from previous films in the James Bond series. Although many elements we have seen in previous films and have come to expect are present (such as the opening pre-credit sequence, fancy gadgets of Q, gorgeous women seducing or seduced by Bond, powerful villains, and a climax in which some huge complex blows up), the several differences stand out.

The villain of the story is no longer a maniacal cartoon character bent on world domination. He is a real-life modern villain who *is* dominating part of the world and who only wants to expand his dominion with new franchises which he sells for 100 million dollars each. What makes this story most frightening is that several Carlos Sanchezes do exist. This one, captured in the first scene, subsequently escapes and exacts his revenge on Lighter by murdering his bride and maiming the agent.

The hero of this story is no longer a cartoon character either. Bond has some real-life motivation: vengeance. When he finds out what has happened to his friend, he uses all of his resources to single-mindedly pursue Sanchez in order to eliminate him. His obsession causes him to lose sight of his duties and abandon his mission. Consequently, he is forced to resign his commission, he gets his license to kill revoked, and he ends up being captured by his own people. By some twist of fate, he manages to turn this to his advantage.

Due to the nature of the story, *License to Kill* is one of the most intense of the eighteen James Bond films with the most graphic, disgusting, disturbing violence of any of its predecessors. Too many people are killed in too many different, horrible ways by the sadistic Sanchez. The intensity left my heart pounding and my jaws aching from gnashing my teeth.

Thankfully, however, two characters provide some comic relief. The character Q, creator of all of 007's amazing gadgets, who usually makes only a brief appearance in the films, takes on an expanded role as Bond's "uncle." Wayne Newton, in his acting debut as Professor Joe, also gives us a chance to relax and laugh. Through him, the film takes the opportunity to poke fun at television evangelists.

Five different actors have portrayed James Bond in one of the most enduring series in film history (eighteen installments over a period of twenty-seven years). Dalton may or may not turn out to be the best Bond, but *License to Kill* is not only one of the best James Bond movies, it is a good movie in general. Because it has an interesting plot, characters you can relate to, nonstop action that keeps your attention, and suspense, not a single point in the film drags. It is a movie not only for the avid Bond fan, but for a larger audience. I highly recommend this movie to anyone, provided they can stomach the violence.

Sample 6B (John)

Fatal Attraction, a dynamic film directed by Adrian Lyne, makes use of a familiar plot. Michael Douglas plays Dan Gallagher, a successful lawyer, happily married, with a six-year-old daughter. Alex, an attractive editor played by Glenn Close, seduces Gallagher while his family is away. The audience begins to see a change in the traditional plot as they realize Alex's insanity. When Gallagher tries to leave her apartment, Alex slashes her wrists in an attempt to keep him there. After he leaves, she resorts to terrorizing his family trying to get him back.

The chemistry between Close and Douglas overwhelms the viewer and contributes a great deal to the success of the movie. Even from their first casual meeting at a business party, it is evident that they will get together. At their second meeting, Gallagher, happily married with no indications of problems, risks everything just to be with her. In a way, this is shocking to the viewer. His life is perfect— his job is going well, he loves his wife and daughter, and they adore him. Yet the audience expects Alex and Gallagher to get together. There is an attraction between them, depicted excellently by Close and Douglas. The speech and eye contact between them bring this attraction to life on the screen.

Although Douglas and Close are considered co-stars, Close steals the show with her transition from previous good-girl parts to the psychotic villainess that the audience comes to hate. Faced with a very different role, she portrays Alex with a passion that is evident on the screen. She combines violent gestures with an eerie calmness that really haunts the audience. Because Alex is so complex, Close must, in a sense, play two characters. At times Alex appears vulnerable and fragile. Yet, for the most part she is the psycho, obsessed with Gallagher and willing to do anything to get him. Close is not alone, however, in the portrayal of the opposite sides of Alex. Lyne, director, works with the costumers to make the side of Alex being portrayed obvious. For example, when she is the invincible psycho, she has blood-red fingernails, an untamed curly mane, and a rough sallow complexion. In contrast, the unguarded vulnerable Alex dresses perfectly and has a well-groomed hairstyle and flawless makeup.

Not only does Close perform well, but Anne Archer also does an outstanding job with the supporting role of Douglas's wife. She is very convincing as she tries to be strong and protect her family. At one point she even threatens to kill Alex if she comes near her family. However, Alex continues to terrorize the family, and the strength and rationality of the wife subside. Alex's lunatic antics cause her to go into hysterics. Eventually, she realizes that to protect her family she must be strong and remain calm, and she regains her strength.

Those expecting a superb performance by Douglas will probably be disappointed. His role, more or less, is to initiate the action. The female roles are so strong that his character fades into the background. He becomes a pawn, reacting only to their actions.

Clearly, for an easy-to-follow thriller, *Fatal Attraction* is very thought-provoking. Lyne has used subtle symbols that only the alert audience will discover. These symbols enhance the ending and make it even more climactic and unpredictable. Still the audience tries to guess the ending. They are moved to talk to Alex as their hatred for her grows and to Gallagher as he makes mistakes that lead to an unpredictable ending. The audience also ponders the origin of Alex's insanity and the motivation of Gallagher to have the affair.

This movie shows dramatically the ill effects of an extramarital affair. The attraction between Alex and Gallagher does become fatal. All parties involved experience grief as a result of the fling. The movie points out the seriousness of having affairs and tries to discourage viewers from participating in them. In my opinion, the movie is a great choice for two hours of suspense and action.

Sample 6C (Constance)

A laser piercing the darkness, a video about German warfare, a humongous detailed pig floating above you, all elements of surprise used to shock a typical audience? Yes—if you are at a Pink Floyd concert.

What first began as a song played in the darkness soon evolved into a show designed to play with your mind. Pink Floyd on its first concert tour in seven years gave audiences what they were looking for, a show that seemed to combine sound with sight and to please all senses. For instance when they performed "Money" they gave the audience a video showing gold bars, coins, and Wall Street scenes, all of which reinforced the meaning behind the song.

When Pink Floyd first announced their coming visit to Lexington, fans dashed out to buy tickets and the concert was soon sold out. However, this was a new Pink Floyd, one consisting of just three members, David Gilmour, Nick Mason, and Richard Wright. Roger Waters, the largest force behind the group, had quit. Many speculated about whether or not Pink Floyd would be the same without Waters—they were, in fact, superb. Although Waters contributed a lot to Pink Floyd, he had gotten too big for his pants. Pink Floyd indeed adjusted well to this loss.

Learning to Fly is their first album without Waters and also the theme of the concert. Both album and concert are outstanding. Many of the songs performed during the concert were instrumental and allowed one's imagination to speculate about the meaning behind the song. Pink Floyd took advantage of this factor and focused our minds on what Pink Floyd wanted us to feel and took our breath away. At one point when Pink Floyd came back from a break they stunned the audience with a larger-than-life pig that was very real and seemed to loom above everyone. Who would have even thought of a flying pig as a special effect but Pink Floyd did and it was well worth it. Audiences were shocked! There were other effects as well, fireworks, symbolic videos, and a laser show that created different designs by using the audience as a background. This combination was very pleasing.

This was truly a psychedelic concert. There were many videos that forced the mind's eye to participate. As "Learning to Fly" was played in the background, the video took us on a journey into a young man's dreams about flight. The young man kept dreaming about being on a stretcher that rolled down a hall and eventually took flight. When the young man awoke his nightmare came true—he was flying and the audience, as well, along with him. The song itself came to an end in the background. The audience woke up. It was an unforgettable concert and the best I have ever been to. A long dry spell passed between Pink Floyd tours and many wondered what had become of them. Now they are back, I hope, for good.

Sample 6D (Mike)

There are many different ways to judge a rock and roll concert. You can look at it from a strictly musical standpoint, or you can also take into consideration the "stage presence," or visual quality, of the musician(s). You also may wish to take the volume of the music and the light show, if there even is one, into account when reviewing a concert.

The Pink Floyd show excelled in nearly all aspects. The only big drawback of the concert was the absence of Roger Waters, who sang nearly all of Pink Floyd's early songs. He wasn't there simply because he isn't a member of the band anymore. David Gilmour, the lead guitarist and now vocalist, did, however, do a commendable job of singing Waters's visual songs. Richard Wright and Nick Mason, the other members of Pink Floyd, were also there along with several other non-Floyd musicians that are touring with them this time.

Since all of the regular instrumentalists were present, the music was superb. The sound was nearly identical to Pink Floyd's recorded music, unlike some concerts in which the music sounds nothing like the albums. Pink Floyd used a quadrophonic speaker system, which was a set of four speakers, one on each side of Rupp [Arena], at this show that greatly enhanced both the volume of the music and stereo-type of music Pink Floyd specializes in. The vocals, of course, slightly lacked because the usual singer was not there.

Although the songs were done extremely well, the most memorable aspect of the concert was the light show and special effects. Pink Floyd certainly took advantage of modern technology and put it to work in a truly awesome laser display. During nearly each song of the concert lasers were fired from all directions and reflected off mirrors, creating a virtual "laser web" over the audience. The web did not remain the same, however, but changed in shape quite frequently.

Behind the stage hung a screen that looked like a gigantic trampoline mat. The screen displayed intricate laser designs that somehow seemed to fit the mood of each song, but occasionally showed real video footage. The only time actual film was played on the screen was when Floyd played songs from their new album, *Learning to Fly.*

Once during the second half of the show when they were playing songs from their *Animals* LP a giant inflatable pig was sent out over the audience by cables. This pig, which must have cost literally thousands of dollars to make, was about 15 feet tall and 30 feet long with glowing red eyes. It had been made perfectly, proportionally correct with some dark patches that made it look like it had been rolling around in its sty. The best part of the "pig experience" was that all of a sudden there was a huge pig standing beside the stage; it was bizarre how something that large could simply come out of nowhere.

It was worth it just to go see the pig; the music and light show were also quite impressive. Pink Floyd concerts have always been very extravagant, but this one was a little more so because this is, more than likely, their final tour. All and all it was a great show that you really should try to see, if you get the chance.

Sample 6E (Christina)

25 Years with The Who

Last night was one 25th anniversary party that many won't soon forget. It was the anniversary of Pete Townshend, Roger Daltrey, and John Entwistle, also known as "The Who," and to celebrate, they put on a three-and-a-half-hour show to a sold out crowd at Sullivan Stadium.

Boston was just one of the stops on The Who's 25-city tour to celebrate 25 years of rocking and rolling together, and they were welcomed back after a 7-year absence from the road with a roaring crowd in the pouring rain to see The Who perform.

The rain did delay the concert for a half an hour, but all the waiting was worth it. The Who opened the show with a 45-minute set of all songs from "Tommy," the rock opera that made them famous, closing this set with the hit "Pinball Wizard." Next Pete Townshend, with acoustic guitar in hand, performed some of his own solo hits, especially ones from his new album "Iron Man," while the rest of the band took a breather.

The Who played just about all of their hits, but what added a nice touch to the show was a mixed bag of Who tunes that aren't as popular and some cover tunes including a bluesy version of Bo Diddley's "I'm a Man." For being away from the road for 7 years, The Who played and sounded as if they have been doing this every day.

To replace drummer Keith Moon, who died in 1978, the band added 12 musicians including a horn section, backup singers, a drummer and percussionist, a keyboardist, and a guitarist to play electric guitar while Townshend used mostly acoustic.

The Who has a huge stage setup that featured 2 diamond vision screens on either side of the stage. The screens gave everyone at the show a good view of the band, even the fans in the rafters could see what was going on on stage. Three banners on each side of the stage kept rolling down and changing pictures to go with the theme of the songs the group sang, and the final pictures spelled out "The Who."

The band encored twice, and their final song was their cover of "Summertime Blues." Then they finally left the stage, leaving their fans screaming for more, even as the stadium lights went on.

The Who say that this is their final tour. There was no new album to go with the tour; it was only to celebrate their anniversary. But The Who proved to all of us that after 25 years, they can still rock and roll with the best of them.

Discussion Questions

1. What criteria have each of these writers used to evaluate their subjects? How clearly do they establish these criteria for their readers?

2. Which of the two reviews of the same rock concert is more interesting or useful to you? What has the writer of that review done to be interesting and useful?

CHAPTER SEVEN

The Process
of Handling Mechanics

Mechanics is a word used for the "smallest" features of a piece of writing, features that occur within and between individual words. These features include spelling, punctuation, capitalization, abbreviations, and the use of numbers. Mechanics also includes matters of *format,* the physical layout of a piece of writing on a page.

In some ways, mechanics is the least important feature of written language. Spoken language, after all, does without mechanical features entirely (making up for them, admittedly, with certain vocal features). Even in written language, standardized mechanics is a relatively recent development. Centuries of writers did centuries of good, effective work with no concern whatever for consistent spelling, capitalization, or punctuation.

But in another way, mechanics is the most important feature of writing. Because spelling, punctuation, and other mechanical features *have* become largely standardized, readers tend to have very strong expectations about them. When these expectations do not get met—when *friend*, for example, is spelled *freind,* or when a comma is used to join two sentences without a conjunction, then readers tend to get annoyed and to discredit the piece of writing.

Mechanics is thus like the finish on a piece of furniture. A good coat of varnish cannot make up for bad wood or woodworking underneath; neither can successful mechanics make up for unsuccessful content or organization or paragraphs or sentences or words. But a bad coat of varnish can keep a well-crafted piece of furniture from being bought, and unsuccessful mechanics can keep an otherwise successful piece of writing from reaching its reader.

This chapter tells you how to use mechanics more successfully in your writing, at all three stages of the writing process.

Predrafting: Almost Ignoring Mechanics

At the predrafting stage, the best thing you can do about mechanical concerns is to ignore them—almost. Because any writing you do at this stage is generally for *your* eyes only, whether it's spelled or punctuated correctly usually doesn't matter. So with a few exceptions, don't even think about mechanics at this stage. The exceptions:

1. As you gather information for the *content* of your writing, be careful to record accurately the spelling of all proper names. For example, if you are interviewing a Mr. Johnson, make sure, at that time, to confirm that his name is spelled *J-o-h-n-s-o-n*, not *Jonson* or *Johnston*. It may be difficult to find out at the drafting or postdrafting stage.

2. If the information you are collecting is from a printed source, and if there is any possibility that you may want to quote it directly, make sure that you record it *exactly*, including the spelling (or even the misspelling) of each word, and including all punctuation marks. (If you are quoting material that includes an error, you should use the Latin word *sic*, explained later in this chapter.) Remember also to record the necessary bibliographical information so that you don't waste time later searching for the correct title of your source, its author, page numbers, and the like. Being careful about certain details only makes good sense.

3. If your predrafting work is going to be seen by someone else, then you may have to pay more attention to mechanics than you would otherwise. A teacher or fellow student, for example, may be reading your notes or outline for the purpose of helping you with your writing process; in such a case, that reader may find it easier to comment on your content or organization if sloppy mechanics don't get in the way.

Drafting: Using Mechanics

Even at the drafting stage, you needn't worry much about mechanics. In fact, overconcern for mechanics at this stage can be harmful to the writing process and the resulting written product, for at least three reasons.

First, excessive attention to such features as spelling and punctuation can interfere with the business of getting words and sentences written. As discussed in the introduction, such attention pits your internal editor against your internal writer and keeps either from doing its work effectively. The drafting stage becomes slow and tedious, and you can easily lose sight of your overall situation, content, and organization.

Second, a premature concern for mechanics can trick you into thinking the writing process is over before it really is. If, during the drafting stage, you invest a lot of time in making sure your spelling, punctuation, and other mechanical features are correct, you may not be as willing as you should be to revise your work at the postdrafting stage. Because the piece of writing looks too neat to be a "rough draft," you might be fooled into thinking it is a finished piece of work.

Third, if you *do* overcome this problem, and *are* willing to make real revisions at the postdrafting stage, then words and punctuation marks are bound to change. As they change, any time you've spent worrying about spelling and punctuation at the drafting stage has been wasted.

Of course, all this does not mean that you should be deliberately careless with mechanics while you draft. Even if you consider yourself a "bad" speller or punctuator, you already know how to spell most words and punctuate most sentences. So when correct mechanics comes fairly automatically to you, of course you should go ahead and use it correctly: there is no point in making unnecessary work for yourself later. And when you are copying proper names or direct quotations from your notes, take time to get them correct. But when correct spelling or punctuation doesn't come automatically, don't stop to worry about it. If you don't know the correct spelling of a word, just write it the way it first occurs to you, and keep going. (If you are afraid that you might forget to correct it later, draw a circle around it to remind you.) If you aren't sure about a punctuation mark, just draw a dash—or anything—and keep going.

In short, give yourself permission to be wrong at the drafting stage. You will have time later to be right.

Postdrafting: Checking Mechanics

Checking the mechanics of your piece of writing, another aspect of Grice's "manner" of expression, is what you do at the end of the writing process. Now is the time to look closely at your spelling, punctuation, use of apostrophes and hyphens, and other mechanics like abbreviations, capitalizations, and numbers. If you have approached your writing systematically, as we hope you have, you probably already know the kinds of mechanical errors that give you the most trouble. If so, you may want to read selectively, concentrating on those parts that will be most helpful to you as a writer.

SPELLING

If, like many people, you have never been a very good speller, it is not your fault. As an English speaker, you have inherited what is probably the world's most difficult language to spell. Speakers of Japanese or Spanish or Russian have much less trouble spelling: their languages have a much more direct correspondence between a word's spelling and its pronunciation. English lacks this degree of correspondence.

People learning English as a second language have to struggle, for example, with the six different pronunciations of *ough* in *bough, bought, cough, tough, though*, and *through*. And although most native speakers soon conquer *that* problem, many never master the opposite problem of words pronounced the same but spelled differently, such as *stationary* and *stationery*, *compliment* and *complement*, or *its* and *it's*.

The difficulties of spelling English result from several historical phenomena. One is the fact that English takes most of its words from two major language families—Germanic and Italic—each with its own pronunciation and spelling practices. Another is the sometimes extreme changes that have occurred in English pronunciation without corresponding changes in spelling: the spelling of *knight*, for example, made sense when the word was pronounced "kuh-nig-t" in the medieval period, but ceased to make sense when the pronunciation shifted to "nite." A third reason for the odd spelling of English is the rather confused and "sloppy" way English spellings got regularized just a few hundred years ago, when a revolution in printing technology led to different printers spelling similar words in very different ways. Finally, English spelling is difficult because nobody is really making the "rules"; spelling, like much else, is a matter of conventions and choices.

Conventions and Choices. The idea of "choices" in spelling may seem strange to you. You may have been taught, all your life, that any word has only one correct spelling. But a great many words can be spelled more than one way; in fact, a whole book has been written just listing the alternative spellings in the five leading American dictionaries (Emery, Donald W. *Variant Spellings in Modern American Dictionaries*. Rev. ed. Urbana, IL: National Council of Teachers of English, 1973). Admittedly, many of these words are relatively unusual borrowings from languages that do not share our alphabet; for example, the five dictionaries list nine different English spellings for the Arabic word sometimes spelled *genie*. But there are other, more common, words about which writers have always disagreed and will continue to do so: *kidnapped* and *kidnaped*, for instance, both have their adherents, and the dictionaries reflect this difference.

Realize, of course, that by far, most English words have only one conventional spelling, and you should use it. But be open-minded to the fact that many words give you choices. To be safe and consistent in making those choices, pick a reputable dictionary (one of those listed in Chapter Six) and use the first spelling given for any questionable word. Remember, of course, that such decisions are best made at the postdrafting stage, not as interruptions during drafting.

"Rules." Because English spelling is so irregular, there are not many rules that govern it. But four rules have proved helpful to many writers. If you have problems spelling the words covered by any or all of these rules, then memorizing the appropriate rules may be worthwhile for you. At first, you will want to save these rules for the postdrafting stage of your writing process; gradually, they will become automatic for you and help you spell more words correctly as you draft.

Rule 1: "*I* before *E*" Rule

This rule is usually stated as a poem:

I before *e*, except after *c*,
Or when sounded like *a*, as in *neighbor* or *weigh*.

This rule, which covers almost all *ie* and *ei* words in English, simply says that the *i* usually comes first, except when the combination follows a *c* or has a "long *a*" sound. Common exceptions include

ancient	conscience	either
financier	foreign	height
leisure	neither	science
seize	species	their
	weird	

Rule 2: "Silent *E*" Rule

Drop "silent *e*" before suffixes beginning with a vowel.

Thus *have* becomes *having, prove* becomes *provable,* and *sincere* becomes *sincerity.*

The largest group of exceptions are words in which the silent *e* is preceded by a *c* or *g*. In such words, the *e* must be retained before suffixes beginning with *a, o,* or *u* to keep the *c* or *g* "soft." Thus *replace* becomes *replaceable,* and *courage* becomes *courageous.*

Also note that an *e* is considered "silent" only when it follows a consonant, so keep the final *e* in words like *agree,* even when adding a suffix like *-able.*

Rule 3: "*Y* to *I*" Rule

When a word ends in *y* preceded by a consonant, change the *y* to *i* before adding a suffix.

Thus *marry* becomes *married,* and *happy* becomes *happiness.*

The major exception is the suffix *-ing*. When adding it, don't change a *y* to *i*; the English language resists having two *i*'s together. *Hurry* becomes *hurrying.*

Rule 4: Double Consonant Rule

This rule is the most complicated of the four, but perhaps the most helpful:

When a word ends in one vowel followed by one consonant,

and

when the accent is on the final syllable,

and

when the suffix begins with a vowel,

then

double the final consonant before adding the suffix.

Thus, *stop* becomes *stopping*, and *occur* becomes *occurred*. *Eat*, however, becomes *eating* (there are two vowels before the final consonant); *edit* becomes *editor* (the accent is not on the final syllable); and *commit* becomes *commitment* (the suffix begins with a consonant).

Be careful to recognize that *w* and *y* often act as vowels at the ends of words and thus don't double in words like *playing* and *knowable*. Also note that the consonant *x* is not doubled, so *fix* becomes *fixing*.

Exercise

Use the preceding rules to find and correct any spelling errors in the following sentences from sample papers.

1.   Each student is allowed only five referal slips per day, so make sure that you choose your jobs carefully. (sample 1B)

2.   Negative situations can either greatly reduce or highly increase one's will to acheive those goals. (sample 3B)

3.   One with the ability to jump over his fence, the other with the clumsyness to trip. (sample 3C)

4.   In the middle of my fourth grade year, my parents decided that the education I was receiving was not adequate. (sample 3D)

5.   Rome contains art gallerys, ancient ruins, and many other tourist sites, but one particular site which impresses tourists is St. Peter's Cathedral. (sample 2A)

6.   The Berlin Wall was built about three decades ago, separateing East and West Berlin. (sample 2E)

7.   Although my son, Josh, and I have experienced some trying times, I have never regreted having him. (sample 4A)

8.   It was an unforgettable concert and the best I have ever been to. (sample 6A)

9.   The Pink Floyd show of Sunday, November 8, 1987, exceled in nearly all aspects. (sample 6B)

10.   They should not be decieved into believing that legal alcohol sales are necessary in order to bring growth and prosperity to the county. (sample 5G)

Tools. Although these four rules are very useful to many writers, they clearly don't solve all, or even most, spelling problems. For the remaining problems, the following postdrafting tools may help:

Tool 1: Reading Backward

Many so-called spelling errors are really only proofreading errors; they result from a failure to recognize what may have just been typing mistakes or "slips of the pen." We often fail to recognize such misspelled words because we are focusing our attention on what our drafts say, not on how individual words are spelled.

To overcome this tendency, many professional proofreaders read pages backward, starting with the last word on each page and reading to the top. If you force yourself to do so, you will find yourself looking at each word *as a word*, not as part of a larger meaning, and you will be much more likely to catch spelling mistakes.

Tool 2: Tallying Problems

As you proofread your draft, look up each word that you have any doubt about, and (this is important) place a pencil mark beside it in the margin of your dictionary. These marks will help you find a word when you look it up again (and you *will* look it up again). But more important, they will give you a running tally of the words you have trouble spelling, and such a tally—because it is personalized for you—will be far more useful than any list of "problem words" that this book could provide.

Use the tally by setting yourself a limit: three marks, perhaps, or five. When you reach the limit, you will know that you could use your time more efficiently by memorizing that word's spelling, not by continuing to look it up repeatedly.

Of course, you could also use your writer's journal to record those "problem" words in your writing. Writing the word with the correct spelling is one way of *learning* to spell it correctly.

Tool 3: Inventing "Tricks"

When you need to memorize the spelling of a word, don't just try to memorize the letters in order. Instead, make up a mnemonic device, or "trick," to help you learn the word. As with all mnemonic devices, the sillier or stranger it is, the better.

For example, if you have trouble spelling the word *conscience*, you might imagine that convicts would have time to make a science out of it, so you could think of the word as *con-science*. Or you might remember the two *m*'s in *recommendation* by imagining two *memos* of recommendation. Or the ending of *attendance* by thinking of attendance at a *dance*. But the best tricks for you will be ones you make up yourself.

Exercise

Review the words you have misspelled in the papers you have written, and in your journal write the correct spelling of each word. Is there a pattern to the words you frequently misspell?

PUNCTUATION

For many writers, punctuation is more difficult than spelling, probably because there seems to be even less agreement about what is "correct." It is true that we have fewer conventions to fall back on for punctuation than for spelling, and the result can be confusion. But that fact has its positive side, too. If there are fewer conventions to fall back on, there are fewer conventions to learn—and many more acceptable choices as a result. In fact, there are actually so few punctuation rules in English that almost all of them can be reduced to a simple chart, based on the work of William Irmscher.

Punctuation Conventions

	To END:	To SEPARATE:	To INTRODUCE:	To ENCLOSE:
PERIOD	Statements and commands			
EXCLAMATION POINT	Exclamations			
QUESTION MARK	Questions			
COMMA(S)		Sentences connected with *and, but, or, nor, for, so, yet* Items in a series Coordinate adjectives Some modifying phrases and clauses	Direct quotations	"Nonrestrictive" words, phrases, and clauses
SEMICOLON		Sentences connected without *and, but, or, nor, for, so, yet* Items with internal commas		
COLON			Specifics, block quotations	
DASH		Major shifts in thought Special emphasis	Generaliza-tions	Major interruptions

Punctuation Conventions

	To END:	To SEPARATE:	To INTRODUCE:	To ENCLOSE:
PARENTHESES				Explanations
BRACKETS				Comments within quotations
QUOTATION MARKS				Direct quotations
				Words used in special ways
				Titles of *parts* of publications

Down the left column of the chart are the ten commonest punctuation marks. Across the top are the four basic uses of punctuation: to end sentences, to separate parts of sentences, to introduce things, and to enclose things. As you see, the chart has a lot of blank space: most punctuation marks have fairly limited uses. The conventions that do appear on the chart are relatively few, and you probably know most of them already. You can use this chart, and the following explanation of it, to identify those punctuation conventions and choices that still cause you problems and learn to solve those problems at the postdrafting stage of your writing.

Ending Sentences. This first use of punctuation is by far the easiest, and it probably gives you very little trouble. Periods, of course, are used to end statements and commands, exclamation points are used to end exclamations, and question marks are used to end questions. Several matters, however, are worth remembering:

1. When you use ellipsis dots (. . .) to indicate an omission at the end of a direct quotation, remember to add a fourth period to end the sentence. (Notice that the period falls inside the closing quotation mark.)

A recent article in *Time* reported that "teen clinics are bringing needed medical care to many who could not otherwise afford it. . . ."

2. Do not overuse exclamation points. When they occur too often in a piece of writing, they lose their impact.

3. When, for the sake of courtesy, you phrase a request as a question, decide whether it is really a question or not. If it really is a question (like "May I please meet with you to discuss the position?" in a job application letter), end it with a question mark. If not (like "Will you please complete all items on the form" in a memo to employees), a period is usually acceptable and less confusing.

4. When you insert a question within another sentence, you may insert a question mark with it:

Why was Stonehenge built? we all asked ourselves.

5. When a quoted question or exclamation comes at the end of a sentence, do not use a period along with the question mark or exclamation point:

The interviewer asked, "Where were you born?"

Separating Parts of Sentences. As the chart shows, three punctuation marks are used to separate parts of sentences from each other. The dash—the least common—is used when a major shift in subject matter occurs within a sentence or when some part of the sentence warrants special emphasis:

We approached the building and—wait! What was that we heard behind us?

The arrangements were made and, of course, this she knew would drive me out of her son's life; and it did—we separated. (sample 4A)

The semicolon confuses many beginning writers but is actually very simple, because it has only two major uses. One is to separate two sentences that have been joined together *without* the use of a coordinating conjunction (*and, but, or, nor, for, so, yet*). Note that all the other relationship signals discussed in Chapter Four are not on this list; if you connect two sentences, and the second begins with a word not on the list of coordinating conjunctions, be sure to use a semicolon.

Your program must include a theme for the camp; also, it must include . . . . (sample 1A)

One might think that Ceralvo has always been simply a rural residential area; however, the buildings there today are actually the remains of a thriving city of another era. (sample 2C)

The only other common use of the semicolon is to separate groups of words that would normally be separated by commas but which already have commas *within* the groups of words. For example, this sentence includes a series of three items:

> Our party included a guide, who was an Oxford undergraduate; three German secondary students, who had joined us for the day; and the members of our class.

Because some of the items in the series have their own internal commas, semicolons are used instead of commas to separate the three items.

The third punctuation mark used to separate parts of sentences is the comma. Although some uses of the comma are governed by fairly strict conventions, other uses are matters of free choice. As a writer, you need to learn which are which. First, consider five basic conventional uses of the comma to separate:

1. Use a comma to separate sentences that have been connected with a coordinate conjunction (*and, but, or, nor, for, so, yet*). The comma, of course, goes before the conjunction:

> English 131 *is* a challenging course, but it teaches you how to hone your writing skills. (sample 7A)

> Each paper was an exercise in persuasion, for I also had to convince my readers why my views were valid. (sample 7A)

But don't simply place a comma before *any* coordinating conjunction in your sentence. You use a comma before a coordinating conjunction to separate sentences, not parts of sentences. For example, no comma is needed before the conjunction *and* in the following sentence:

> Writing isn't simply thinking about your topic once and then writing down your thoughts. (sample 7A)

2. Use a comma to separate items in a series, whether they are words, phrases, or even clauses. Writers differ on whether to put a comma before the word *and* or the word *or* in a series; most newspapers, for example, do not use a comma before the conjunction, whereas most book publishers do. But unless you know for sure that you should leave such a comma out, you will be safer to put it in.

The art museums, ancient ruins, and fountains are just as much fun to explore. (sample 2A)

Each member exchanged papers with another member, read the draft, and gave their opinions and suggestions about the paper. (sample 7B)

3. Use a comma to separate "coordinate adjectives," adjectives that *separately* modify a noun. As a test, see if you can put the word *and* between the adjectives; if so, separate them with a comma:

The part seen by most tourists is a tall, cold, gray wall. . . . (sample 2E)

A handsome, tuxedo-clad man climbs down a steel cable. . . . (sample 6A)

However, if an adjective modifies the combination of the next adjective and the noun, do not separate the adjectives with a comma. You will find that you cannot put the word *and* between such adjectives:

. . . the winding gravel road that leads to Ceralvo . . . (sample 2C)

The villain of the story is no longer a maniacal cartoon character bent on world domination. (sample 6A)

4. Use a comma to separate some modifying phrases and clauses from the rest of the sentence. Specifically,

a. Put a comma after dependent clauses that begin sentences.

Because I wrote clearly and effectively, my Children's Literature instructor knew that I understood the material. (sample 7A)

Although we all have opinions, we do not very often take the time to put them down on paper. (sample 7D)

b. Put a comma after participial phrases (phrases based on an *-ing* or *-ed* verb) that begin sentences.

Faced with a very difficult role, she portrays Alex with a passion that is evident on the screen. (sample 6B)

Being a beginning college student, you may wonder how a university

level writing course is different from other writing courses. . . .
(sample 7B)

c. Put a comma after "long" prepositional phrases that begin sentences.
(You will have to decide for yourself whether such a phrase is long
enough to need a comma.)

In your editorial concerning "the possibilities of what Oldham County
could become," you suggested changing the county from "dry" to
"wet" in order to attract new businesses. (sample 5B)

At the end of this course, I learned very valuable lessons that
improved my writing and that will help me throughout college and
my career. (sample 7B)

d. Put a comma before "nonrestrictive" phrases and clauses that end
sentences. Modifiers are nonrestrictive if they simply add information
about the word they modify, not restrict it to a particular case.

RESTRICTIVE (no comma): My research may someday save the lives of
others who suffer with the dreaded disease called cancer. (sample 2B)
(The clause beginning with *who* restricts the word *others* to a
particular group.)

NONRESTRICTIVE (comma): Lastly, you must attend the state meeting,
which is held one weekend in early spring. (sample 1A)
(There is only one state meeting, so the final clause simply adds
information about when it is held.)

5. Use a comma to separate most introductory "relationship signals"
from the rest of a sentence. Specifically, use commas after most relationship
signals *except* coordinate conjunctions (*and, but, or, nor, for, so, yet*).

However, there are always new goals to be set. (sample 3D)

Furthermore, the rule states that no one can park after midnight.
(sample 5C)

In addition to these five conventional uses of the comma to separate
parts of sentences, there are other uses that involve free choice by the writer.
As you read the writing of others, you may want to pay occasional attention
to how commas are used; in this way, you will begin to sense how commas
can help the readability of the written product.

Introducing Parts of Sentences. Only three punctuation marks are usually used to introduce sentence parts: the comma, colon, and dash.

Commas are used to introduce direct quotations:

> I was within five feet of her when she put out her hand abruptly and said, "Leave me alone! I'm so mad at those *stoopid* Yankees!" (sample 5I)

Dashes are used to introduce generalizations that follow specifics, usually several specifics:

> Choice of dealer, choice of model, and choice of time of year—these are the three best ways to save.

Colons are used to introduce specifics *after* a generalization. Thus the colon is the only punctuation mark that functions as a specific relationship signal, as defined in Chapter Four.

> The deregulation of telephone service had an important effect: it gave consumers a choice of long-distance phone companies.

Colons are also used to introduce block quotations (quotations of more than eight lines or so), lists, and the like. These, of course, also qualify as specifics after a generalization.

> As I mentioned earlier, I do sympathize with those of you who are about to take W131, and I offer the following suggestions:
>
> 1. . . . .
>
> 2. . . . .
>
> 3. . . . . (sample 7A)

Enclosing Sentences or Their Parts. Punctuation marks used to enclose are always used in pairs. As the diagram shows, these marks are commas, dashes, parentheses, brackets, and quotation marks.

Commas enclose nonrestrictive words, phrases, or clauses, used either as modifiers or appositives:

> RESTRICTIVE (no commas): You can buy an input wire that connects the portable model to your home stereo for under $10. (sample 1C) (The clause beginning with *that* restricts the meaning of *wire* to a specific kind.)

> NONRESTRICTIVE (commas): The third model, which may be the most versatile, is similar to the "Walkman." . . . (sample 1C)
> (The clause beginning with *which* simply adds information about the third model.)

Dashes enclose major interruptions in the meanings of sentences; they can also be used instead of commas around nonrestrictive phrases or clauses that contain other commas. They should be used rarely, except in informal writing.

> These services—including not only normal telephone transmission but also data transmission for business, industry, and government—vary from company to company.

Parentheses enclose explanations. If the material within the parentheses is one or more complete sentences, the punctuation at the end of the material should be inside the parentheses. If the enclosed material is only part of a sentence, any end punctuation should be outside.

> Five different actors have portrayed James Bond in one of the most enduring series in film history (eighteen installments over a period of twenty-seven years). (sample 6A)

> You can find long-distance companies listed in your phone book. (Look under "Telephone Companies" in the yellow pages.)

> Most have toll-free numbers (with "800" prefixes).

Brackets are used to enclose comments within quotations. When you are quoting someone else but need to add corrections or explanations of your own, put brackets around your additions so that your readers will know that they were not part of the original quoted material.

> One expert on telephone service has written, "The results of this action [deregulation] have been a mixed blessing for the American consumer."

One special use of brackets within quotations is to enclose the Latin word *sic*. Used in brackets, this word, meaning "thus," signals a mistake in the original quoted source, so that readers won't think that the error was in your copying.

> The expert continued, "Even by 1886 [*sic*], problems with telephone deregulation were arising."

Quotation marks are used, of course, to enclose direct quotations, as shown in the two previous examples. They are also used to enclose words or phrases used in special ways: ironically or technically, for example.

For some consumers, these problems called into question the assumptions of the "Reagan revolution."

Finally, quotation marks are used to enclose the titles of *parts* of published works. That is, they enclose names of newspaper and magazine articles, short stories, poems, songs, and the like. Titles of *whole* works—books, magazines, newspapers, record albums, films—are usually underlined in handwritten or typewritten material, and italicized in print.

One common problem in using quotation marks is knowing where to put other punctuation marks that accompany them. Remember these rules, on which almost all writers agree.

1. Always put periods and commas *inside* closing quotation marks, regardless of logic. (See the periods in both of the two previous examples.)

2. Always puts colons and semicolons *outside* closing quotation marks.

3. Put question marks and exclamation points inside or outside, depending on the meaning of the sentence: if the quotation is itself a question or exclamation, the mark goes inside; otherwise, it goes outside.

Exercise

Copy the following sentences, making any changes in punctuation that will make the sentences more conventional or more effective:

1.   Luckily, however, those events supplied the basis for my decision to become a genetic engineer and they have inspired me to strive towards reaching my goal. (sample 3B)

2.   You probably have heard that Rome contains beautiful history but until you experience it yourself you will not realize the truth of this statement. (sample 2A)

3.   Minding their own business they hurry through the crumbling buildings as soldiers suspiciously glance about. (sample 2E)

4.   One might think that Ceralvo has always been simply a rural residential area, however, the buildings there today are actually the remains of a thriving city of another era. (sample 2C)

5.   The instructor also created an atmosphere of creativity, and welcomed our comments and opinions throughout the semester. (sample 7D)

6.   I now consider writer, reader, and subject, I narrow my focus and decide what I want to say, before I sit down to write. (sample 7D)

7.   Miller Park has always been the playing site of Campbellsville's Little League baseball games, which sometimes last beyond midnight. (sample 5C)

8.   Many speculated about whether or not Pink Floyd would be the same without Waters—they were, in fact, superb. (sample 6C)

9.   For example, when she is the invincible psycho she has blood red fingernails, an untamed curly mane and a rough sallow complexion. (sample 6B)

10.   As also stated in "Newsweek", the lottery is a unique way of drawing money from citizens, "for it lays taxes only on the willing". (sample 5H)

OTHER MECHANICAL CONCERNS

Apostrophe. An apostrophe is a mark of punctuation most commonly used to show possession of a noun or indefinite pronoun. When the noun in possession is singular, an apostrophe (') is added, followed by an *s*. (But if the singular noun ends in *s*, writers disagree about whether to add only an apostrophe, as in *Tess' purse*, or an apostrophe and an *s*, as in *Tess's purse*. Most seem to favor the latter.)

. . . in any apartment building a person's guests are not asked to leave at a certain time. (sample 5B)

This child's life would certainly not be ended. . . . (sample 4A)

When the noun in possession is plural, ending in *s*, only an apostrophe is added after the *s*. (But if the plural noun does not end in *s*, add an apostrophe and *s*, as in *women's gloves* and *children's games*.)

My parents' lack of communication and support has left a scar on me that can never be erased. (sample 4B)

The computer's program could only be changed by rewiring it. (sample 4C)

An apostrophe is also used in place of omitted letters in contractions:

Last night was one 25th anniversary party that many won't soon forget. (sample 6E) (*will not → won't*)

It doesn't matter how long I've lived in Indiana, or how much of its hard water I drink. (sample 5I) (*does not → doesn't; I have → I've*)

Finally, an apostrophe is used to show the plural of numbers and letters:

During the mid–1980's, water travel was the most popular form of transportation. . . . (sample 2C)

When she writes, Amy reverses her *f*'s and *s*'s.

Hyphen. The hyphen is a mark of punctuation used to join words together in a variety of situations. Some common uses are as follows:

- To join parts of compound words. (When you doubt whether a word is hyphenated, always check your dictionary.)

    mother-in-law   *self-conscious*
    cross-reference   *mail-order*

- To join words used as a single adjective before a noun. (Note that when an adjective is combined with a word ending in -*ly*, no hyphen is used, as in *the badly burned piece of toast*.)

A Coast Guard helicopter swoops down on a small single-engine plane piloted by Carlos Sanchez. . . . (sample 6A)

. . . they stunned the audience with a larger-than-life pig. . . . (sample 6C)

- To join words in compound numbers between twenty-one and ninety-nine and in fractions.

    twenty-nine
    two-thirds

- To divide a word between syllables when the word runs over the end of a line of type. If you do not know where a syllable ends, always check your dictionary. In the following sentence, for example, *depend-*

able, which has three syllables, *de-pend-able,* can be hyphenated as follows:

> The office worker was courteous, efficient and dependable.

or

> The office worker was courteous, efficient, and dependable.

Capitalization. The convention of capitalizing personal and geographical names and the first words of sentences is virtually universal among writers of English. Beyond that, however, there is wide choice. Some writers and publications, following what has become known as "up-style," capitalize most nouns that stand for specific persons, places, or things, whether or not a proper noun is attached.

> Dr. Alvarez was recently selected as President of the University.

Other writers and publications, following what has become known as "down-style," tend to capitalize *only* names, not attached words.

> For the past five years, president Alvarez was academic affairs dean of Gutenburg college.

Most writers and publications follow a style somewhere in between. Such a "middle style" is probably the best course for you to follow. In general, you will meet most of your readers' expectations, thus increasing the readability of your writing, if you capitalize the following:

1. Personal names and initials.

    Eleanor Roosevelt

    T. S. Eliot

Some names of non-English origin have parts that are not capitalized. For such names, check a reputable reference book.

    Maurice de Vlaminck

    John von Neumann

2. Titles that precede a name.

    Dr. Troxel

    President Kennedy

Titles that follow a name, however, are usually not capitalized.

Patricia Troxel, doctor

John F. Kennedy, president of the United States

3. Academic degrees and their abbreviations.

Doctor of Philosophy
Ph.D.
M.D.

General terms for degrees, such as *bachelor's* and *master's*, are usually not capitalized.

4. Family relationships, when used as, or with, names.

Uncle Karl
Please, Mother

Such terms used as common nouns are usually not capitalized.

his uncle
my mother

5. Place names.

Rocky Mountains
North Africa
Ecuador

Accompanying adjectives of direction, however, are usually not capitalized.

southern Iowa
eastern Kentucky

But if you are referring to a specific geographical region, you do capitalize.

Susan lives in the Midwest.

He attended undergraduate school in the East.

6. Names of buildings, monuments, and the like.

Statue of Liberty
Sears Tower

7. Names of governmental bodies, educational institutions, businesses, and other organizations.

the Federal Communications Commission
Columbia University
Prentice Hall, Inc.

Common nouns for these bodies are not capitalized when used alone.

the commission
the university
the corporation

8. Names of days of the week, months of the year, and holidays.

Monday
September
Thanksgiving Day

Seasons, however, are not usually capitalized.

summer
fall

9. Names of deities (including pronouns referring to the deity, such as *He, His, Him*), revered persons, religious groups, and important religious events.

Allah
Buddha
the Church of England
the Exodus

10. Names of ships, aircraft, and spacecraft.

Titanic
Spirit of St. Louis
Sputnik

Note that such names are also italicized (underlined in handwriting or typing).

11. Brand names of products or services.

Kellogg's Rice Krispies
WordPerfect

12. The first and last words in titles of created works (books, periodicals, articles, poems, plays, songs, paintings, etc.), as well as all nouns, pronouns, verbs, adjectives, adverbs, and subordinate conjunctions. Prepositions,

coordinate conjunctions, and articles should not be capitalized, unless they are the first or last word in the title.

The Old Man and the Sea

Much Ado about Nothing

New England Journal of Medicine

Numbers. The decision to make about numbers is whether to write them in words or figures. Again, conventions vary widely, but the following "rules" are generally safe:

1. Use words for numbers less than 100.

two

ninety-eight

2. Use figures for exact numbers of 100 or more.

124

1,387

3. If you are discussing quantities of the same item both above and below 100, use figures.

The chain has expanded from 2 restaurants to 157.

4. Do not begin a sentence with figures; use words, or rewrite the sentence.

Four hundred seven veterans were present.

or

There were 407 veterans present.

5. Use figures for dates.

He has been here since December 8, 1986.

or

He has been here since 8 December 1986.

6. Use figures for page numbers.

Read pages 7–28 for Thursday.

7. Use words for approximate numbers.

More than forty thousand letters were received.

8. Use figures for percentages, followed by the word *percent*.

The lot was only 40 percent full.

Abbreviations. In general, avoid abbreviations; complete words will almost always be more readable. The following abbreviations, however, are used so often that they will cause no problems for your readers.

1. *Mr., Mrs., Ms., Dr.,* and *Rev.*

2. *Co.* and *Inc.,* when used as parts of company names.

3. *St., Ave.,* and other abbreviations after street names.

4. *U.S.* (note the periods).

5. Abbreviations for states, when following city names.

6. A few very familiar abbreviations and acronyms for governmental agencies, corporations, and other organizations.

FBI

IBM

YWCA

Formats. If you are using this book in a course, your instructor may specify formats for the final copies of your written work. In the absence of such specifications, the following guidelines will probably be acceptable.

1. If you are handwriting your paper, use lined white paper, $8\frac{1}{2} \times 11$ inches, write on every other line, and clearly distinguish between uppercase and lowercase letters. If you are typing, use white bond paper, $8\frac{1}{2} \times 11$ inches, and type on every other line.

2. Write or type on only one side of each sheet.

3. Leave 1-inch margins at the top, bottom, and sides.

4. Center the title of your paper at the top of the first page, remembering to capitalize the first and last word and all other words except articles (*a, an, the*), prepositions, and coordinate conjunctions. Do *not* underline the title, enclose it in quotation marks, or place a period after it.

5. Use blue or black ink (or typewriter or printer ribbon).

6. Write your name and the page number in the upper-right corner of each page after the first.

For business letter formats, see the letters among the sample papers in this book.

Exercises

A. Revise the following sentences from the sample papers, correcting any errors in the use of apostrophes, hyphens, capitalization, abbreviation, or numbers.

1.   Before I made my decision, I took a 300 level literature course required for English majors. . . . (sample 7A)

2.   In L390, Children's Literature, I read 27 books and wrote critiques for each one. (sample 7A)

3.   When I realized we were all in the same boat, we could either sink or swim, my self confidence began to grow. (sample 7C)

4.   The goal is to improve your own writing style, not the instructors, so forget about grades and just do your best. (sample 7C)

5.   I am certain that incoming Freshmen who are dreading this course will be pleasantly surprised. (sample 7D)

6.   When he finds out what has happened to his friend, he uses all of his resources to single mindedly pursue Sanchez in order to eliminate him. (sample 6A)

7.   Boston was just one of the stops on The Whos 25 city tour to celebrate 25 years of rocking and rolling together, and they were welcomed back after a 7 year absence from the road with a roaring crowd. . . . (sample 6D)

8.   Unlike most hoosiers who were weaned on many hours of televised high school basketball games, I grew up in the northeast, in a home where professional and midget wrestling were watched. (sample 5I)

9.   I looked at Mr Werner straight in the eyes. . . . (sample 5I)

10.   Therefore, lets lay the blame where it belongs, on Congress and not on President Reagan. (sample 5F)

B. In your journal, keep a list of the common mechanical errors in your writing. Write the sentence containing the error, your corrected version of the sentence, and a brief explanation of the error. Review this material in your journal before you revise your next paper.

Assignment 7: Reflecting on the Writing Course

Assignment: In this final essay, you are asked to reflect on your learning experiences over the course of the semester, and on the relevance of those experiences to the writing tasks you can expect in other courses in your college career. Address your essay to students who have not yet enrolled in English composition.

This writing assignment gives you an opportunity to reflect on your learning and to begin thinking about the kinds of writing you will be asked to do in other courses. To what extent have your experiences in English composition prepared you for future writing tasks? Unlike the other writing assignments, however, it specifies a particular writing situation. In what ways can your own experiences in this course be informative and instructive to students who will, at some future time, be taking the same course?

It may be helpful for you to begin talking with faculty and students in your prospective major, and in courses outside your major, and collecting information about specific kinds of writing assignments. What do these assignments ask you to do? What skills do they require? You might also consider what you learned about yourself as a writer and about writing as process, product, and power. Clearly, there are many aspects of the course that you could discuss in your essay, but you should focus on those that you think are most important or most relevant to your purpose.

Sample Papers

Sample 7A (Nancy)

What I Learned in W131

I sympathize with those of you who are about to take English W131. Many of you are reluctant to take 131 because you feel it has absolutely nothing to do with your majors. Let's face it, the truth is that many of us fear writing. As students, we know that writing is supposed to reflect what we think. But when we write our papers, we panic and only concentrate on using perfect grammar. Then we submit our first drafts as final products. Our fear produces weak papers.

Well, having just completed 131, I can tell you there is nothing to fear. English W131 *is* a challenging course, but it teaches you how to hone your writing skills. If you apply what you learn in 131 to your writing for other courses, then you will write better papers for the remainder of your academic careers. You will also lose some of your anxiety about writing, and this will enable you to develop your writing skills.

It will come as a surprise to many of you that there is actually a process in writing. Writing isn't simply thinking about your topic once and then writing down your thoughts. If only it were that simple! Writing is a process that requires much thought and planning before you begin your paper. It also demands that you revise and rewrite several times before you arrive at a good final draft.

Now imagine learning about this writing process after years of writing your own way and doing just fine, thanks very much. Add to that a group of peers reading your papers and commenting on them in class. Multiply that with not receiving a single grade from the professor until the end of the course, after you submit what *you* think are your four best papers. That equals English 131. Even though having wisdom teeth pulled sounds like more fun, 131 isn't as bad an ordeal.

At first, the students in my group were timid, and their comments about my papers were gentle. They were just as frightened of criticism as I was. We all figured that if we wrote nice things about each other's papers, then we would receive nice criticism. This changed during the first few weeks.

Because we received feedback from our professor only after final drafts were submitted, we learned to rely on each other to correct and edit our papers. Most of the students in my group developed a keen editorial eye. But learning how to work with a group of other students who were as unsure about their skills as I was about my own, was frustrating. Even with the professor's encouraging words and guidance, and our textbook, it took us a while to trust each other's skills and good grammatical instincts. It is said that a common adversary will bring people together. Well, what brought our group together were the assignments and all the revisions!

The papers I found most challenging were the process paper, the autobiography, and this paper on academic writing. Our first paper, the process, was my baptism into academic writing. It was the first time I forced myself to think carefully and thoroughly about my subject and my writing process. It was also the first time I learned that clarity in writing begins with a definite writing situation—writer, reader, subject, and purpose.

The autobiography paper insisted that I keep an audience in mind. This was very difficult because I first wrote my autobiography without accomplishing my purpose—to inspire secretaries to return to school. The final draft of that paper didn't work because it didn't address secretaries. Unfortunately, this meant I had to go back and start from the beginning.

And this paper, on academic writing, demands that I demonstrate the skills I've learned, and address those of you who are about to take W131. Although these papers were the most difficult for me, *all* of the papers assigned in 131 were exercises in developing, examining, and writing ideas clearly.

The result of W131 is that my writing process has changed. Before this class, I would simply write a paper and then make minor changes. Now I immerse myself in my topic and think about the position I wish to take. I prewrite ideas, phrases, and sentences, and I make an informal outline. Only *after* I perform that ritual do I begin to write, and eventually rewrite.

With a double major, English and Spanish, I expect to write hundreds and thousands of words in the next two years. My advisor, Professor _____ from the English Department, counseled me about the kinds of writing required in courses in my majors. Most of my writing will be essays and papers on a variety of topics. I am not frightened by the prospect of two years of revisions, rewrites, and reams of wasted paper. English 131 has prepared me for what lies ahead.

Now it may appear that I'm a pinhead to have a double major, but I didn't foolishly commit to this insanity. Before I made my decision, I took a 300 level literature course required for English majors to see if I had the right stuff. (For those of you who are still taking 100 and 200 level courses, enjoy them while you can!) I have never read or written so much in my life. In L390, Children's Literature, I read 27 books and wrote critiques for each one. Some of you may think that children's books are short and quick to read. That's what I thought too. But much of the great children's literature was first written for adults. Therefore, the genre is sophisticated and the stories can be *lengthy*. I had W131 the same semester, so I was ready for my literature course.

Before writing each critique, I thought about the book I read. I researched the subject, formed an opinion, and then wrote my observations about the book. After I completed a rough draft, I put it aside for some time. In the meantime, I thought more about my critique and what I wanted to say. When I returned to the rough draft, I read it, edited it, and then rewrote it. New ideas were added and sound ones were developed in the second, third, and fourth drafts. I earned good grades and received positive comments on my critiques. This convinced me to pursue the double major. It also showed me how 131 worked.

Because I wrote clearly and effectively, my Children's Literature instructor knew that I understood the material. Writing the critiques for L390 forced me to examine the literature and form my own opinion about the genre. Each paper was an exercise in persuasion, for I also had to convince my instructor why my views were valid.

This is why English 131 is a required course. Whether you are a Business, Computer Science, History, or Art major, you need to write papers that will show the knowledge you have acquired in your discipline. Those papers will be opportunities for you to express your views, to question material, to pass on information to your professors, or to formulate your own new ideas. We learn through writing.

As I mentioned earlier, I do sympathize with those of you who are about to take W131, and I offer the following suggestions:

First, lose your fear of others reading your papers. All of the students in 131 are in the same situation. Relax and get to know the students in your work group. The group must agree that each member will attend class regularly and give constructive criticism on the papers. At the end of the semester you'll be amazed at how much everyone has improved.

Second, read and study literature that interests you. For example, if you are interested in sports, you probably know that some of the most beautiful prose is created in that genre. Ask yourself why an essay or a story is compelling. Read each sentence. Notice the flow from one idea to the next. Each sentence is a link in a chain. It interests you because the thought is lucid. It engages you, which brings me to my third and final suggestion.

Keep in mind that your papers should engage the reader. By this I don't mean to exhaust your reader with sentences that each strain to be in the literary hall of fame. Nor should you embarrass yourself and write every sentence for a laugh. Instead, at the end of your paper ask yourself if you enjoyed reading it. Did your paper accomplish its purpose? If you answer no to either question, then you need to work on it some more.

Even though I have completed English 131, I still have much to learn about writing. Good writing is a skill that takes years to perfect. I console myself by thinking about all the revisions best-selling authors, journalists, presidents of corporations, and even professors have to do before they finally get a good draft. Revise and rewrite are forever emblazoned in my brain. Even now, as I write this paper to a close, I am aware of my writing process, my audience and my purpose.

Sample 7B (Carol)

Success in W131

Being a beginning college student, you may wonder how a university level writing course is different from other writing courses you have taken in the past or you may be saying, "Oh no! not another writing class!" Those were the same thoughts that went through my mind the first day of this class. At the end of this course, I learned very valuable lessons that improved my writing and that will help me throughout college and my career.

One way this course has helped me was with the help of collaborative groups. The collaborative group, comprised of four to five people, was used for evaluating the drafts of our work. Each member exchanged papers with another member, read the draft, and gave their opinions and suggestions about the paper. In the beginning, this was difficult to do because no one felt qualified to evaluate and give suggestions to another person about his paper. As the semester advanced and we began learning more about the writing situation and focusing the paper on one particular issue, we became more comfortable about evaluating another person's paper.

Another way this course has helped me was the role of the teacher. In my opinion, Professor _____ allowed me to progress as a writer by not restricting the class to his style of writing. Instead, he allowed us to develop our own style of writing. He did this by not putting comments on the final drafts of our papers. At first, this was intimidating because no one knew what was right or wrong with their paper; but that was the "plan": to develop our skills as writers. Through the exercises we did in our textbook and with the help of our collaborative groups, we were learning the writing process without any strict teacher intervention.

Nevertheless, W131 has served as the foundation for writing in my future and current courses. In my major, history, I am presently taking a course in which we take essay tests. Because of W131, I have learned how to focus my topic and organize the essay. In the future I plan to pursue a law career. Law schools suggests that you take many writing courses while you are in college. In law school, I will have to learn how to write legal briefs and in my final year of law school, I may have to write research papers for some courses.

As a result of W131, I have become a more confident writer. I have been able to express my opinions more clearly and in a more organized way. This course has helped me for my future courses and assignments for the rest of my college career and law school.

Sample 7C (Marcie)

The Secret of My Success

Are you dreading Freshman Composition? Don't. While we are all uncertain of our ability as writers, it is important to our success in college that we develop writing skills. I would like to suggest that you keep an open mind and let me share some of the experiences I had in English W131.

My first day of class I took stock of just who the other students were. Are they grown whiz kids? Must be brains. No, they were young, married, black and white people, just like you and me. They were just as unsure of themselves and brimming with anxiety. The instructor, hoping to ease some of the tension, begins by filling us in on what will be expected during the semester. There will be daily journal entries. (What's that?) Collaborative groups. (Who are they?) No instructor feedback. (What do you mean?) No grades until the end of the semester. (No way!) What on earth am I doing here? Am I going to be my own instructor?

As I reflect on that first day of class, I can't believe I'm here. The semester's at an end, and this class has been one of the most personally rewarding experiences I've ever had. It's true. Every Freshman lives through W131. But not all will benefit. Remember that open mind? It's your ticket to success. Let go of your fear and get to work understanding the concept of the course. I did. When I realized we were all in the same boat, we could either sink or swim, my self-confidence began to grow.

Understanding what is expected of you in this class may help to ease some of your anxiety. One of the course requirements that I had difficulty comprehending at first was the daily journal entries. Let's not confuse a diary with a journal. A diary is a listing of the days events and activities that have happened while the journal is thoughts and ideas that have sparked our interest and that can be used as a source for future writing material. It is quite fulfilling evaluating your day and finding something in it that challenges the mind. This practice has proved to be the importance of reflection.

The collaborative groups were four to six people working together critiquing each other's work and were almost the demise of my future in W131. I was afraid for the other people to read my work, fearful of criticism. But I soon learned the importance of sharing opinions and of reevaluating my work, a hard lesson to learn. Because grades are not assigned until the end of the semester, these groups became our only feedback on progress being made with each assignment. True feelings of trust among fellow students emerge due to being part of the collaborative group.

Lack of instructor feedback and no grade until semester's end can cause tremendous strain on the student-instructor relationship. Do not let this affect your attitude, however. While the concept may be new, it is actually a lesson in real life. The goal is to improve our own writing style, not the instructor's, so forget about grades and just do your best. Do it for yourself.

Don't let the term "English Composition" intimidate you. It is simply writing, a means of communicating by the written word. Throughout college, as well as life, it will significantly impact on how we get our message across. In my major, Nursing, I will be expected to perform a number of writing skills, and W131 helped to prepare me for these assignments.

One assignment in Nursing, for example, will be to write a paper on the nursing process. Understanding the importance of sequencing each step and gearing it to the appropriate reader and situation will enable me to step right into the assignment already understanding the process concept. Before W131, I did not realize that most things have a process and that in order to understand the concept you must know what it is. In fact, in every course I have taken so far, there is a process. Where have I been? To really comprehend what a process is, you will need to take English Composition.

Another assignment in Nursing will be to write Patient Care Plans, the plan on how and when treatment will be managed for a patient in my care. This assignment will require organizational skills and also proper sequencing. I have learned there are questions that must be asked in order to have proper organization. Again W131 has provided the ground rules for this. When preparing my patients for treatment, I will need to determine what it is I have to do, why I have to do it, where it will be done, and by whom. Learning to ask the appropriate questions leaves little chance for error in preparing for the care of my patients.

My effectiveness as a nurse will benefit from the interpersonal skills gained from being in the collaborative group. The group afforded me the opportunity to experience constructive criticism as a positive influence and to learn from it. I now realize the importance of hearing other opinions and reevaluating my own.

One of the final assignments in Nursing will be correspondence with future employers and preparing a resume. My writing skills will be the first factor about me that will have to sell. If I cannot express my ideas in writing, I will not get my foot in the door for an interview. I must have confidence in my skills as a writer and this course has boosted my self-esteem in this area.

The impact of W131 on my future success as a student and nurse is evident. Let the seed of success grow for you as it has for me. Accept the responsibility. Before you step into a class that will require writing skills, get prepared. Sign up for English Composition, W131, as soon as possible. It could be the secret of your success.

Sample 7D (Kathy)

English Composition: A Pleasant Surprise!

I began English Composition this semester wondering if this new type of class was going to improve my skills and prepare me for academic writing. This class was, after all, an experimental class with an unpublished textbook. In retrospect, I am pleased with the progress that I have made and the knowledge that I have gained. In the following essay I will outline parts of the course which I believe to be beneficial and state how they will help prepare me, and other incoming Freshmen students, for future academic writing.

The writing situation has always been somewhat elusive to me. After speaking with other students this seems to be a universal problem. English Composition has shown me how to identify my reading audience, narrow the subject matter, and define the purpose of the essay. These subjects will be especially helpful when I begin writing treatment plans for patients in my Nursing clinicals. In writing treatment plans the nurse must be able to focus on one patient, write for a specific audience, the medical staff, and for the well-being of her patient. All of the essays written this semester have given me experience in these areas.

The essay stating my opinion was also a valuable part of the class to me. Although we all have opinions, we do not very often take the time to put them down on paper. This essay not only gave me the chance to do that, I also had to substantiate my opinions. Graduate nurses have informed me that as a Nursing student I will be asked to evaluate a patient's condition, state my opinion, and back it up with facts.

Describing a place, object, or situation is something we are all asked to do in our daily lives. It is also something I will be asked to do in Nursing. Describing a patient's appearance or condition is an extremely important part of being a Nurse. The essay on description gave me the opportunity to expand my knowledge on the alternative ways to describe something. Sense of touch, taste, smell, and sight are obvious ways to describe something. But I also learned that I can describe something by a sense of feeling, how it feels to be somewhere, spiritually and emotionally. I believe this broadened my perspective on description.

Thinking back over the class structure, I am impressed with how different the class works now as opposed to how it began. At the start of the semester everyone was concerned with stating opinions on a fellow student's assignment. The class was divided up into groups to discuss and critique each other's papers. As the class has progressed this fear has diminished. Our confidence in our opinions and the knowledge we have gained made us feel more confident to respond to a classmate's paper. We have come to trust the people in our groups and value their advice and opinions.

The role of the instructor in this course is very different from other classes that I have attended. All of the students were surprised to discover we would not receive comments or letter grades on completed assignments until the second or third revision of the paper. Although this seemed frustrating in the beginning, I now see it as beneficial for the most part. By not receiving letter grades, or comments, the responsibility for learning and revising was put on the shoulders of the student and not the instructor. This forced us as writers to dig deeper into our own thoughts and come up with our own ideas. The instructor also created an atmosphere of creativity, and welcomed our comments and opinions throughout the semester.

My role as a writer has also expanded over the last few months. I think more carefully about each sentence that I put down. I make sure it is a valid point and relative to the subject matter. My revisions are carefully thought out; each change is made for a specific reason. The process of organization and the structure of a paper is something I think about prior to writing. In the past, I did not consider this until after the first draft.

My writing process is similar now as in the beginning of the semester. I still think a great deal before I begin writing, but now I have more specific thoughts to guide me. I now consider writer, reader, and subject; I narrow my focus and decide what I want to say, before I sit down to write.

In addition to all these things I think my confidence as a writer is what has grown the most. I believe that I can meet any writing challenge that is presented to me in the future. By utilizing the knowledge that I have gained this semester and applying hard work, I believe my future compositions will be creative, organized and informative.

I am certain that incoming Freshmen who are dreading this course will be pleasantly surprised. It is not the standard classroom setting. It is a class where you can explore your own talents and thoughts, and learn how to put them down on paper effectively.

Discussion Questions

1. Of these four papers, which do you think are most informative and instructive to the intended readers, students who have not yet taken the writing course? Why?

2. Some students working on this assignment felt the writing situation was too restrictive. What restrictions does the writing situation pose in a paper of this kind, in which the writer is asked to reflect on his or her learning?

Index